ROUTLEDGE LIBRARY EDITIONS:
THE MEDIEVAL WORLD

Volume 3

ORAL POETICS IN MIDDLE ENGLISH POETRY

ORAL POETICS IN MIDDLE ENGLISH POETRY

Edited by
MARK C. AMODIO
WITH THE ASSISTANCE OF
SARAH GRAY MILLER

Routledge
Taylor & Francis Group
LONDON AND NEW YORK

First published in 1994 by Garland Publishing, Inc.

This edition first published in 2020
by Routledge
2 Park Square, Milton Park, Abingdon, Oxon OX14 4RN

and by Routledge
52 Vanderbilt Avenue, New York, NY 10017

Routledge is an imprint of the Taylor & Francis Group, an informa business

British Library Cataloguing in Publication Data
A catalogue record for this book is available from the British Library

ISBN: 978-0-367-22090-7 (Set)
ISBN: 978-0-429-27322-3 (Set) (ebk)
ISBN: 978-0-367-18565-7 (Volume 3) (hbk)
ISBN: 978-0-429-19683-6 (Volume 3) (ebk)

Publisher's Note
The publisher has gone to great lengths to ensure the quality of this reprint but points out that some imperfections in the original copies may be apparent.

Disclaimer
The publisher has made every effort to trace copyright holders and would welcome correspondence from those they have been unable to trace.

ORAL POETICS IN MIDDLE ENGLISH POETRY

edited by

Mark C. Amodio

with the assistance of

Sarah Gray Miller

GARLAND PUBLISHING, INC.
New York & London / 1994

Library of Congress Cataloging-in-Publication Data

Oral poetics in Middle English poetry / edited by Mark C. Amodio.
p. cm. — (Albert Bates Lord studies in oral tradition ; vol. 13) (Garland reference library of the humanities ; vol. 1595)
ISBN 0-8153-0830-2 (alk. paper)
1. English poetry—Middle English, 1100–1500—History and criticism. 2. Oral-formulaic analysis. 3. Oral tradition—England. I. Amodio, Mark. II. Series. III. Series: Garland reference library of the humanities ; vol. 1595.
PR317.07207 1994
821'.109—dc20 94–9803
CIP

Printed on acid-free, 250-year-life paper
Manufactured in the United States of America

For my children,

Madeleine Phoebe
and
Lucas Antonio

General Editor's Foreword

John Miles Foley

The purpose of the Albert Bates Lord Studies in Oral Tradition, with its companion the journal *Oral Tradition*, is to bring before an interdisciplinary constituency essays, monographs, and collections that, in focusing on one or more oral or oral-derived traditions, offer insights that can be useful for investigators in many of the more than one hundred language areas now influenced by this field. Thus earlier volumes have treated, for example, orality and the Hebrew *Mishnah* (Jacob Neusner), *Beowulf* and shamanism (Stephen Glosecki), the Hispanic ballad (Ruth Webber, editor), Marcel Jousse's *The Oral Style* (Edgard Sienaert and Richard Whitaker, translators), the Middle English romances (Murray McGillivray), Turkic oral epic (Karl Reichl), identification in Homeric epic (Carolyn Higbie, editor), and African trickster tales (Zinta Konrad). Future books in this series will include a study of the Brother Peter folktale tradition from Guatemala as well as occasional collections of articles on a variety of areas. The overall aim is to initiate and sustain conversations among scholars who, because of the categories according to which we are segregated in modern academia, seldom if ever have a chance to talk to one another. With this goal in mind, we extend a warm invitation to new voices to join the conversation—both as readers of these and other volumes and, hopefully, as authors with contributions to the ongoing discourse.

This thirteenth volume in the Lord series, edited and introduced by Mark C. Amodio, presents a work of many hands on a single focused topic: the nature and importance of oral tradition for Middle English "literature." The quotation marks used in the last sentence set the boundaries of the term *literature* not only typographically but conceptually. In peeling away the layers of our contemporary sensibility, we come first to the long-recognized truism that literary works of the medieval period are assimilated to modern literature only at the considerable price of submerging from view a significant part of their genesis and continuing identity. Textuality in the Middle Ages is simply not congruent with the post-Gutenberg, mass paperback, and now electronic textuality of our time: behind even the most trustworthy and handsome variorum edition of a medieval work lie the unsettling divergences among manuscripts (not to mention the nagging problems of their authority and use), starkly different notions of authorship, and not least the matter of the reception of these texts. How were they created? How were they read? How were they performed? And how were they experienced by their audiences and readers?

Most of these riddles have been with us for some time, but the next layer of our sensibility has been laid bare only relatively recently. This is, of course, the question of the relationship between oral tradition—as a medium of composition, performance, reception, or some combination of these—and Middle English "literature" as we have it. In many ways the question is much more difficult for post-Conquest works than for the poetry of the Anglo-Saxon period that chronologically precedes it. Old English maintained an oral traditional register, a homeostatic idiom that nonetheless also responded to the cultural need to translate and to create Christian narrative and lyric poetry; on balance, whether a given Anglo-Saxon poem was actually composed orally or in writing proves less important than the fact that it was made and experienced under certain significative assumptions on the part of both maker and audience. Middle English verse, on the other hand, knew no such single expressive (and perceptual) medium. Additionally, even more than their Old English counterparts, the post-Conquest poets spoke in a plurality of voices, identifying a wide spectrum of genres, sources, translations, and textualities. A universalist model for oral tradition and literature—with or without the quotation marks—always runs the risk of reductionism, but in respect to Middle English verse it amounts to little more than an outright distortion.

What then has been the history of scholarship on the issue—more accurately, *issues*—of oral tradition in post-Conquest England? In his introduction to the collection, Amodio offers an expert discussion of what may be seen as the gradual problematization of orality and literacy in works of verbal art from this period, showing how early typographies proved too exclusive to explain the heterogeneity of relevant texts and bringing to bear the new and potentially productive concepts of "vocality" and developing literacy. Amodio goes on to illustrate the complexity of the interpretive challenge by considering the case of Laȝamon's *Brut*, which presents the critic with multiple interweavings of literacy and oral-traditional structure and reference. After a brief but exemplary discussion of the poem's major features in the context, he concludes as follows: "[a]cknowledging the tension which informs the medieval oral-literate continuum will enable us to understand more clearly both the mix of oral and literate poetics we discover in a poem such as the *Brut* as well as the 'cultural diglossia' central to medieval English society" (21). Concepts such as *tension, continuum,* and—one that Amodio does not happen to mention—*persistence* mark the path toward a suitably plastic and pluralized model of oral tradition in the verbal art of post-Conquest England.

Aiding and abetting Amodio in establishing a new interpretive paradigm for Middle English poetry is a cast of specialists in appropriately diverse areas. Their individual efforts are capably summarized by Sarah Gray Miller (29-37), and I will not anticipate that heroic catalogue here. Suffice it to say that, in addition to the editor's own enlightening comments on the *Brut*, this volume presents nine essays touching on Chaucer's *Canterbury Tales* (with special attention given to *The Franklin's Tale, Sir Thopas,* and the *Melibee*); on the medieval romances of the *Seege of Troy, Robert of Cisyle, King Horn, Havelock the Dane, Sir Gawain and the Green Knight,* and *Amis and Amiloun*; on the Alliterative *Morte Arthure*; and on Robert Mannyng of Brunne's *Handlying Synne.* All of the contributors—Leslie K. Arnovick, Nancy Mason Bradbury, John M. Ganim, Britton J. Harwood, Dave Henderson, Seth Lerer, Alexandra Hennessey Olsen, Ward Parks, and Donna Lynne Rondolone—have, in the plurality of their voices, echoed Amodio's call for a new oral poetics, a suitably complex poetics for a complex "literature."

Center for Studies in Oral Tradition
University of Missouri, Columbia

Acknowledgments

I would like to thank, first of all, the contributors to this volume; without their interest, patience, and good will this collection would never have come to be. Thanks are also due to Jennifer Berzansky (Vassar '95) for all the help she provided during the final stages of production and to John Miles Foley for his always sound advice on editorial matters large and small. I am especially grateful to Sarah Gray Miller for her invaluable assistance; she was involved in all aspects of this project from its early stages, both as my research assistant and, during the summer of 1992, as a Ford Scholar. This book was funded in part by generous grants from the Vassar College committee on research and the Ford Scholars' Program.

Contents

Introduction: Oral Poetics in Post-Conquest England

Mark C. Amodio

I

The topic addressed in this collection is not new: the oral tradition's possible influence on the vernacular poetry produced during the Middle English period has been a subject of scholarly discussion since the late nineteenth century (Parks, "Oral-Formulaic Theory" 638). But despite the early attention to its possible orality, Middle English literature has consistently been situated at the very periphery of oral studies.[1] As oral theory has developed over the past thirty-five years, our knowledge of many ancient, medieval, and contemporary oral traditions has greatly increased but because there has been no systematic or sustained effort made to chart the influence of the oral tradition in the years following the Norman Conquest, there has been no corresponding progress in our

[1]Parks has demonstrated the impressive chronological scope of the scholarly discourse devoted to the oral tradition's influence on Middle English poetry, but the number of scholarly works on it remains small–the thorough bibliography appended to his survey lists some twenty-five books and approximately one hundred thirty-five articles, many of which touch only incidentally on the topic ("Oral-Formulaic Theory" 683-94). To this list one could add several more recent studies (see, for example, several of the essays in Doane and Pasternack's collection) but their number remains small.

understanding of orality in the Middle English period. While it has become almost axiomatic to assert that some sort of oral tradition informs the written one which comes to supplant it during the Middle Ages,[2] the precise nature of this tradition remains largely unexamined even when it is being consciously invoked.[3]

There are many reasons why investigations of the oral tradition in post-Conquest England hover on the margins of literary and cultural studies: of these, the more important are the tacit equation of literacy with literary excellence; the widely held assumption that the cultural and political ascendancy of 'learned' written tradition relegates the oral to some sort of shadowy, vaguely defined, 'popular' one;[4] difficulty in sorting out the complex and confusing relationship between memorial

[2]Doane offers the following succinct articulation of this view and of the central problem that attends it: "it is known–though rarely is the knowledge effective–that nearly all vernacular texts and many Latin ones (e.g., saints' lives, liturgy) preserved from the Middle Ages down to the thirteenth century and beyond are merely traces of an existence that was normally vocalized" (xii). And Spearing, after acknowledging that Old English poetry "was undoubtedly at one stage orally composed" argues that even though "[w]e have no direct evidence of an oral stage in the development of Middle English alliterative poetry . . . it represents essentially a later stage in the Old English tradition, and it retains a considerable formulaic content" (23).

[3]For example, Grudin concludes her recent discussion of closure in the *Canterbury Tales* by arguing that the "consciously imitated oral quality" of some of the tales "shows Chaucer's pronounced interest in the social interactions of discourse" (1163). Many other such statements which depend upon similar broadly defined notions of 'orality' could easily be added here. My point is not that Grudin and others are mistaken but simply that the terms 'oral' and 'orality' are often employed in ways that range from loose (as in Grudin's case) to uninformed.

[4]Consider, for example, the following statement of Bäuml's: "[w]hen writing became the accepted method for the transmission of knowledge, the function of poetry shifted: it ceased to be predominantly didactic and became predominantly aesthetic. The leading classes of society looked to the written word, and no longer to oral poetry, as transmitting the cement of their society. When a society becomes literate in this basically modern sense, oral poetry *sinks* to the illiterate, i.e. the *disadvantaged* in such a society" ("Unmaking of the Hero" 89; emphasis his). Ólason, in discussing the ballad tradition, offers a similar view. He notes that Mrs. Brown, "a highly literate" singer whose ballads appear in the Child edition, "partook of two traditions, which she kept apart in her mind: the literate culture and standard English of her day, and a lower-class culture transmitted in the local dialect" (118).

transmission and productive oral composition;[5] and the belief that "textual transmission through oral channels is . . . corruptive" (Reichl 262).[6] In addition, the implicit literacy of Middle English authors, the presence of indisputable written sources for many extant Middle English poems, and the undeniable textuality of the poems themselves have all seriously impeded our ability not just to understand but even to perceive the specialized character of the oral tradition in post-Conquest England.[7]

The highly literate nature of the English Middle Ages has proved to be a nearly insurmountable problem to the investigation of orality in the period in large part because the dominant theoretical model for investigating oral poetry remains that first articulated by Milman Parry and subsequently expanded by the late Albert B. Lord. In its influential 'classical' form (as it appears in Parry's works and especially in Lord's seminal book, *The Singer of Tales*), the theory insists that only those poems composed by pre-literates under the highly specialized demands of oral performance can be labelled 'oral.'[8] As a result of laying such stress upon these criteria, the theory unduly privileged what we ought perhaps to label 'high-context' orality while denying the possibility of a meaningful oral influence on any poetry which did not

[5]For recent studies of the role memory plays in oral transmission, see Olsen's contribution to this collection; Lord ("Merging of Two Worlds"); Finnegan (52-87); Jabbour; McGillivray; and Quinn and Hall. Carruthers has recently considered the nature and broad cultural role of memory in the Middle Ages.

[6]Pearsall offers an extreme reading of the multiformity which characterizes texts produced within oral societies when he suggests that although "[t]here was probably an orally transmitted alliterative verse, . . . its products, when written down, would have the debauched character of the *Prophecies*" (6). He continues in this vein by asserting that "[a]ll the evidence we have suggests that oral transmission makes wretched what it touches, and that the longer the process the more debased the product. . . . There is no mystery about oral transmission, and I should make it clear that I am not invoking the higher mysteries of oral formulaic composition, which are even more irrelevant to Middle English than to Old English alliterative verse" (idem). For a fuller and more reasoned treatment of the question of "oral transmission as a predominantly degenerative process" (Finnegan 142), see Finnegan (134-69).

[7]See further Bäuml's important discussion of medieval literacy and illiteracy ("Varieties and Consequences").

[8]For a fuller discussion of the scope and history of this theory, see Foley (*Theory of Oral Composition*).

strictly conform to the model which Lord set forth in *Singer*.[9] Lord's well known and highly influential assertion that the "techniques [of oral and literate composition] are . . . contradictory and mutually exclusive" (*Singer* 129) neatly articulates what for many oral theorists is the fundamental belief that "orality and literacy [are] differing mentalities" which mark discrete "states of mind and . . . stages of culture" (Stock, *Listening* 6).

Much of the opposition to the early, uncritical, and often overly exuberant applications of the Parry/Lord theory had less to do with the nature of the broad theoretical claims made concerning the orality of some medieval English poetry than with the polemics necessitated by adhering to what Brian Stock has labeled the "strong thesis" of oral composition. Because the oral and the literate were believed to occupy discrete cognitive spheres, the appearance of verbal formulas and such things as oral traditional themes and type-scenes were taken as reliable indicators of the orality of many medieval texts.[10] In arguing against this view, Larry D. Benson noted that many (if not most) of the pronouncements regarding the orality of Old English poetry were sharply at odds with both the demonstrable formularity of texts composed in writing and the fact that all the texts believed to have been composed orally survive only in written form. Rather than ignoring or attempting to explain away the many important and inescapable links between the oral and the literate, recent work on oral, or to be more precise, oral-derived[11] texts has shown that the investigation of the putative orality of any ancient or medieval text must be carried out along twin axes: one demonstrably oral and the other in fact written. And as a

[9]Foley has recently considered the necessarily performative aspect of oral poetries ("Word-Power"). Ong ("Medieval Textualization"); Stock (*Implications* 12-87); Bäuml ("Varieties and Consequences"); and Ziolkowski are among those who have recently argued for a more complex relationship between orality and literacy than the 'classical' Parry-Lord theory admits.

[10]Magoun's "The Oral-Formulaic Character of Anglo-Saxon Narrative Poetry" remains the *locus classicus* of this view. Consider, for example, his often cited assertion that "the recurrence in a given poem of an appreciable number of formulas or formulaic phrases brands the latter as oral, just as the lack of such repetitions marks a poem as composed in a lettered tradition. Oral poetry, it may be safely said, is composed entirely of formulas, large and small, while lettered poetry is never formulaic" (190). For early and influential work on oral traditional themes, see Magoun ("Beasts of Battle"); and Greenfield.

[11]See Foley (*Traditional Oral Epic* 1-51) for a fuller discussion of this important term.

result, a far more nuanced view (what Stock terms the "weak thesis") of the relationship between orality and literacy has emerged, one that eschews the binarism characteristic of the strong thesis and instead "attempts to account for the interaction of the oral and the written after the initial step [towards literacy] is taken" (Stock, *Listening* 5-6). The advantages of the weak thesis are twofold: first, it reflects the reality of the medieval oral-literate nexus much more accurately than the strong thesis can because "[i]t assumes that a knowledge of writing is not completely new. More writing is merely being introduced into a society that already has some texts" (*Listening* 6); and second, it places the intersection of orality and literacy squarely in the center of the complex social, economic, linguistic, and political dynamic of the Middle Ages.

That orality and literacy exist along a continuum and are integral and interrelated parts of a subtle and complex cultural change rather than (largely) unrelated moments of cultural evolution has become increasingly clear, but in acknowledging this we need also to admit that the continuum's theoretical termini are marked by real and substantial cognitive differences. At one end of the oral-literate continuum lies what Walter Ong has called a primary oral culture, one that is absolutely innocent of writing and the specialized habits of mind that it entails.[12] In such a culture, oral poets, far from being mere entertainers, serve as "[t]he repositories of learning, of the knowledge necessary for the preservation of the fabric of society" (Bäuml, "Unmaking of the Hero" 89). Although many more examples could be easily adduced here from a wide variety of cultures, one need only consider the powerful reassertion of human "communitas" which informs the reconciliation of Priam and Akhilleus in the final book of the *Iliad*[13] or the well-known catalogue of ships contained in book II of the same poem to glimpse the broad, significant, and culturally central role oral poets play within pre-literate societies.[14] But even within those societies which are well on their way to being (or are already) highly literate, we often discover that oral poets continue to fulfill significant functions. For example, the role of the scops in *Beowulf* attests to their continuing im-

[12]Ong defines "primary orality" as "the pristine orality of cultures with no knowledge of writing" ("Medieval Textualization" 1). But Doane correctly cautions us against uncritically accepting the existence of such a culture because "primary orality is forever inaccessible to us (if it is not merely mythical)" (xiii).

[13]Foley argues this at greater length in *Immanent Art* (135-89).

[14]See further Havelock; Lord (esp. *Singer*); and Foley (esp. *Immanent Art*).

portance in an increasingly literate society: to cite just a few instances, the news of Grendel's attacks upon Heorot spreads "gyddum geōmore" (151a) 'sadly in songs'[15] and the songs composed on the morning following Beowulf's dispatching of Grendel and the one sung at the Geat's funeral serve the traditional function of keeping Beowulf's heroic accomplishments alive, something of no small importance to the pre-literate heroic society depicted within the poem.[16] This is not to suggest that *Beowulf* supplies unambiguous evidence that an oral tradition was still active when the poem was committed to manuscript some time during the tenth or perhaps even eleventh century;[17] rather the various performances by scops in the poem witness the importance still attached to the *idea* of traditional oral production and transmission in the literate culture of the Anglo-Saxons and further serve to remind us that throughout the Anglo-Saxon period and even through the more widely literate later Middle Ages, literary reception remained primarily (and perhaps for a very large segment of society, exclusively) aural, not ocular. As A.N. Doane has argued, medieval "[t]exts were written to be heard—whatever the mechanisms of their original production" (xii).[18]

The "vocality"[19] of medieval texts is especially important in a primary oral culture because the poet is not marked by the absence we

[15]I cite Klaeber's edition of *Beowulf.*

[16]Lerer, in suggesting that "[t]hose scenes of bardic performance or social response long understood to be the heart of Anglo-Saxon self-representation are, when seen in broader contexts, framed by presentations of the written text, and function more as tropes than as unmediated versions of historical reality" (4) offers a far different picture of the scop's role.

[17]For more detailed discussions on the date of *Beowulf*'s composition, see Kiernan and the essays collected in Chase. Niles offers a succinct account of the issue and suggests that the poem may have been composed as late as the tenth century (Beowulf 96-117).

[18]For discussions of reading in the Middle Ages, see Clanchy (202-30, esp. 214-20); Chaytor (5-21); Saenger ("Silent Reading"; "Separation of words"); and Illich (35-39). Ziolkowski succinctly notes that "the act of reading itself was both intensely oral and visual: a text was read not simply through being scanned with the eyes, but also through being mouthed or sounded aloud" (195-96). See also Parks ("Song, Text" 107-108 and n7). We should recall with Bäuml, however, the important difference "between a traditional 'performance' on the part of an oral poet and a reading of a text by a minstrel" ("Varieties and Consequences" 245).

[19]The term is Zumthor's. Schaefer notes that "[i]n *La lettre et la voix* Zumthor definitively explains *vocality* as the realm in which the 'physical aspect of medieval texts, their mode of existence as objects of sensorial perception' unfolds"

have come habitually to associate with post-medieval literary production but by his or (more rarely) her immediate physical presence: without the poet there is no poem. The "text" an oral poet produces is truly dynamic because it is always and only public[20] and it enjoys a most ephemeral and temporally circumscribed existence because it is "In his substaunce . . . but air" (*House of Fame* 768).[21] Residing only within the collective memory of those present while it is performed, the oral text leaves behind no trace once the final reverberations of the poet's voice die out. And because it is always necessarily composed under the exigencies of performance, poetry produced within a primary oral culture is highly protean.[22]

At the equally theoretical opposite end of the oral-literate continuum lies a culture that is fully literate, one in which orality does not figure at all in the creation, transmission, and reception of texts. In such a society, "culturally essential knowledge is transmitted in writing, and whoever has no ready access to it is . . . disadvantaged in respect to his ability to carry out social functions requiring such access" (Bäuml, "Varieties and Consequences" 243). In addition, both the production and reception of texts within such a literate culture are intensely private and highly idiosyncratic endeavors.[23] The texts this culture produces are unconventional in the most technical sense of that term; that is, whereas orally produced texts are of necessity rooted in and perhaps even determined by a highly specialized, conventional discourse, one shared deeply by both poets and audiences, fully literate texts spring from the imaginative well of an author who consciously and carefully molds his or her thoughts according to his or her tastes, inclination, education, etc.[24] While a certain degree of orality attends even those texts

("Hearing from Books" 118; citing Zumthor 21). See also Schaefer ("Alterities").

[20]On the important relationship the performer in an oral culture has with his audience, see Lord (*Singer*); and Foley ("Traditional Oral Audience").

[21]I cite Benson's edition of Chaucer's poetry throughout.

[22]On this aspect of oral poetry see Lord (*Singer* 26-29). Finnegan (52-87) advances an alternative view of the role of performance in oral cultures.

[23]A good deal of post-structuralist critical discourse has been devoted to this topic. On the idiosyncratic nature of literary reception in a literate culture, see Fish and the essays collected in Tompkins.

[24]Foley has recently attempted to clarify the differences between "oral traditional and textual modes" of composition by distinguishing between "inherent" and "conferred" meaning. See further his important discussion in *Immanent Art* (esp. xiv ff.).

produced in highly literate societies—for example, authors may employ a variety of narrative voices within their texts and they frequently give public readings—, the compositional process remains exclusively private. Literary reception is similarly private: authors write and readers read in isolation. The texts produced in a fully literate culture have an attendant fixity forever denied the truly oral text; Chaucer's well-known and very modern sounding excoriation of sloppy scribal practice in "Adam Scriveyn" would be meaningless in a pre-literate society in which texts exist *as* variants, not fixed, *author*ized, monolithic entities capable of being compared to some known standard and corrupted in transmission:[25]

> Adam scriveyn, if ever it thee bifalle
> Boece or Troylus for to wryten newe,
> Under thy long lokkes thou most have the scalle,
> But after my makyng thow wryte more trewe;
> So ofte adaye I mot thy werk renewe,
> It to correcte and eke to rubbe and scrape,
> And al is thorugh thy negligence and rape.
>
> (Benson 650)

The differences between what we can reductively, if conveniently, label the 'oral' and the 'literate' minds are profound, but the likelihood of discovering a culture which unambiguously embodies either model remains remote because primary oral cultures are rare indeed and even highly literate cultures such as the one within which we operate are deeply affected by oral habits of mind in that "oral discourse surrounds and conditions the use of written texts" (Olson and Torrance 1). Although at one time ancient and medieval texts were regularly pronounced as being demonstrably "oral" (this despite the inescapable physical evidence of the codices which contained them), one is hard pressed to discover similar statements in the work of contemporary oral theorists.[26] Indeed, the categorical distinction between the

[25]See also Chaucer's comments in the *Troilus* (V. 1793-98). For discussions of Chaucer's modernity, see Sanders; and Travis.

[26]But see Creed's careful and tentative acknowledgment that his "working hypothesis" concerning *Beowulf* is that "the poem that has come down to us in Cotton Vitellius A. XV is a copy of a recording of a performance" (194). Niles sounds a similar note when he comments that he sees "no reason to preclude the possibility of our text of *Beowulf* being the work of a self-dictating poet, or perhaps, a gifted author steeped in oral tradition, yet schooled in the arts of an ad-

"oral" and the "literate" which had provided the very foundation of oral theory has been largely abandoned and a new model has emerged, one that acknowledges the ineluctable, perhaps sustaining, tension between and interdependency of the 'oral' and 'literate' minds. Far from sounding the "death knell" of oral composition, to use Lord's well known phrase, the onset of literacy marks the beginning of a powerful, flexible (and still continuing) interaction between orality and literacy.[27] The chirographic tradition which emerges and gains increasing cultural importance throughout the medieval period does not simply and immediately replace the older oral one which it comes to supplant but rather merges with it to form a partnership which has yet to be fully understood. As Stock, in arguing that "[t]here is . . . no clear point of transition from a nonliterate to a literate society" notes (*Implications* 9), oral habits of mind persist even within increasingly literate societies (idem 42-87).[28] And Rosalind Thomas, in a comment that applies equally well to medieval England, contends that in ancient Greece

> [t]he mere presence of writing [was] not enough to prompt its widespread use. Moreover, written and oral methods of communication or validation may exist side by side for a considerable time after the influx of writing. The old oral methods [were] not abandoned immediately, if indeed at all.
>
> (34)

The technology of writing may, as Ong observes, reduce the "dynamism of sound to quiescent space" (*Orality* 82), but in so doing it merely muffles rather than throttles the continued articulation of oral poetics; what emerge from the vernacular manuscript culture of the English Middle Ages are, to borrow a phrase from John Miles Foley, "texts that speak to readers who hear."

The manner of poetic production changes as literacy gains ground—put simply, what had been public and communal becomes pri-

---

vanced literary culture as well" ("Anglo-Saxon Oral Poetics" 365). Most recently, Niles has argued that the poem may be the product of what he labels an "oral poetry act" ("Oral Poetry Acts" and "*Beowulf* in Literary History" 101-06). Cf. also Duggan's argument that our text of the *Chanson de Roland* is a recording from oral songs.

[27]Lord himself moved more and more towards this position in the years preceding his death (see esp. "Merging").

[28]See also Clanchy.

vate and idiosyncratic—but the shift from producing poetry exclusively during public performance with all its attendant pressures and demands (see Lord, *Singer*; Finnegan) to producing it privately and in writing does not entail a concomitant and equally dramatic alteration in poetic articulation. As the four poems generally attributed to Cynewulf attest, some of the extant Old English poetry which conforms to the oral traditional model may well have been produced by highly literate poets.[29] And traces of oral tradition may be found in *writings* as diverse as a poem by Catullus, the *Nibelungenlied*,[30] Milton's *Paradise Lost*, and even contemporary descriptions of battles fought during the American Civil War. Scholars trained in oral-formulaic rhetoric[31] may well be able to detect the vestiges of the beasts of battle typical scene in the following lines from *Paradise Lost*:

> [Death] with delight . . . snuff'd the smell
> Of mortal change on Earth. As when a flock
> Of ravenous Fowl, though many a League remote,
> Against the day of Battle, to a Field,
> Where Armies lie encampt, come flying, lur'd
> With scent of living Carcasses design'd
> For death, the following day, in bloody fight.
> (X 272-78)[32]

The many descriptions of light flashing off the rifle stocks and fixed bayonets of approaching armies in a contemporary historian's account of the Civil War recall, if they do not descend from (at whatever remove), the flashing objects which figure so prominently in the hero on the beach story pattern common to Old English oral and oral-derived poems.[33] Stripped as they are of their traditional context and entirely

[29]See esp. Olsen and Schaefer on Cynewulf. The poems *The Fates of the Apostles*, *Juliana*, *Christ II*, and *Elene* are attributed to him because they all appear to bear the runic "signature" 'Cynewulf.'

[30]For a discussion of the oral-formulaic context of Catullus *Poem 5*, see Renoir ("Oral Theme" and *Key* 41-44); for the *Nibelungenlied* see Renoir ("Oral-Formulaic Theme Survival").

[31]Renoir discusses this notion at greater length in *A Key to Old Poems* (49-104).

[32]I cite Hughes's edition of *Paradise Lost*.

[33]Flashing objects also seem to figure in the affective dynamics of *Paradise Lost*. Consider the following: the legions of God, on their way to engage Satan's forces

removed from the tradition within which they developed, these scenes nevertheless appear to retain a good deal of what Alain Renoir would term their "affective impact";[34] the carrion beasts mentioned in *Paradise Lost* will indeed preside over the fallen on the battlefield, as their Anglo-Saxon counterparts frequently do, and Shelby Foote's recurrent references to the brightness of the muzzles and bayonets borne by approaching opposing armies focus our attention on the bloody uses to which both rifle and, more grimly, bayonet will be shortly put.[35]

What these and other related vestiges of the oral tradition suggest is not that an active oral poetics underlies the works in which they appear; rather they point to the inherent organizational power which attends some oral traditional narrative elements. Although the 'classical' formulation of the oral theory laid heavy stress upon the necessity of composition within performance, it is highly unlikely that any of our extant Old English poems (with the possible exception of Cædmon's *Hymn*) are recordings of actual performances.[36] Given the state of developing literacy in Anglo-Saxon England[37] and the probable presence of an active oral tradition during the period, we may be justified in speculating that some written Old English poems are only slightly removed from their oral versions, although, of course, we will never be able to know for sure just how close any given text is to its oral predecessors. When we move beyond the Conquest, however, speculation regarding the putative oral foundations of any given piece of vernacular

---

stretcht [far]
In battailous aspect, and nearer view
Bristl'd with upright beams innumerable
Of rigid Spears, and Helmets throng'd, and Shields . . . .
(VI 80-83)

[34]Or to adopt Foley's terminology, these vestiges of the oral tradition retain some degree of their "traditional referentiality" despite their distance from the tradition.

[35]An audience whose horizon of expectations derived from the Old English oral-formulaic tradition would have no trouble identifying and correctly 'reading' these elements: both the carrion beasts and the shining objects have been shown to be significant indicators of a slaughterous encounter (Crowne; Renoir, *Key* 96-104). The soundtracks that accompany certain genres of contemporary movies provide a modern analogue to this aspect of medieval oral poetics. Although examples could be multiplied almost at will, consider only the ominous music which precedes each of the shark's attacks in the thriller, *Jaws*.

[36]But see Lerer's important reconsideration of the Cædmon story (33-48).

[37]See esp. O'Keeffe; and Lerer.

poetry becomes even more problematic. Whether or not the oral tradition was active during the Anglo-Saxon period is certainly arguable, but the Middle English period, witnessing as it does the steady and widespread rise of the literate authorial consciousness which comes to dominate literary production in our culture, appears to be clearly removed from the world of oral composition.[38] This shift towards literate composition may be nowhere more clearly illustrated than in the sudden appearance of different verse types following the Conquest. The formal variety which comes to characterize Middle English versification signals an important change not only in how authors articulate poetry but in how they conceive it: throughout the Anglo-Saxon period, the poetry's formal homogeneity suggests that it could only be articulated within the confines of the four-beat alliterative line so familiar to all students of Old English poetry. As A.J. Bliss has noted, "[o]ne of the most striking characteristics of OE poetry is its extreme uniformity," a uniformity which leads him to suggest that "for all intents and purposes there is only one metre" (23).[39] But the years following the Conquest witness a radical alteration in "the metrical principles that had prevailed for four centuries" (Cable 54). The metrical changes evident from the late Anglo-Saxon period on are attended by a "significant change in mode of composition and performance" (Cable 54-55) and mark the beginning of what will eventually be the complete reconfiguration of English poetic meter.[40] Although there may be no demonstrable link between changes in poetic form and shifting authorial consciousness, the breakdown of classical Old English meter is (perhaps more than coinci-

[38]Literacy spread rapidly during the period but, as Stock reminds us, "[d]own to the age of print and in many regions long afterwards, literacy remained the exception rather than the rule. Despite primary schools, cheap paper, spectacles, and the growing body of legal and administrative material, the masses of both town and countryside as late as the Reformation remained relatively indifferent to writing" (*Implications* 13). See also Bäuml's discussion of the differences between medieval and modern literacy ("Varieties and Consequences").

[39]However, as Bliss and many others have noted, some metrical variation did exist in Old English poetry: hypermetric and rhyming passages occur with some frequency, and the existence of the *Riming Poem* witnesses that the dominant poetic form could be expanded to embrace a different one. See further Donoghue ("Meter") and the works cited therein.

[40]As a way of illustrating one possible change that arises from the breakdown of 'classical' Old English meter, Cable turns to *Durham*, a poem which "shows a clear break from the classical meter of Old English poetry" (52), that, he argues, results from the poet's "misreading" (54) of the classical meter.

dentally) concomitant with the development of the post-traditional, literate author.

II

Within the English poetic tradition, Laȝamon, the author of the Middle English *Brut*—one of the earliest poems to appear in English following the Norman Conquest[41]—stands as the first unambiguous example of the literate authorial consciousness which emerges as a result of the cultural shift from orality to literacy. Although not much is known about the details of his life,[42] there is little doubt that Laȝamon was a literate author who was a proficient reader of at least two, and perhaps three, languages. The chief evidence for this is the poem's relationship to its primary text, the French *Roman de Brut* of Robert Wace, but Laȝamon himself points to both his linguistic ability and the literate nature of his endeavor. In the poem's prologue, after explicitly naming himself (something an oral poet need never do for he and his poem are inseparable),[43] Laȝamon states that his desire to tell the history of the kings of England impelled him to journey far and wide throughout the country in search of textual exemplars. After much searching, he continues, he finally acquired three suitable ones, one written in English, one in Latin, and one in French:

> He nom þa Englisca boc;   þa makede Seint Bede
> An-oþer he nom on Latin;   þe makede Seinte Albin
> And þe feire Austin . . .
> Boc he nom þe þridde;   leide þer amidden
> Þa makede a Frenchis clerc;
> Wace wes ihoten;   þe wel couþe writen.
>
> (16-21)[44]

[41]The poem appears to have been composed sometime between 1185 and 1216. Le Saux (1-13) provides a useful summary of the arguments concerning the poem's date.

[42]What little we do know of his life, coming as it does in the poem's prologue, must be treated with due caution.

[43]On this point, see Nagy.

[44]I cite Brook and Leslie's edition of the *Brut* throughout. All translations of the *Brut* are mine unless otherwise noted.

'He took the English book which St. Bede made and another he took in Latin, which St. Albin and the fair Austin made . . . . The third book he took, which he laid amid the others, was made by a French clerk named Wace who well knew how to write.'

Having presented us with this very clear model of literate—even scholarly—behavior, Laȝamon anchors his text yet more firmly to a literate poetics by briefly describing the mechanics underlying its physical production:

> Feþeren he nom mid fingren; 7 fiede on boc-felle.
> 7 þa soþere word; sette to-gadere.
> 7 þa þre boc; þrumde to are.
>
> (25-27)

'He seized a feather with his fingers and wrote on the book-skin, and those true words set together, and those three books compressed to one.'

The illuminated ornamental initial representing a monk busily engaged in copying or perhaps composing a text which marks the prologue's beginning in British Library MS Cotton Caligula A.ix, Laȝamon's figuring of his text as a "boc" to be "rede" by his audience, the fundamentally intertextual nature of his own compositional process,[45] and the demonstrable and far-reaching influence his chief source exerts over the poem's narrative shape complete the situation of the *Brut* within a highly self-conscious, literate poetics still recognizable to and shared by us today.

Yet certain aspects of the text's thematics, lexicon, syntax, metrics, and physical encoding in the manuscript paradoxically compel us to read against the accurate and careful depictions of literate production the poet and illuminator offer us. As a full treatment of all these matters lies beyond the scope of this introduction, in considering the text's mix of oral and literate poetics I will focus here only upon the physical evidence the Caligula manuscript affords us and that version's relationship to its primary source.[46]

[45]See Parks ("Song, Text" 106-108 and nn.) for a fuller discussion of the term "intertextuality."

[46]Recent studies of the poem's diction, lexicon, and syntax include Stanley; Iwasaki; and Amodio. British Library MS Cotton Otho C.xiii contains a version

In calling attention to the residual orality apparent in Old English manuscripts, Katherine O'Brien O'Keeffe has established that the manner in which vernacular poetry is physically encoded evidences the close, dynamic relationship between orality and developing literacy in the Anglo-Saxon period.[47] As we move beyond the Anglo-Saxon period, however, the representation of verse in manuscripts becomes quite fixed and we have no trouble discovering the antecedents of our contemporary conventions in manuscripts appearing soon after the Norman Conquest. Such things as spelling, punctuation, and capitalization do not become fully regularized until well after the medieval period draws to a close, but in terms of spatialization, that is, the identification of poetry as poetry through its specialized situation on the manuscript page, modern practice descends directly from that which dominates in the Middle English period. But even though they generally witness a higher degree of incipient textuality than their Anglo-Saxon predecessors, manuscripts of Middle English poems often prove important in helping us evaluate a text's poetics, especially when, as in the case of the *Brut*, the conflict between a poem's internal evidence (e.g., its indebtedness to written sources) and its physical encoding forces us to read the one against the other.

British Library MS Cotton Caligula A.ix is generally believed to date from the first half of the thirteenth century, a time when the conventions of representing vernacular poetry were still in flux. Presented in double columns throughout and written in two alternating hands, the *Brut* is, significantly, not formatted as poetry, an important matter which often goes unremarked.[48] Although it possesses punctuation which seems to mark half-lines,[49] the poem is represented in blocks of prose extending from the right to left margin in each column. By way

---

of the *Brut* that is generally believed to be somewhat later than that preserved in Caligula.

[47]See O'Keeffe (esp. 1-46). Kiernan also discusses the relationship between vernacular and Latin poetry ("Reading Cædmon's 'Hymn'").

[48]For example, neither Madden nor Le Saux mentions this in describing the Caligula version. Donoghue, citing Blake's remark that "the boundaries between poetry and prose were more flexible at that time" ("Laȝamon's Ambivalence" 538; citing Blake 120), reminds us that the "traditional distinction between verse and prose in this transitional period has come into question" (idem), but he too passes silently over the poem's physical encoding.

[49]Donoghue has recently argued that the poem is "copied with punctuation that distinguishes the caesura and the end of the full line" ("Laȝamon's Ambivalence" 539).

of contrast, the *Hule and Niȝtengale*, a poem roughly contemporary with the *Brut* which shows heavy French influence in its lexicon and meter, is clearly lineated as poetry.[50] That each line of verse in the *Hule* ends with a point followed by significant blank space further underscores its poetic status.

The *Brut*'s manuscript encoding fails to mark it unambiguously as poetry, but there seems little doubt as to how Laȝamon conceives his project. Following the prologue, the poem proper begins with the statement that "Nv seið mid loft-songe þe wes on leoden preost / al swa þe boc spekeð; þe he to bisne inom" (36-37), lines which a recent translator, Donald Bzdyl, renders as "Now Layamon, who was a priest in the land, will tell in stately words all that he found in his exemplars" (35). But translating the well attested Middle English compound "loft-song" as "stately words" instead of as "song of praise" suppresses Laȝamon's awareness of the orality which informs his endeavor.[51] And translating the line "al swa þe boc spekeð" as "all that he found in his exemplars" instead of the more literal "all that the books speak" further muffles the text's oral poetics.[52] It seems highly unlikely that this particular occurrence of what has been labelled the "trope of the Talking Book" (Gates 131) is meant to invoke the sort of fictional oral tradition which, for example, the poet of the much later *Sir Gawain and the Green Knight* strives to recall in using both this trope and the "I heard" formula so frequently found in Old English oral-derived poetry.[53] Even though the *Gawain*-poet consciously attempts to maintain the "fiction of oral transmission . . . throughout the poem," by its conclusion the poem's authority shifts away from the oral and becomes firmly and finally anchored in "the best boke of romaunce" (Ganim 71). In sharp

[50]The version of the *Hule* to which I refer here occupies folios 233-46 of British Library MS Cotton Caligula A.ix and is presented in facsimile in Ker. Interestingly, the *Brut*, a poem whose apparent 'Englishness' has long attracted scholarly comment, occupies the first 192 leaves of the same codex (Madden I xxxiv).

[51]Donoghue's translation of this phrase (539) accords with mine in echoing the *MED* citation for the compound 'lof-song' (L.5, 1147).

[52]Madden translates these lines less eloquently but more accurately as "Now saith with lofty song *he* who was priest on earth (*or* in *the* land) 'all' as the books speak that he took for pattern" (I 4).

[53]The talking book trope occurs in lines 690-91 of *Sir Gawain*: "Mony wylsum way he rode / Þe bok as I herde say." The other two references to books emphasize their written nature (2521; 2523). I cite Davis's edition of *Sir Gawain*. See also Parks ("Traditional Narrator").

contrast to the *Gawain*-poet, Laȝamon does not strip the oral tradition of its traditionality by cultivating it as, to use Franz Bäuml's formulation, "an implicit fictional 'character' of literacy" ("Unmaking of the Hero" 43); for Laȝamon, the link between oral and written poetic articulation has yet to be severed.

The *Brut*'s relationship to Wace's twelfth-century French *Roman de Brut* sheds further light on its oral poetics. Itself heavily dependent upon Geoffrey of Monmouth's *Historia Regum Britanniae*, the *Roman de Brut* has so influenced the shape of the *Brut*'s narrative that it seems entirely plausible that Laȝamon worked directly from a copy of the French text. The two poems' narratives correspond so closely that, as J.S.P. Tatlock has noted, it seems that Laȝamon "almost never inserts wholly new episodes or incidents" but rather amplifies "what he has found in Wace" (489). Håkan Ringbom similarly argues that "the completely new matter added by Lawman (i.e. episodes not even hinted at in Wace) amounts, at most, to a few hundred lines" (105).[54] Yet the order of events is virtually all that the English poet takes from the French text; Laȝamon "amplifies" his source by more than doubling its length.[55] He rejects Wace's highly regular octosyllabic couplets, substituting instead a versification whose principles have yet to be absolutely classified: Daniel Donoghue argues that the poem's meter "is looser than classical Old English verse and conforms somewhat to John C. Pope's definition of Ælfric's rhythmical prose" but adds that this definition fits only imperfectly because "within the same passage Laȝamon's verse form can show variations in the number of stressed syllables, in alliterative patterns, and in the use of rhyme" (539). The poem's metrical variations are considerable: sometimes verses conform to the model of the Old English four-beat alliterative line, sometimes they evidence tail-rhyme (if, following Frederic Madden, we print the text in short lines) or internal rhyme (if, following the poem's modern editors, G.L. Brook and Roy F. Leslie, we print it in long lines), sometimes verses rhyme and alliterate, and sometimes they do neither. Laȝamon also employs a conservative, highly traditional native lexicon very reminiscent of that employed in Old English oral-derived poetry. Even

[54]On the *Brut*'s relationship to its sources see Ringbom; Le Saux; and Donahue (68-162).

[55]Le Saux, however, argues for a close correspondence between Laȝamon's half-lines and Wace's octosyllabic couplets and suggests that Laȝamon's additions may be much smaller than previously believed (24-58).

though the *Brut* was composed during a time when French was radically reshaping the English word-stock, the poem's lexicon is strikingly free of French influence; by one count, both manuscripts of the poem, totalling approximately 30,000 long lines of poetry, contain only some 150 words of French derivation (Monroe).[56]

Rather than appealing, as is frequently done, solely to the poet's politics or his supposedly antiquarian sentiments as a way of explaining the *Brut*'s poetics,[57] we ought to consider as well the powerful influence oral poetics continued to exert over poetic articulation well into the Middle English period. For Laȝamon, as perhaps for many other Anglo-Saxon scribes/poets who were "conditioned by formulaic conventions" (O'Keeffe 41), poetic thought and poetic articulation are inextricably linked to a simultaneously determining and enabling oral poetics.[58] As a consideration of the *Brut*'s relationship to its primary source makes clear, Laȝamon does not merely and slavishly translate the *Roman de Brut*; rather, he recreates it. And in recreating it he employs the only poetic idiom at his disposal, that which descends from the English oral tradition. That he should so ably transform a metrically and lexically alien text into something so recognizably English is not surprising because the idiom of oral tradition—its thematics, diction, etc.—is

> not simply . . . [one] that allows convenient oral composition but [is] the equivalent of a critical methodology, evolved and practiced by a 'school' or 'interpretive community' unified by the act of (re-)making and (re-)reading traditional verbal art.
>
> (Foley, "Texts That Speak" 150)[59]

[56]Madden estimates that the Caligula MS contains less than fifty words of demonstrably French origin (xxii). Monroe discovers ninety-four words of French derivation in Caligula and a further sixty-four in Otho, making, he says, "a grand total of 158" (567).

[57]For the most recent study in this vein, see Donoghue ("Laȝamon's Ambivalence"). The best discussion of the poet's supposed antiquarianism remains Stanley. For a contrasting view of this matter, see Amodio ("Some Notes" 190-93).

[58]Le Saux has advanced the promising argument that Laȝamon's text is a "dynamic-equivalence translation," that is "one concerning which a bilingual and bicultural person can justifiably say, 'That is the way we would say it'" (26; citing Nida 166) but she offers no in-depth account of the poem's poetics.

[59]In arguing for the communal nature of the oral tradition's idiom, Foley thus develops Fish's notion that "the meanings and texts produced by an interpretive

To be a part of this community, Laȝamon need not have been tutored by an oral scop, nor need he even have been exposed to an active oral tradition.[60] O'Keeffe illuminates the process by which oral poetics may be preserved and transmitted through non-oral channels when she argues that the many "metrically, syntactically and semantically appropriate" variants contained in the manuscripts of Cædmon's *Hymn* bespeak "a . . . state between pure orality and pure literacy whose evidence is a *reading process* which applies oral techniques for the reception of a message to the decoding of a written text" (41; emphasis mine).[61] These "oral techniques" are not consciously cultivated as such: rather they result from the scribes/poets being "conditioned by formulaic conventions" (idem) as a consequence of their experience with oral and oral-derived texts, whether they read, copied, or took them down from dictation. Such conditioning occurred because the central affective, metonymic character of the oral tradition (something which insured its continued survival before the introduction of writing) does not vanish once the texts become encoded in manuscripts. The notion of "ballad competence" which Vésteinn Ólason derives from Chomskyan linguistics, recalling as it does Lord's seminal comments on the "grammar" of oral tradition (*Singer* 35-36), is most instructive here.[62] In considering how "Tristrams kvæði" could so completely adhere to the contours of the Icelandic ballad tradition despite being based on a written French "roman," Ólason suggests that when it

> was composed by someone who had either read the saga or heard it read or faithfully retold, what might be called ballad competence must have been alive in the Icelandic community; either the original composer had mastered it, or it was sufficiently alive in the audience to result in the adaptation of the song to ballad norms.
> (122)

---

community . . . do not proceed from an isolated individual but from a public and conventional point of view" (14). Cf. further Foley's comments in "Orality, Textuality" (esp. 38) on the nature and character of oral traditional idiom.

[60]For what is still the best account of how living oral traditions are transmitted across generations, see Lord (*Singer* 13-30).

[61]For an extended but largely unconvincing critique of the theory O'Keeffe advances, see Moffat (esp. 810-14.).

[62]See also Kellogg.

Laȝamon, in contrast, does not bring us as fully into the world of the medieval English oral tradition; his "oral traditional competence" is limited and in many ways reflects his situation at (if not beyond) the absolute limits of an active oral poetics (in the classical, performance-based sense).

The distinction Brian Stock draws between "traditional" and "traditionalistic" action may well prove most helpful as we attempt to sort out the complex poetics of the *Brut* and many other pre- and post-Conquest vernacular poems. "Traditional action," Stock explains, "is substantive. It consists of the habitual pursuit of inherited forms of conduct, which are taken to be society's norm. Traditionalistic action, by contrast, is the self-conscious affirmation of traditional norms. It is the establishment of such norms as articulated models for current and future behavior" (*Listening* 164). Although we should by no means wholly discount the possibility that Laȝamon engaged in "traditionalistic" action by *consciously* attempting to recreate the Anglo-Saxon poetic tradition based on his careful reading of Old English poetry and his absorption of the poetic principles informing it,[63] if we see him as a "traditional" poet, in Stock's sense of the term, we shall, as Renoir has remarked, "spare ourselves the frustration of looking for things that are not there while overlooking those that are" ("Oral-Formulaic Rhetoric" 135).

As I have tried to suggest briefly above, the complex weave of the *Brut*'s poetics evidences that the cultural shift from orality to literacy "is not a discrete and decisive shift but [is] rather a continuum of change" (Machan 229). This shift is not, as the romantic, evolutionary view suggests, a simple, clear-cut, and, most importantly, unidirectional movement towards social and cultural development but a dynamic and

[63]He may have had access to the library at Worcester which appears to have contained a sizable collection of Anglo-Saxon manuscripts during the twelfth and thirteenth centuries (Donoghue, "Laȝamon's Ambivalence" 541). But even if he did read extensively in these manuscripts, we would do well to remember that the codification of the Old English poetic system is fairly recent: no contemporary Anglo-Saxon account of the principles informing Old English verse has been discovered yet. For the view that Laȝamon's syntax is not the product of conscious archaizing on the poet's part, see Amodio ("Some Notes" 190-93). In contrast to the *Brut*'s "traditional" versification, the versification of *Sir Gawain and the Green Knight*, because it appears to have been "consciously selected from the fund of traditional knowledge in order to serve present needs" and thus stands as the "self-conscious affirmation of traditional norms" (Stock, *Listening* 164), is clearly "traditionalistic."

complicated process; both before and especially after the Conquest, orality and literacy interact and intersect in a host of complex and "vital ways, sometimes cooperatively, sometimes conflictively" (Doane xiii). Acknowledging the tension which informs the medieval oral-literate continuum will enable us to understand more clearly both the mix of oral and literate poetics we discover in a poem such as the *Brut* as well as the "cultural diglossia" central to medieval English society.[64]

III

Despite coming under intense cultural, linguistic, and perhaps political pressure, the oral poetics which provides a foundation for much of our extant Old English poetry does not vanish in the years following the Norman Conquest. But before we can arrive at a fuller understanding of the English oral tradition in the post-Conquest period a great deal of work needs to be done and some basic questions of influence (if the poets are working outside a firmly established and productive oral tradition, how are the mechanics of the tradition passed along?), of production (if the poem is composed without the attendant pressures of performance, what role do oral traditional metrics, formulas, type-scenes, etc. play?), of transmission (were poems read from manuscripts, were memorized versions recited, etc.?), of reception (do shifts in production and transmission result in a concomitant shift in the audience's horizon of expectations, or does it remain fairly stable? does the audience's role in shaping the narrative diminish or disappear completely?), and of definition (what does the phrase "oral tradition" mean in the increasingly literate context of the post-Conquest period?), to name but a few, all need to be answered. In considering these and many other issues from a rich variety of perspectives, the essays which follow seriously challenge some fundamental assumptions concerning the context and composition of English literature during one of the most important but least understood periods in English literary history.

Department of English
Vassar College

[64]See Stock (*Implications* 12-87); and Ziolkowski.

Works Cited

Amodio, Mark C. "Some Notes on Laȝamon's Use of the Synthetic Genitive." *Studia Neophilologica* 59 (1987): 187-94.

—. "Laȝamon's Anglo-Saxon Lexicon and Diction." *Poetica* 28 (1988): 48-59.

Bäuml, Franz. "The Unmaking of the Hero: Some Critical Implications of the Transition from Oral to Written Epic." *The Epic in Medieval Society*. Ed. Harald Scholler. Tübingen: Verlag, 1977. 86-99.

—. "Varieties and Consequences of Medieval Literacy and Illiteracy." *Speculum* 55 (1980): 237-65.

Benson, Larry D. ed. *The Riverside Chaucer*. 3rd ed. Boston: Houghton, 1987.

Bliss, Alan J. "An Introduction to Old English Metre." Intr. Daniel Donoghue. *OEN Subsidia* 20 (1993).

Brook, G.L and R.F. Leslie, eds. *Laȝamon*: Brut. EETS os 263, 277. Oxford: Oxford UP, 1963, 1978.

Bzdyl, Donald G., trans. *Layamon's* Brut. Binghamton: Medieval & Renaissance Texts and Studies, 1989.

Cable, Thomas. *The English Alliterative Tradition*. Philadelphia: U of Pennsylvania P, 1991.

Carruthers, Mary. *The Book of Memory: A Study of Memory in Medieval Culture*. Cambridge: Cambridge UP, 1990.

Chase, Colin, ed. *The Dating of* Beowulf. Toronto: U of Toronto P, 1981.

Chaytor, H.J. *From Script to Print: An Introduction to Medieval Literature*. Cambridge: Cambridge UP, 1945.

Clanchy, M.T. *From Memory to Written Record: England 1066-1307*. Cambridge, MA: Harvard UP, 1979.

Creed, Robert P. "The *Beowulf*-Poet: Master of Sound-Patterning." *Oral Traditional Literature: A Festschrift for Albert Bates*

Lord. Ed. John Miles Foley. Columbus: Slavica, 1981. 194-216.

Crowne, David K. "The Hero on the Beach: An Example of Composition by Theme in Anglo-Saxon Poetry." *Neuphilologische Mitteilungen* 61 (1960): 362-72.

Davis, Norman, ed. *Sir Gawain and the Green Knight*. 2nd ed. Oxford: Clarendon, 1967.

Doane, A.N. "Introduction." *Vox intexta: Orality and Textuality in the Middle Ages*. Ed. A.N. Doane and Carol Braun Pasternack. Madison: U of Wisconsin P, 1991. xi-xiii.

Donahue, Dennis P. *Lawman's* Brut, *An Early Arthurian Poem: A Study of Middle English Formulaic Composition*. Lewiston: Mellen, 1991.

Donoghue, Daniel. "Laȝamon's Ambivalence." *Speculum* 65 (1990): 537-63.

—. "Old English Meter." *ANQ* ns 3 (1990): 69-74.

Duggan, Joseph J. The Song of Roland: *Formulaic Style and Poetic Craft*. Berkeley: U of California P, 1973.

Finnegan, Ruth. *Oral Poetry: Its Nature, Significance and Social Context*. 1977. Bloomington: Indiana UP, 1992.

Fish, Stanley. *Is There a Text in This Class?* Cambridge, MA: Harvard UP, 1980.

Foley, John Miles. "The Traditional Oral Audience." *Balkan Studies* 18 (1977): 145-54.

—. "Reading the Oral Traditional Text: Aesthetics of Creation and Response." *Comparative Research on Oral Traditions: A Memorial for Milman Parry*. Ed. John Miles Foley. Columbus: Slavica, 1987. 185-212.

—. *The Theory of Oral Composition: History and Methodology*. Bloomington: Indiana UP, 1988.

—. *Traditional Oral Epic: The* Odyssey, Beowulf, *and the Serbo-Croatian Return Song*. Berkeley: U of California P, 1990.

—. *Immanent Art: From Structure to Meaning in Traditional Oral Epic*. Bloomington: Indiana UP, 1991.

—. "Orality, Textuality, and Interpretation." *Vox intexta: Orality and Textuality in the Middle Ages*. Ed. A.N. Doane and Carol Braun Pasternack. Madison: U of Wisconsin P, 1991. 34-45.

—. "Texts That Speak To Readers Who Hear: Old English Poetry and the Languages of Oral Tradition." *Speaking Two Languages:*

Traditional Disciplines and Contemporary Theory in Medieval Studies. Ed. Allen J. Frantzen. Albany: State U of New York P, 1991. 141-56.

—. "Word-Power, Performance, and Tradition." *Journal of American Folklore* 105 (1992): 275-301.

Foote, Shelby. *The Civil War: A Narrative*. 3 vols. New York: Random House, 1963.

Ganim, John M. *Style and Consciousness in Middle English Narrative*. Princeton: Princeton UP, 1983.

Gates, Henry Louis, Jr. *The Signifying Monkey*. Oxford: Oxford UP, 1988.

Greenfield, Stanley B. "The Formulaic Expression of the Theme of 'Exile' in Anglo-Saxon Poetry." *Speculum* 30 (1955): 200-06.

Grudin, Michaela Paasche. "Discourse and the Problem of Closure in the *Canterbury Tales*." *PMLA* 107 (1992): 1157-67.

Havelock, Eric A. *Preface to Plato*. Cambridge, MA: Harvard UP, 1963.

Hughes, Merritt Y., ed. *Paradise Lost*. New York: Macmillan, 1962.

Illich, Ivan. "A plea for research on lay literacy." *Literacy and Orality*. Ed. David R. Olson and Nancy Torrance. Cambridge: Cambridge UP, 1991. 28-46.

Irving, Edward B., Jr. *Rereading* Beowulf. Philadelphia: U of Pennsylvania P, 1989.

Iwasaki, Haruo. "A Peculiar Feature in the Word-Order of Layamon's *Brut*." *Geibun-Kenkyu* 26 (1968): 64-77.

—. "A Few Notes on the Vocabulary of Laȝamon's *Brut*." *Poetica* 24 (1986): 1-15.

Jabbour, Alan. "Memorial Transmission in Old English Poetry." *Chaucer Review* 3 (1969): 174-90.

Kellogg, Robert L. "The South Germanic Oral Tradition." *Franciplegius: Medieval and Linguistic Studies in Honor of Francis Peabody Magoun, Jr.* Ed. Jess B. Bessinger, Jr. and Robert P. Creed. New York: New York UP, 1965. 66-74.

Ker, N.R., ed. The Owl and the Nightingale: *Reproduced in Facsimile from the Surviving Manuscripts Jesus College Oxford 29 and British Museum Cotton Caligula A.ix*. EETS ns 251. London: Oxford UP, 1963.

Kiernan, Kevin S. Beowulf *and the* Beowulf *Manuscript*. New Brunswick: Rutgers UP, 1981.

—. "Reading Cædmon's "Hymn" with Someone Else's Glosses." *Representations* 32 (1990): 157-74.

Klaeber, Friederich, ed. Beowulf *and the* Fight at Finnsburg. 3rd ed. Lexington: Heath, 1950.

Lerer, Seth. *Literacy and Power in Anglo-Saxon Literature*. Lincoln: U of Nebraska P, 1991.

Le Saux, Françoise. *Layamon's* Brut: *The Poem and its Sources*. Cambridge: Brewer, 1989.

Lord, Albert B. *The Singer of Tales*. Cambridge, MA: Harvard UP, 1960.

—. "The Merging of Two Worlds: Oral and Written Poetry as Carriers of Ancient Values." *Oral Tradition in Literature*. Ed. John Miles Foley. Columbia: U of Missouri P, 1986. 19-64.

—. "The Nature of Oral Poetry." *Comparative Research on Oral Traditions: A Memorial for Milman Parry*. Ed. John Miles Foley. Columbus: Slavica, 1987. 313-49.

McGillivray, Murray. *Memorization in the Transmission of the Middle English Romances*. New York: Garland, 1990.

Machan, Tim William. "Editing, Orality, and Late Middle English Texts." *Vox intexta: Orality and Textuality in the Middle Ages*. Ed. A.N. Doane and Carol Braun Pasternack. Madison: U of Wisconsin P, 1991. 229-45.

Madden, Frederic, ed. *Laȝamons* Brut. 3 vols. London: Taylor, 1847.

Magoun, Francis Peabody, Jr. "The Oral-Formulaic Character of Anglo-Saxon Narrative Poetry." *Speculum* 28 (1953): 446-67. Rpt. in *An Anthology of* Beowulf *Criticism*. Ed. Lewis E. Nicholson. Notre Dame: U of Notre Dame P, 1963. 189-221.

—. "The Theme of the Beasts of Battle in Anglo-Saxon Poetry." *Neuphilologische Mitteilungen* 56 (1955): 81-90.

Moffat, Douglas. "Anglo-Saxon Scribes and Old English Verse." *Speculum* 67 (1992): 805-27.

Monroe, Benton S. "French Words in Laȝamon." *Modern Philology* 4 (1907): 559-67.

Nagy, Gregory. *Pindar's Homer: the lyric possession of an epic past*. Baltimore: Johns Hopkins UP, 1990.

Niles, John D. Beowulf: *The Poem and Its Tradition*. Cambridge, MA: Harvard UP, 1983.

—. "Toward an Anglo-Saxon Oral Poetics." *De Gustibus: Essays for Alain Renoir*. Ed. John Miles Foley. New York: Garland, 1992. 359-77.

—. "Oral Poetry Acts." Div. on Old English Language and Literature, MLA Convention. New York, 27 Dec. 1992.

—. "Locating *Beowulf* in Literary History." *Exemplaria* 5 (1993): 79-109.

O'Keeffe, Katherine O'Brien. *Visible Song: Transitional Literacy in Old English Verse*. Cambridge: Cambridge UP, 1990.

Ólason, Vésteinn. "Literary Backgrounds of the Scandinavian Ballad." *The Ballad and Oral Literature*. Ed. Joseph Harris. Cambridge, MA: Harvard UP, 1991. 116-38.

Olsen, Alexandra Hennessey. *Speech, Song, and Poetic Craft: The Artistry of the Cynewulf Canon*. New York: Lang, 1984.

Olson, David R. and Nancy Torrance. "Introduction." *Literacy and Orality*. Ed. David R. Olson and Nancy Torrance. Cambridge: Cambridge UP, 1991. 1-7.

Ong, Walter J. *Orality and Literacy: The Technologizing of the Word*. London: Methuen, 1982.

—. "Orality, Literacy, and Medieval Textualization." *New Literary History* 16 (1984): 1-12.

Parks, Ward. "The Oral-Formulaic Theory in Middle English Studies." *Oral Tradition* 1 (1986): 636-94.

—. "The Traditional Narrator and the 'I Heard' Formulas in Old English Poetry." *Anglo-Saxon England* 16 (1987): 45-66.

—. "Song, Text, and Cassette: Why We Need Authoritative Audio Editions of Medieval Literary Works." *Oral Tradition* 7 (1992): 102-15.

Pearsall, Derek. "The Origins of the Alliterative Revival." *The Alliterative Tradition in the Fourteenth Century*. Ed. Bernard S. Levy and Paul E. Szarmach. Kent: Kent State UP, 1981.

Quinn, William A. and Audley S. Hall. *Jongleur: A Modified Theory of Oral Improvisation and Its Effects on the Performance and Transmission of Middle English Romance*. Washington, DC: UP of America, 1982.

Reichl, Karl. "The Middle English Popular Romance." *The Ballad and Oral Literature*. Ed. Joseph Harris. Cambridge, MA: Harvard UP, 1991. 243-68.

Renoir, Alain. "Oral-Formulaic Theme Survival: A Possible Instance in the *Nibelungenlied.*" *Neuphilologische Mitteilungen* 65 (1964): 70-75.

—. "Oral Theme and Written Texts." *Neuphilologische Mitteilungen* 77 (1976): 337-46.

—. "Oral-Formulaic Rhetoric and the Interpretation of Literary Texts." *Oral Tradition in Literature*. Ed. John Miles Foley. Columbia: U of Missouri P, 1986. 103-35.

—. *A Key to Old Poems: The Oral-Formulaic Approach to the Interpretation of West-Germanic Verse*. University Park: Pennsylvania State UP, 1988.

Ringbom, Håkan. *Studies in the Narrative Techniques of* Beowulf *and Lawman's* Brut. *Acta Academiae Aboensis*, ser. A 36, 1968.

Saenger, Paul. "Silent Reading: Its Impact on Late Medieval Script and Society." *Viator* 13 (1982): 367-414.

—. "The separation of words and the physiology of reading." *Literacy and Orality*. Ed. David R. Olson and Nancy Torrance. Cambridge: Cambridge UP, 1991. 198-214.

Sanders, Barry. "Lie it as it plays: Chaucer becomes an author." *Literacy and Orality*. Ed. David R. Olson and Nancy Torrance. Cambridge: Cambridge UP, 1991. 111-28.

Schaefer, Ursula. "Hearing from Books: The Rise of Fictionality in Old English Poetry." *Vox intexta: Orality and Textuality in the Middle Ages*. Ed. A.N. Doane and Carol Braun Pasternack. Madison: U of Wisconsin P, 1991. 117-36.

—. "Alterities: On Methodology in Medieval Literary Studies." *Oral Tradition* 8 (1993): 187-214.

Spearing, A.C. *Criticism and Medieval Poetry*. New York: Barnes and Noble, 1972.

Stanley, E.G. "Laȝamon's Antiquarian Sentiments." *Medium Ævum* 38 (1969): 23-37.

Stock, Brian. *The Implications of Literacy: Written Language and Models of Interpretation in the Eleventh and Twelfth Centuries*. Princeton: Princeton UP, 1983.

—. *Listening for the Text: On the Uses of the Past*. Baltimore: Johns Hopkins UP, 1990.

Tatlock, J.S.P. *The Legendary History of Britain*. Berkeley: U of California P, 1950.

Thomas, Rosalind. *Oral tradition and written record in classical Athens*. Cambridge: Cambridge UP, 1989.
Tompkins, Jane P., ed. *Reader-Response Criticism*. Baltimore: Johns Hopkins UP, 1980.
Travis, Peter W. "Affective Criticism, the Pilgrimage of Reading, and Medieval English Literature." *Medieval Texts and Contemporary Readers*. Ed. Laurie A. Finke and Martin B. Shichtman. Ithaca: Cornell UP, 1987. 201-15.
Ziolkowski, Jan. "Cultural Diglossia and the Nature of Medieval Latin Literature." *The Ballad and Oral Literature*. Ed. Joseph Harris. Cambridge, MA: Harvard UP, 1991. 193-213.
Zumthor, Paul. *La lettre et la voix: De la "littérature" médiévale*. Paris: Éd. Seuil, 1987.

Introduction to the Individual Contributions

Sarah Gray Miller

Few modern scholars will deny the influence of oral tradition on Middle English literature, and many agree that the shift from orality to literacy was a gradual one, not to be viewed in the strict black and white terms of yesterday. Despite this general consensus, Mark C. Amodio, in his introduction to the collection, argues that "Middle English literature has consistently been situated at the very periphery of oral studies" (1), and it is this deficiency that the contributors to *Oral Poetics in Middle English Poetry* attempt to redress. Though their topics range from the romance genre to Chaucer's *Canterbury Tales*, the following essays share the aims of exploring, defining, and tracing the complex relationship between the emerging literate tradition and its receding oral ancestor in the centuries following the Norman Conquest.

In "Literacy, Orality, and the Poetics of Middle English Romance," the first of three essays devoted to the romance, Nancy Mason Bradbury works through two important lines of inquiry in an effort to diffuse the literate bias which has caused many to dismiss the Middle English romances. After first asking how we go about discerning the oral nature of a given romance (since the only records of the genre are, of course, written), Bradbury develops a new set of tools which will enable critics in a literate society to understand more fully the orality informing many Middle English romances.

Bradbury stresses the importance of medieval sources which repeatedly mention minstrel recitation and calls upon manuscript variation that appears to be the result of memorial transmission instead of scribal emendation. She grants that the scribe does appeal to memory when transcribing page by page but argues that this could not account for what Murray McGillivray refers to as "memorial transfer," the process by which passages "at a considerable remove from one another" are conflated (46). Bradbury also suggests comparing the piece in question with one that we know is written and illustrates her claims by considering variations evident in the multiple manuscripts of the *Seege* or *Batayle of Troye*.

After pointing to the biases, literate and otherwise, which have kept many from situating memorial transmission in its proper cultural setting, Bradbury suggests that a knowledge of oral-formulaic theory and an understanding of the extratextual resonances that accompany an oral performance will curb the prejudices of the literate critic. She proposes that critics pay close attention to the use of "resinging," a narrative device through which the same event is related at different times and from different perspectives, arguing that we ought to view this not as inept repetition but a "mark of skill." Bradbury also illustrates the need for an increased awareness of the methods used in Middle English romances to emphasize the "emotional core of a received story" (62). Employing these suggestions as a starting point, Bradbury ultimately calls for a new poetics of the Middle English romance, in which critics must lay aside their "postwar aesthetic judgments" (64) in order to view the romances through the "lens" of orality.

Alexandra Hennessey Olsen similarly examines the relationship between oral transmission and the Middle English romance but focuses her attention on a specific example in "Oral Tradition in the Middle English Romance: The Case of *Robert of Cisyle*." Olsen, using the older Vernon manuscript of *Robert* as a control, studies the variations in the Trinity Dublin abridgement and the longer Cambridge version as a way of uncovering the residual orality informing the romance. But before attempting this, Olsen first carefully distinguishes between oral improvisation and scribal emendation: as she argues, oral improvisors "substituted words when they forgot the exact wording of a line but remembered the sense of it" (73), whereas scribal variations tend to reveal the scribe's aesthetic preferences. Through her detailed study of the treatment of the poem's rhyming couplets in the abridged and received versions of the poem, Olsen convincingly establishes that the variations among the manuscripts arise from changes made during oral recitation, which were later recorded.

In the final essay concerning the Middle English romance, "Tradition and Heroism in the Middle English Romances," Dave Henderson also examines the "transitional texts" of this genre, which range from the very traditional, or more formulaic works to the less traditional, or more literate ones. Employing *King Horn*, *Havelok the Dane*, and *Sir Gawain and the Green Knight*, he sets up a framework for determining the degree of traditionality in a given text. Though Henderson, like Bradbury and Olsen, examines the use of performative techniques in these texts, he shifts the focus toward the different meanings and characterizations that accompany varying degrees of traditionality.

Both *Horn* and *Havelok*, with their dependence on such things as the return song narrative pattern and the technique of poetic variation, typify the traditional romance. According to Henderson, more important than the use of poetic devices in determining traditionality, however, is the characterization of the heroes in these texts. Both Horn and Havelok are flawless and, therefore, heavy, one-dimensional characters. Henderson locates *Gawain*, a much more ambiguous romance, on the opposite end of the spectrum. Unlike *Horn* and *Havelok*, *Gawain* abandons the traditional heroic code and focuses on the imperfections and self-doubt of its hero. Furthermore, the definitions of good and evil are more sophisticated in *Gawain*: the Green Knight is not only an atypical villain, he's somewhat likable.

Henderson is quick to admit that not all of the Middle English romances are so easily classified, but demonstrates how the extremes of *Horn* and *Havelok* and *Gawain* can be applied to other works. *Amis and Amiloun*, for example, upholds the traditional heroic definition of true friendship, yet the plot also includes religious allegory and such ambiguous moments as the undeserved punishment of several characters. Thus *Amis and Amiloun*, like most other Middle English romances, falls somewhere between *Horn* and *Havelok* and *Gawain* on the spectrum of traditionality.

In "The Devil's Writing Lesson," John M. Ganim explores the dynamic interplay between orality and literacy as it surfaces in the tension between popular and official culture in the early fourteenth century. By focusing initially on a scene in Robert Mannyng of Brunne's *Handlyng Synne* involving "janglyng" in church and the failed efforts of a devil to transcribe the gossip, Ganim illustrates the ways the poem "coopt[s] the anarchic urges of popular culture to the moral guardianship of official culture, at the same time that the excesses of official culture are moderated by the festive laughter of popular culture" (114). *Handlyng Synne*'s status as a confession manual makes its relationship to speech especially important, and Ganim depicts confession as a pointed instance of the official culture's attempt to control the popular culture, as the former appropriates the orality of the latter in an effort to moderate it. Although speech in Mannyng's narratives is very powerful (it possesses the ability to thwart the devil, after all), Ganim concludes that the aim of Mannyng's narratives is not to glorify the spoken word but to demonstrate the need for controlling it.

The following essays by Leslie K. Arnovick, Ward Parks, and Seth Lerer share a common focus in that they all explore some of the ways in which the oral tradition functions in Chaucer's *Canterbury Tales*, yet each takes a sharply different perspective on this issue. Arnovick, in "Dorigen's Promise and Scholars Premise: The Orality of the Speech Act in the *Franklin's Tale*," examines the conversation between Dorigen and Aurelius in the garden, a moment of dialogue within the larger dialogue among the pilgrims. Employing the intersecting "oral realms" of linguistic, legal, and folkloric tradition, Arnovick attempts to discern whether or not Dorigen's speech actually constitutes a promise to Aurelius. In applying speech act theory to the dialogue between Dorigen and Aurelius, Arnovick demonstrates the need for examining the larger discourse surrounding Dorigen's so-called promise. What appears to be Dorigen's "pledge," Arnovick argues, is merely "a secondary speech act embedded within the first" (134). Though Dorigen's "promise" appears linguistically sound, Arnovick llustrates the necessity of looking beyond "the conventionalized form of her 'pledge' in lines 997-98" (130).

Placing Dorigen's speech against the social background of legal tradition, Arnovick proves that Dorigen could not have been legally bound to commit adultery and that rashly made promises were not considered legally binding contracts. Furthermore, Arnovick, by situating Dorigen's dilemma within the folkloric tradition, explains that the rash promise in the *Franklin's Tale* "allies itself with motifs and tales exploring the power of language" (141). Thus, the folk audience's familiarity with the outcome of this kind of tale greatly diminishes the seriousness of the pledge for them; they know at the outset that Dorigen will not have to keep her "promise" to Aurelius. The evidence available for coming to terms with Dorigen's speech is ultimately contradictory and ambiguous, but Arnovick adds, this may be the point. Chaucer may be revealing "as he does so many times elsewhere, the ambiguity of something so seemingly certain"(142-43).

In "Oral Tradition and the *Canterbury Tales*," Ward Parks also examines the question of orality in the *Canterbury Tales* and suggests that the work be viewed as "a literate author's representation of the proceedings of an oral tradition" (150). After all, Parks explains, the work is presented as the written record of stories composed spontaneously and told aloud, and many of the tales contain formulaic elements reminiscent of oral poetic performances. Emphasizing the probability that Chaucer came into contact with various oral traditions, Parks notes that, at the very least, Chaucer wrote in a period in which the oral poetic tradition remained interwoven with the growing trend toward literacy. Although Chaucer undoubtedly leans toward the literate side of this spectrum, Parks argues that Chaucer's relationship to orality is complex, being "sometimes sympathetic and sometimes critical" (158). In order to illustrate the ways in which orality and literacy interact within the *Tales*, Parks turns to *Sir Thopas* because it satirizes the English metrical romance, a genre which "was more deeply rooted in orality than was the continental literary tradition out of which Chaucer's own work for the most part grows" (158).

In demonstrating the differences between an oral performance and a literary work, Parks points out that in an oral performance certain inconsistencies are easily passed over but, when permanently fixed in a text, they stand as glaring mistakes. Because much of an oral performance depends on recollections shared by poet and audience which are outside the actual performance, once the poem becomes textualized and is "stripped of its extratextual resonances, [it] is liable to seem disconnected and full of holes" to the reader (163). This, Parks claims, is what happens in *Sir Thopas*: Chaucer places oral-derived styles and formulas in a textual setting where they become open to criticism.

Thopas' storyteller repeatedly fails to organize narrative formulas into a coherent tale, and stock themes set up expectations that the story never fulfills. Some of these inconsistencies may not have seriously damaged an oral performance, but "the textualization of an originally oral form of poetic narrative has ruptured that consensus that would supply a traditional coherency overriding temporary narrative breakdowns" (166). The tale of *Sir Thopas* ultimately falls to pieces, and Parks argues that the storyteller's failure causes the breakdown of the story to look like the breakdown of the oral-derived formulaic style, a style that "[t]o Chaucer and a growing class of literate brethren . . . had become cliché" (166). This tension between literacy and orality is evident throughout the *Tales* and can be seen in the *General Prologue*, where a literate and learned Chaucer positions himself as the mere recorder of oral performance. "Thus," Parks writes, "wittingly or unwittingly, the orality-literacy dynamic with all its cultural resonances insinuates itself into the basic conceit on which the *Canterbury Tales* is founded" (173).

In the final essay devoted to the notion of orality in the *Canterbury Tales*, "'Now holde youre mouth': The Romance of Orality in the *Thopas-Melibee* Section of the *Canterbury Tales*," Seth Lerer also examines this "orality-literacy dynamic" as it applies to *Sir Thopas*, but he contrasts *Thopas*, which he characterizes as a parody of rambling orality, with the *Melibee*, a more serious and literary tale. In arguing that the *Thopas* becomes a story more concerned with its narrator than its protagonist, Lerer claims that the storyteller's constant interruptions and his reliance on stereotypical devices direct the audience's attention away from the story at hand. Central to Lerer's analysis of *Thopas* is the concept of *inventio*, or "finding," a term with which Chaucer would have been familiar: *inventio* refers to "the rhetorical discovery of topics as well as the narrative discovery of objects" (186). The *Thopas*, then, may be seen as a romance of *inventio*, in which both narrator and Thopas "go in search of something they will never find" (188).

For Lerer, the move from the *Thopas* to the *Melibee* embodies the growth from childish orality to the more serious literacy of adulthood. In *Thopas*, both its protagonist and its narrator appear childlike when reprimanded by the giant Olifaunt and Harry Bailly, respectively, and the childish nature of the tale is reinforced by the fact that the medieval romance narrative belongs, according to Lerer, to the "categories of boys' books" (191). The *Melibee*, in contrast, is an adult story more written than told. Here, the narrator recedes behind the action of the story, and, within the tale, Prudence not only reads but quotes from literary sources: "it would appear that Prudence can barely open her mouth without quoting a text or citing an authority" (196). The stress then is placed not just upon reading, but reading "appropriatively," as Prudence has the ability to match the quotation with the situation at hand. Thus, Lerer concludes, the adult Prudence and the invisible narrator of her story have outgrown the once giant Harry Bailly, who does not understand the *Melibee* and now appears "far beneath the Chaucerian narrator in self-awareness" (198).

In "*Wyrchipe*: The Clash of Oral-Heroic and Literate-Ricardian Ideals in the Alliterative *Morte Arthure*," Donna Lynne Rondolone considers the transition from orality to literacy as it emerges in the early-fifteenth century poem, and she credits much of the scholarly disagreement surrounding the poem as arising from the tension between these two very different heroic codes which inform *Morte Arthure*. For Rondolone, this tension is clearly rooted in the larger cultural setting in which the poet composed. She argues that the kinesthetic nature of oral performance and the stress placed on memory keep a member of an oral society from thinking through inner conflict, so he or she works it out through concrete action instead. Furthermore, in an oral setting, people cannot separate ideas from objects or the divine from the human and, consequently, see themselves as undifferentiated from the cosmos. Thus the oral-heroic ideal stresses action, not thought, and god-like self-possession, rather than deference to a higher power. The literate Ricardian ideal, on the other hand, is exemplified in a hero such as Gawain. Rondolone, building upon the work of Eric Havelock and Walter J. Ong, asserts that the advent of literacy removes a large burden from the memory, and the mind evolves "from an embattled contestant into a dispassionate intellect free to reflect and develop the skills of abstraction and analysis" (212). Humanity initially sees itself as separate from the cosmos, and, as religion expands, comes to see itself as powerless against the divine.

As society moves from oral to literate communication, these two separate heroic codes surface in *Morte Arthure*, and Rondolone provides a theoretical framework for this tension in her discussion of *wyrchipe*, which is both an Old and Middle English concept. For the oral hero, *wyrchipe* "is both the integrity of the hero's will, the impenetrability of his self-possession, and others' recognition that the hero's personal power guarantees the integrity and safety of his social order" (224). The word takes on a different meaning, though, in the literate-Ricardian ethic, and is used in relation to God, who "is not defined through concrete action. While his grace has efficacy, we cannot watch it work" (225). Rondolone concludes that, because of its different meanings to oral and literate societies, *wyrchipe* is central to the orality/literacy conflict which, in *Morte Arthure*, ultimately becomes the struggle between the god-like Arthur and the abstract, literate concept of God.

In the final essay in this collection, "The Alliterative *Morte Arthure* As a Witness to Epic," Britton J. Harwood also examines the tensions between orality and literacy that shape the poem. However, unlike Rondolone who sees these tensions emerge in the shifting definition of the hero, Harwood examines the form in which the poet composed, the epic, and its relation to preliterate society.

The Alliterative *Morte Arthure* presents a paradox: although the poet draws on a number of written sources, the poem also seems to have been composed orally. In fact, according to James Johnson and Valerie Krishna, *Morte Arthure* comes closer to meeting Milman Parry's criteria for oral composition (e.g. pervasive parataxis, formulaic density, and formulaic thrift) than *Beowulf* does. Harwood points out, though, that the poet's literacy is evident in his use of formulas, which often indicate the literate habits of planning and consistency. How then, do we reconcile this written work with its oral tendencies? Harwood suggests we view the poem as a written simulacrum of orality and argues that "[i]t seems to be oral because the poet wishes it to appear that way" (247).

Harwood further asserts that the Morte Arthure has the feel of an orally composed work because the poet is imitating both the form and function of epic poetry, which often served as what Havelock called a tribal encyclopedia for preliterate societies. In other words, in the absence of widespread literacy, the epic maintains a culture's social, political, and legal customs, and it does this through digressions which record, or catalogue, important features of a society. Harwood notes that *Morte Arthure* has often been criticized for its digressions, but suggests that they are central to the poem's poetics; it is within the "digressions" that the poet is able to convey a great deal of culturally significant information.

Harwood's comparison of *Morte Arthure* with the written texts from which the poet worked illustrates the ways in which the poem serves to preserve cultural norms in late-medieval England. Each time the poet borrows from and modifies another chronicle, he does so in the interest of explaining and defending the socio-political mores of late fourteenth century England. Harwood asserts that in doing this, the *Morte Arthure*-poet also ends up defending the upper classes against the peasantry. In fact, almost all of the *Morte Arthure*-poet's changes serve the purpose of reinforcing class hierarchies, and Harwood concludes his essay with an examination of class conflict and how it surfaces in two of the poem's episodes: Arthur's fight with the Giant and his dream of the fight between the bear and the dragon. For Harwood, these incidents are particularly significant, perhaps "the foyer of the poem": in fulfilling their acculturating functions, the "fight between dragon and bear is class warfare, interpreted from one side" (277), and the fight with the giant witnesses the poem's ideological triumph "over the peasantry, [while] sublimely ignoring the contradiction that it tries to place a historical group outside culture" (278).

As Amodio has noted above, "a great deal of work needs to be done" (21) on the medieval oral-literate nexus; taken as a whole, the essays which comprise this volume constitue a major step toward understanding the dynamic and complex interplay between orality and literacy in the years following the Norman Conquest.

Vassar College

Literacy, Orality, and the Poetics of Middle English Romance

Nancy Mason Bradbury

Literary scholars are at a point of decision, it seems, in approaching medieval English narrative, especially those anonymous narratives loosely known as the Middle English romances. While one group of scholars investigates the importance of their residual orality, another argues for treating the marks of oral delivery found in these poems as a literary motif, a narrative strategy like any other chosen by a writer to appeal to a private reader.[1] The critics who argue against the importance or likelihood of oral performance are of course correct in pointing out that we have the texts of these tales, while the performances are lost. They are also correct in pointing out that the atmosphere of performance has been encoded into the written text, whether an oral recitation ever took place at all. Because our tools for analysis and our aesthetic preferences are adapted to the written word, our task as critics is certainly simpler if we assume that in fourteenth-century English narrative we have a thor-

[1]For a survey of investigations of residual orality, see Parks ("Oral-Formulaic Theory"). For the myth, fiction, or literary motif argument, see Mehl (8-12); Hirsh (342); Pearsall ("The *Troilus* Frontispiece"); Fewster (22-28); and Taylor (62). Taylor's richly documented argument appeared as mine was completed. For the purposes of this essay, I follow convention in using "Middle English romance" to refer to the large and varied corpus of anonymous narratives written in English between 1225 and 1550. They are listed chronologically in Severs (I: 13-16).

oughly literary product which for historical reasons carries some superficial conventions of oral address.

But a provocative body of scholarship now exists to show that in the Middle Ages the written word and the voice are not to be understood simply as alternative physical means of transmitting the same message. From a growing variety of premises, the conclusion drawn is that oral modes of thought and expression are distinct from written ones in ways important to all aspects of literary study. As long ago as 1957, Northrop Frye argued that the ultimate determinant of genre was the "radical of presentation" or the situation of the author either as speaker to a present audience—"*epos*"— or as a generator of pages to be read by silent readers—"fiction" (246-51). A large and varied corpus, the so-called Middle English romances present notorious problems of genre, and surely one reason for this is their origin in an era in which *epos* was gradually giving way to fiction.[2]

As it forces us to rethink our notions of genre, the new work in literacy and orality requires that we revise our understanding even of concepts as basic as author, audience, and text.[3] The major legacy of the Parry/Lord hypothesis to medieval studies will very likely be its demonstration of the link between orality and multiformity, the simple but crucial recognition that in an oral culture, one finds not variants on a fixed original, but poems and narratives that exist only as variants. Parry's and Lord's discoveries about primary orality require considerable modification, however, to suit the complex interactions of oral and literate modes of thought and expression found in medieval Europe. A useful extension of the vital concept of multiformity into the realm of writing is Paul Zumthor's "mouvance," the continual interaction among versions, the 'fundamental instability' that we find in the written remains of medieval orality (*Essai* 70-74). Another important extension of multiformity into manuscript culture is John Miles Foley's characterization of "traditional referentiality," the way in which what may appear to us to be inartistically repetitive structures in a text can convey a rich fund of extratextual, associative meanings, drawn from the many

[2]For heroic attempts to deal with the generic problems posed by the romances, see Pearsall ("Development of Middle English Romance"); Strohm; Mehl; and Fewster. Fewster's bibliography lists many works seeking to define such subgenres as alliterative romance, tail rhyme romance, and Breton *lai*.

[3]For varying perspectives on this basic argument, see Lord (*Singer*); Jauss; Zumthor (*Introduction*); and Ong.

occurrences of these structures in the tradition as a whole. According to Foley, traditional referentiality persisted in a manuscript culture like that of medieval England because "it offered a dependable and cherished way to summon meaning, a method that was in some aspects inimitable in the incipient world of textuality" (xv).

The tangled threads of literacy and orality are difficult to unwind at the distance of six centuries and more, and the influence of orality of some sort upon any written document is notoriously hard to prove, as is the very existence of an oral tradition when one's records are in writing. There is, however, more than enough evidence to support the modest assertion that the context for the anonymous Middle English romances is not a "basically competent hack professionalism," as one literary history of the period has it (Pearsall, *Poetry* 148), but rather a lively interaction of writing, memory, and limited improvisation. The history of the romances bears out Brian Stock's claim that the great transition in the Middle Ages "was not so much from oral *to* written as from an earlier state, predominantly oral, to various combinations of oral *and* written" (*Implications* 9). By embodying the combined effects of improvisation, memory, performance, and writing, the romances re-enact for us the complexities of late medieval orality and literacy.

Regarding the oral survivals in medieval romance as one literary device among others thus seems an inadequate response to the arguments for the special significance even of residual orality. If, as Stock argues, "the central problem in the Middle Ages is the relation of orality to a world making ever-increasing use of texts" (*Listening* 35), then it seems ill-advised to collapse the reminders of oral ancestry into literary devices. Derek Brewer remarks that "no branch of literature in our history has suffered more from novel-centered theories of reading or expectation than the medieval romances" ("Medieval Literature" 250). If we make no effort to grapple with their oral and traditional affiliations, these narratives, so representative of the era that produced them, will undoubtedly suffer more. But how best to respond to these challenges, which seem to me to be more acknowledged than acted upon? We might follow the lead suggested by Foley:

> Instead of looking at oral and orally derived poems through the interposed lens of literary values and assumptions, and consequently finding aesthetic inquiries stalled, we must begin at a much more fundamental level by

determining how these poems convey meaning.
(xii)

Foley's words raise at least two important issues. First, his argument concerns Homeric and Germanic epic, traditions at considerable remove from the metrical romances of medieval England. Insights about the lasting effects of oral ancestry can only be useful to students of the later Middle Ages if they are situated in appropriate generic, historical, and cultural contexts. What evidence is there that the Middle English romances are orally derived in ways that matter for critical purposes? Second, what lens are we to substitute for the "lens of literary values and assumptions," the only lens that most of us have ever been trained to use? These two questions govern the inquiry that follows.

To begin with the issue of why we might consider the English romances to have been orally derived, we can look briefly at the question of their genesis and transmission. Some romances demonstrably came into English in written form: they translate extant French works almost line by line (Baugh "Middle English Romance"). But, in general, we may have overworked the lost French original as a hypothesis, and written origins do not necessitate exclusively written transmission. Many modern scholars have remained highly skeptical of the role of professional performers in the dissemination of the metrical romances, whether we imagine them reading from manuscripts or reciting from memory (Mehl 7-13 and refs.). This skepticism is in part a reaction against the excesses of romantic medievalism with its uncritical vision of merry minstrels spreading mirth and tales throughout the land. The term "minstrel" itself may be ill-chosen, since in Middle English it generally means "musician" (Greene cxxxv ff.). But a variety of medieval sources, especially devotional works, criticize *disours*, *seggers*, *rymours*, or *geestours* in terms sufficiently specific to show that it is to tellers of secular stories, not simply to musicians and ruffians, that they object. J.A. Burrow responds aptly to what he calls "a distinct counter-romantic bias" on the part of modern scholars against the possibility of oral performance, observing that "if the 'geestour' or 'disour' was as unimportant a person as these writers suggest, it is hard to understand why the sources mention him so often" (*Ricardian Poetry* 13, 146n8).[4]

[4]Chestnutt makes this argument in more detail. See also Edwards, who regards the minstrel as "the prime agent of romance transmission" (93).

It is also hard to imagine why both Robert Mannyng and the author of the *Speculum Vitae* seek so strenuously to disassociate themselves from minstrel recitation if such a practice were not well known to them and to their audiences:

> I mad noght for no disours,
> Ne for no seggers, no harpours . . . .
> (*Chronicle* 75-76)

> I warne ȝow ferst at þe begynning,
> I wil make no veyn spekyng
> Of dedes of armes ne of amours,
> Os don mynstreles and oþer gestours
> Þat make spekyng in many a place
> Of Octouian and Isanbrace
> And of many oþer gestes,—
> And namely whan þei come to festes,
> Ne of Beus of Hamptoun,
> Þat was a knyght of gret renoun,
> Ne of sir Gy of Warewyk
> Al þow it mowe some men like
> . . . .
> For I holde þat nowht bot vanyte.
> (*Speculum Vitae* 35-48)[5]

The *Speculum Vitae* is not the only contemporary source to mention specific romances by name, and a number of these romances survive to us in just the sort of widely-varying manuscript versions that have given rise to the whole question of oral transmission. Although his work on the romances is otherwise exemplary, I do not believe, for example, that sufficient evidence exists to justify Dieter Mehl's argument that the versions of tales specifically described by contemporary sources as oral recitations "could hardly have been like those that were finally written down in some comparatively careful collection, but were probably much shorter and clumsier" (9). The assumption that orally performed versions must necessarily be relatively short and clumsy seems to me to illustrate the modern bias toward familiar, literate means of composition and dissemination.

[5]I cite Furnivall's edition of Robert Mannyng's *Chronicle*. The *Speculum Vitae* as quoted by Baugh ("Middle English Romance" 10). Baugh's article is a particularly important contribution to the questions under discussion here.

Reluctant to grant much importance to oral performers, modern scholars have been even more unwilling to acknowledge memory as an important factor in romance transmission, in part because we tend greatly to underestimate the capacity for memorization possible in a culture far less literate than our own. When Petrarch, whose own memory was probably developed far beyond most of ours, speaks of "a great memory . . . and even greater audacity" as a characteristic of the professional storytellers of his day, he is very likely remarking on a faculty quite extraordinary by modern standards (Baugh, "Middle English Romance" 4). E.B. Vitz calls attention to the outrageous claims made by the interlocutors of the anonymous thirteenth-century *Deux Bourdeurs Ribauds*. Both "bordeurs" or "menestreux" boast of repertoires (known to them *par memoire* and *par cuer*) that are immense by our standards (320), thus providing us with a French counterpart to Petrarch's description of memory surpassed only by audacity. However exaggerated these claims to capacious memory, they point to the importance of that faculty in the transmission and performance of the medieval romance.

An important English reference to memorial transmission comes from Robert Mannyng, an early fourteenth-century cleric from Lincolnshire, who complains about the inept handling of his favorite metrical romance, *Sir Tristrem*. It would be the best of the romances, "if men it sayd as made Thomas" (*Chronicle* 100). Instead, incompetent reciters drop out couplets and obscure the wording:

> But I here it no man so say,
> þat of som copple som is away;
> So þare fayre sayng here beforn
> is þare trauayle nere forlorn.
> (*Chronicle* 101-04)

Mannyng's words show us both that he thinks of *Sir Tristrem* as a fixed text—the new desire for verbatim reproduction is making its way into popular poetry—and that he was accustomed to hearing it recited from memory.

In addition to the testimony of primary sources, we also find that editors and others working closely with individual romances have continually reported variation among manuscript versions that does not appear to them to arise from ordinary errors in scribal copying.[6] Their

[6]The following is a partial list of editors and textual critics who report what they interpret as memorial variation: Kölbing (*Ipomedon* lxv); Hofstrand (152);

observations are based not on impressionistic reactions to a poem's atmosphere but on meticulous comparison of the variations in the available manuscript readings. William Holland's assessment of the versions of *Arthour and Merlin* is that

> there is simply no way to make this situation fit the usual idea of the descent of a literary text . . . . However, the copying at fairly wide intervals of a memorized text, one perhaps passed orally from minstrel to minstrel or taken from dictation for use as a prompt book by a minstrel wishing to learn the text, might be expected to produce this sort of change over a period of time.
>
> (98-99)

He notes further that "the changes consist largely of substitution of one conventional phrase, one formula, for another" (99). A number of scholars have also pointed out variations more likely to be auditory than visual: "in euery steode" for "in heruest tyde"; "mony wyues child" for "meigne, wijf and childe"; or "al by empne" for the place-name "Albyenne" (Smithers, *Alisaunder* II: 11-12).[7]

A problem with this sort of internal evidence, as Murray McGillivray rightly points out (4), is that scribal copying in the Middle Ages had itself a considerable auditory and memorial component. Long ago, H.J. Chaytor's *From Script to Print* made the important point that the scribes themselves vocalized the texts they copied and could create errors that might look to us to be auditory in origin (4-12). Our most influential textual scholars, including Eugene Vinaver, George Kane, and E.T. Donaldson, have all stressed that copyists hold the text in their minds as they turn from exemplar to copy, and, however short the time and the passage involved, alterations both intentional and unintentional do occur.[8] Can we hope to distinguish the short-term memory of a copyist from the longer term memory of a performer?

McGillivray argues that we are on the safest ground if we look for variations in a romance text that involve the conflation of passages

---

Smithers (*Alisaunder* II: 11-12); Duggan (concerning *The Wars of Alexander*); and Krishna. Other cases for nonwritten stages in the transmission of romances are presented by Knight; Reichl; and Quinn and Hall.

[7]For another argument from auditory variation, see Knight.

[8]See Vinaver (354-60); Kane (125-26); and Kane and Donaldson (130-40).

at a considerable remove from one another. A copyist working through an exemplar page by page would be highly unlikely to introduce such variation while a performer with the whole text in memory might easily do so. McGillivray calls such large-scale variation "memorial transfer" and cites examples from four metrical romances: *King Horn*, *Floris and Blancheflur*, *The Seege of Troye*, and *Sir Orfeo*. He notes significantly that these works, all extant in a number of manuscript versions, also contain a high proportion of the kind of small-scale alterations that could indicate either scribal or memorial variation. Small-scale alteration is an ambiguous indicator in itself, since it could indicate the tricks either of a scribe's or of a performer's memory, but in combination with the transposing or conflating of passages at considerable distance from one another, such alterations increase the probability of memorial rather than scribal variation (59-88).

A second means of distinguishing the copyist's short-term recall from the performer's long-term memory is to use a text known to be transmitted in writing as a control. Thus Holland and McGillivray both turn to the wealth of manuscripts of the *Canterbury Tales* for comparative purposes. One common source of variation in romance manuscripts is transposition of the two lines of a rhymed couplet: for example, the Auchinleck couplet "Euerich gode harpour is welcom me to / For mi lordes loue, Sir Orfeo" (A 51-18) appears in Harley 3810 as "For my lordys love, Syr Orpheo, / Al mynstrellys ben welcom me to" (H 468-69). Such transposition of couplet lines would make no difference at all in performance, and it is indeed a common trick of the memory, as I can testify from marking student-memorized passages of Chaucer's couplets, a surprising number of which are similarly "reversible." McGillivray points out that transposition of couplet lines occurs seven times in the version of *Sir Orfeo* found in MS Ashmole 61. In a passage of equivalent length from the *Knight's Tale*, only three manuscripts out of fifty include more than one such transposition and no manuscript exceeds three. Even allowing for the greater cultural prestige that would help to preserve Chaucer's texts and for the greatly increased complexity of thought and style that makes his couplets less subject to transposition without disruption of meaning, the difference is sufficiently striking to suggest different means of transmission (McGillivray 90-91, 94; Holland 98-99). When we weigh contemporary testimony along with the evidence from the state of the texts, there seems little reason for resisting what medieval sources plainly tell us about the role of performance and, at least on occasion, of memory, in the dissemination of the romances.

In fact, although it was formulated in connection with Old English poetry, Alan Jabbour's characterization of a primarily memorial tradition describes admirably the relationship among the versions of the Middle English romances:

> [i]f . . . we discover that in a certain tradition the variants of a song show a history of word-for-word or phrase-by-phrase oral transmission from a known or presumed archetype, we may describe the tradition as memorial. But considerable variation would almost certainly appear in the several texts, such as omission, addition, interpolation from other songs, stylizing, formulizing, or the like. These improvisational traits would compel us to call the tradition "primarily memorial."
>
> (178)

The simultaneous circulation of written texts does not disrupt a memorial tradition as it can an improvisational one. A primarily memorial tradition, again in Jabbour's words, "is capable of interacting comfortably and even profitably with lettered tradition. It entertains roughly the same attitude toward 'the text' found in lettered tradition, for it endeavors to preserve a work in detail as well as in main outline" (181). This description accords both with contemporary testimony and with the state of the romance texts left to us from the later Middle Ages. Jabbour's hypothesis about Old English poetry closely resembles the conclusion that Baugh drew about the transmission of Middle English narrative. Baugh too sees a process of transmission that is essentially textual by the standards of oral-formulaic composition, but very loose and improvisational by the standards of written transmission:

> To a minstrel verbal accuracy is not important so long as he keeps the meter. He is not reciting Shakespeare. He is telling a story. Even if his memory is a good one, he may have occasional lapses, be forced to improvise, may drop out a couplet or a stanza, may substitute a familiar rime-tag or formula without even being aware of it, may alter a particular passage through equally unconscious contamination with a similar incident in some other romance which he is accustomed to recite, may insert at times a couplet or a whole passage if it is part of his general stock of conventional descriptions and incidents, commonplace

> lines and phrases. Of course, he is corrupting the text, but that is a modern notion. The important thing is for him to keep going.
>
> ("Middle English Romance" 29)

Surely Middle English romances circulated both in writing and in memory, and were written down at varying stages of their evolution, with writing frequently serving to "recycle knowledge back into the oral world," as Walter Ong puts it (119).

The early- to mid-fourteenth century English romance called by its manuscripts either the *Seege* or *Batayle of Troye* gives us an unusual opportunity to observe the interaction between fixed text and limited improvisation that Jabbour and Baugh describe as typical of a primarily memorial tradition. This popular retelling of a culturally prestigious matter is particularly interesting from the point of view of orality and textuality.[9] When they are fixed in a single surviving text, the speaker's extranarrative remarks to his listening audience appear to have lost their mobility and their air of improvisation: they seem open to treatment as one kind of literary device among others. But because the *Seege of Troye* exists in four manuscript versions, the remarks indicating oral delivery in this poem never became quite "fossilized." The performer's glib and genial commentary becomes reanimated when we look at the "mouvance" among manuscript versions.

The three earliest versions of the *Seege* are fairly similar; the fourth was quite thoroughly revised in the fifteenth century for a more literate audience.[10] The early versions contain many extranarrative remarks related to performance; they vary considerably from version to version. For example, a series of place-marking couplets divides the narrative into units: "Lordyngis, saun faile, / Thus endith theo iiij bataile." It is hard to imagine why a copyist would move these markers

[9]The *Seege* is one of the four texts studied by McGillivray in connection with memorization, but the argument from the extranarrative remarks that follows is my own, built on suggestions from Barnicle's introduction to her edition. I cite Barnicle's edition of the *Seege* throughout.

[10]The *Seege* occurs in MSS Lincoln's Inn 150 (early fifteenth century), Egerton 2862 (late fourteenth century), Arundel 22 (mid fourteenth century), and Harley 525 (mid fifteenth century). For manuscript information, see Barnicle (ix-xviii) and Guddat-Figge (182-86, 214-15, and 228-31). The dates above are according to Guddat-Figge.

around.[11] Yet one version splits the sixth battle (according to the others) into two, and then leaves the last battle uncounted to make up the difference. Another teller does not recount the fourth and ninth battles, and marks the fifth battle at its beginning instead of its end. He changes the standard wording of the second battle-marking couplet, adding a line that breaks both the meter and the couplet system:

> I telle ȝou sorys, wyth-oute fayle,
> Thus ended the secu[n]de batayle.
> *I now wyl ȝow telle of the iij batayle.*
> (A 815-17; emphasis mine)

In lines unique to that version, the Arundel teller gaily announces his half-way point and very likely a break in the recitation:

> Her ys þe haluyndell of our geste;
> God saue vs, mest and lest.
> ffyl þe cuppe & mak ous glad,
> ffor þe maker þus so bad.
> (A 980-83)

Memorial transmission seems a more likely hypothesis than scribal variation for explaining the origins of extranarrative lines referring to an assembled group and to the progress of the recital.

No one knows just how or why such extranarrative remarks become part of the written texts of a given poem. The theory that they are part of a deliberately cultivated fiction of performance offers little help in this case. First, it does not account for the variation in the wording and placement of these remarks among the three manuscript versions. Second, a writer sophisticated enough to conceive of such a narrative fiction could presumably do better than nine repetitions of the battle-marking "Lordynges, saun faile" couplet. These and similar remarks were not recognized as a deliberately cultivated literary device by the fifteenth-century adapter whose version survives in MS Harley 525. His revisions reveal his attempt to make the poem more literary and sophisticated, and, in the carefully revised portion of his version,

[11]Hardman cites some interesting examples of scribal manipulation of structural divisions and reading units. Most, however, involve the use of rubrics, large capitals, or other extratextual unit-markers, rather than the more radical recasting evident in the versions of the *Seege*, which she does not discuss.

such remarks are consistently excised (Barnicle xxxiii; Hofstrand 121-40).

When and how each version of the narrative in question was committed to writing is impossible to say. Given our distance from the poem's genesis, writer can no longer be distinguished from performer. But the simplest and most plausible explanation for the variation in place-markers and in other extranarrative remarks is that these texts bear the marks of frequent use: they have passed through memories as well as written copies, and have been worn in and adapted to reflect the needs and the improvisations of various tellers. A version of Homer's Catalogue of Ships appears in the *Seege of Troye,* but the wear and tear on the Greek names has been so great that a Homeric poet would be unlikely to recognize such heroes as Sir Polipete of Empy or Sir Podam of Calapy. The *Seege*-tellers handle this (to them) fairly meaningless material almost as though it were a song. They punctuate the mention of each hero with a refrain, but both the names and the use of the refrain vary notably from version to version. If the problems in this catalogue are due in part to memorial lapses, the various tellers of the *Seege* were not the only ones to find it a challenge to memory. A Harvard graduate who by the end of 1986 had memorized nearly twenty-two books of the *Iliad* mentioned the Catalogue of Ships as one of the remaining stumbling blocks in his own performance (Galvin 42-46).

I stress the likelihood and the importance of memorial transmission because it seems to me the most methodologically problematic and least explored of the means of romance provenance. Romances were also read from manuscripts, privately and in company, and I do not mean to discount the obvious importance of written transmission, only to right the balance somewhat in favor of memory. Even many of those most involved with oral-traditional studies have inherited the original biases of Parry and Lord on this issue and are inclined to view memory as an inferior substitute for spontaneous composition in performance.[12] Meanwhile, modern, literate biases may dispose the rest of us to view memorial transmission as only and always an inferior sub-

[12]Because he was so inclined to generalize from his fieldwork with South Slavic epic, Lord originally sought to draw a very sharp line between what he considered true orality—spontaneous oral composition in performance—and traditions involving memory (see *Singer* 128-30). He later qualifies this position somewhat in "Memory, Fixity, and Genre," recognizing that the role of memory would vary by tradition and by genre. In "Perspectives," he acknowledges the existence of transitional texts.

stitute for writing—surely not the case in a performance-oriented genre. While we are learning more about the importance of memory to the most learned levels of medieval culture,[13] we know comparatively little about its role in popular entertainment. The uses of memory are both culture-specific and genre-specific, and we cannot generalize to late medieval romance either from modern literate cultures such as our own or from a modern, preliterate, epic tradition such as Parry and Lord studied in Yugoslavia. Rather, we need to view memory as a means of transmission with its own advantages and disadvantages within its generic and cultural setting. If we conclude that memory served as an important alternative to writing as a means of transmitting romances, this circumstance is a further argument for locating these narratives at the relatively unexplored borders of medieval literacy and orality.

In turning now to consider the way in which their existence on the borders of literacy and orality affects the artistry of the English romances, I limit my discussion to three criteria that would make possible more informed judgments about the aesthetic value of these narratives. The first criterion is a matter of style and the formula; the second and third concern narrative technique. All three are attempts to respond to the romances as arising from a complex context in which they might be read privately, read aloud from manuscripts by members of the household, and both read aloud from manuscripts and recited from memory by professional performers. The techniques I describe can be appreciated by ear or by eye; they testify to the flexibility and the transitional nature of the context that gave rise to them.

A major objection to the Middle English romances as literature has of course been to their repetitious and "uninventive" style. Such objections proliferated under the growing influence of the New Criticism in the period of the second World War and following. An increasing preoccupation with "close reading" had begun to make itself felt in British universities in the late twenties with the work of F.D. Leavis and I.A. Richards (Eagleton 30-46). Like any change in critical methodology, the advent of the New Criticism led to preferences for certain kinds of texts over others. While many earlier critics had emphasized the storytelling talents of the English romance writers, Laura Hibbard

[13]Calls for attention to the importance of memory in medieval culture include the recent works by Coleman and Carruthers and a conference held at New York University in 1991: "*Memoria*: The Memory Culture of the Middle Ages and the Renaissance."

Loomis in 1942 turned critical discussion toward romance style, which she described as characterized by "well-worn clichés," "stereotyped formulas of expression," and "stock phrases" (607-08). These features led to her judgment that the authors of the romances in the Auchinleck collection were the equivalents of modern "literary hacks" (608). The assumption that the romances are 'hackwork' has had a lasting effect on critical assessment of their style.

One result of the recent study of oral as opposed to literary style has been to show that the densely textured, startlingly original, complex literary language treasured by the New Critics is the product of a long written tradition: it can only be appreciated by someone who can pause, reflect, and reread. Oral poetry cultivates its own aesthetic effects, many of which are not readily apparent to modern literates. The applicability of oral-formulaic studies to the formulaic language of poems transmitted by writing and memory is still under debate, and few scholars still share Parry's and Lord's original optimism about formula density as a necessary indicator of oral composition. Alain Renoir has argued, however, that our knowledge of the formula can help us to evaluate written and memorized works that employ a strongly traditional, shared poetic language. Following Stanley Greenfield and Foley, Renoir argues that for an audience who knows the tradition, a formulaic expression can convey with stunning economy a freight of associations carried over from previous contexts. Greenfield, Renoir, and Foley all argue that an essential part of studying these poems is recontextualizing their style, as best we can, by studying the extant occurrences of the phrases in question in other works belonging to the same generic and stylistic tradition.

In his most recent work, *Immanent Art,* Foley makes the further argument that this carrying over of meaning from previous contexts is in fact the essence of oral-traditional art: oral poetry and its near descendants in the realm of writing operate from a principle of metonymy in which the occurrence of a formula in a particular narrative draws upon or, more accurately, is contiguous with all other occurrences. Thus he claims that meaning is "immanent" throughout an oral tradition. Although Foley does not discuss his choice of the term "metonymy," he is presumably adopting the Structuralist distinction between the metonymic and metaphoric axes of language. This distinction, brought to prominence by Roman Jakobson, departs from the classical rhetorical notion of metonymy as a subspecies of metaphor and instead represents metaphor and metonymy as polar opposites, the first reliant upon the similarity between two necessarily distinct entities and the second upon the contiguity of the parts or aspects of one single entity.[14] If oral and orally-derived texts do indeed operate metonymically, if each occurrence of a formulaic expression derives its meaning from its living connection to the other occurrences within that tradition with which the auditor is familiar, then the need to study the occurrences that happen to survive becomes all the more urgent. According to Foley,

> [t]he ability to (re-)instill what may appear, from a literary perspective, to be repetitive, mechanical structures with the referentiality they command under the aegis of tradition allows an audience to respond faithfully to the signals encoded in the text and thus to assist in fashioning an aesthetically coherent work.
>
> (47)

The arguments I have just outlined are based on examples from oral and orally-derived epic—Homeric, Germanic, and South Slavic—but they may be fruitfully applied to "what may appear, from a literary perspective, to be repetitive, mechanical structures" in the English romances. While neither densely textured nor original, and distinctly ill-suited to psychological probing or to philosophical dispute, such repeated language, when skillfully used, can convey the social and cultural concerns that lie at the heart of a traditional society. My example for the moment is the late-medieval and early-modern outlaw tradition that includes the *Tale of Gamelyn* and the later Robin Hood ballads.[15] The shared language of these works is well-stocked with greet-

[14]The literary implications of Jakobson's distinction are further explored by Lodge.

[15]See note 1 above for my use of the term "romance" to refer to works like *Gamelyn*. Since I am not claiming that the romances were composed spontaneously in performance, I have not tried to provide and defend a rigorous definition of their formulaic language. I simply draw upon the widely recognized fact that the language is repetitive of itself and of other works in the same tradition and that stereotyped phrases are regularly used in similar contexts. Although I cannot make the case here, I think that in this particular tradition, formulaic language is much more systematic and functional than in many other romances—more like the formulae of an improvisational tradition. The language of the outlaw tradition resembles that described by Andersen for the British ballad in general (see esp. 35-36).

ings, leave-takings, challenges, and agonistic encounters—in other words, those encounters that have a ritual or formulaic quality even in real life. These encounters frequently involve questions of public identity, as these "greetings" demonstrate:

> "who is thy fader
> and who is thy sire?"
>
> (*Gamelyn* 221)

> "Yonge men," sayde Gamelyn
> "by ȝour lewte,
> What man is ȝour maister
> that ȝe with be?"
>
> (*Gamelyn* 657-58)

> "Who is thy maister?" sayde the knyght;
> Johnn sayde, "Robyn Hode"
>
> (*Gest of Robyn Hode* st. 26)

> "Say me nowe, wight yonge man,
> What is nowe thy name?
> In what countre were thou borne,
> And where is thy wonynge wane?"
>
> (*Gest* st. 148)[16]

The challenge implied in these inquiries—the agonistic tone—is characteristic of orally communicated poetry, where testing, flyting, riddling, and other forms of "facing off" are common.[17] *Gamelyn*, the *Gest of Robyn Hode*, and a whole series of later ballads are devoted to hostile challenges and ultimate reconciliation between Robin (the "king of outlaws" in the earlier *Gamelyn*) and various strangers who eventually join his band, indicating that the assertion of one's adult identity to potentially hostile listeners is a critical issue in these works. Consequently, the teller's traditional language is well-stocked with the

[16]I cite Skeat's edition of *Gamelyn* but follow Burrow in printing ballad stanzas rather than the long lines of Skeat's edition (see "*Sir Thopas* in the Sixteenth Century" 73). I cite Child's edition of the *Gest of Robyn Hode* and the other outlaw ballads throughout.

[17]For other examples of introductory challenges, see Baugh ("Improvisation" 425-26) and Schmirgel's list in the appendix to Kölbing's edition of *Sir Beues of Hamptoun* (li). For an agonistic tone as characteristic of oral poetry, see Ong (43-45); and Parks (*Verbal Dueling* 42-48 and 96-99). For formulas and social ritual, see Wittig (*Structures* 41-46).

vocabulary of tension-filled, face-to-face encounters. Each time he uses it, an audience competent in the tradition hears not just an isolated request for a particular piece of information, but a fundamental challenge that must be met, usually with blows as well as words, before the outsider is admitted to the society of the greenwood. Each new exchange imports metonymically (in Foley's sense of the term) the significance of previous exchanges. In Greenfield's words, "a whole host of overtones springs into action" (205).

While the seeking and asserting of one's identity are common issues in works with folktale plots, more specific to these greenwood outlaw tales is the false declaration of identity, where the social outcast steps into the role of the authorities who enforce his exile. Here too the language is stereotyped to the point of ritual. Little John overpowers a porter (actually a jailer) and turns the tables:

> "Now wil I be porter," seid Litul John,
> "And take þe keyes in honde."
> (*Robin Hood and the Monk* st. 71)

Adam Bell, the hero of another outlaw ballad (Child #116), announces his assumed role in similar language, with the same oralist emphasis on keys as concrete evidence of authority:

> "Now am I porter," sayd Adam Bell;
> "Se, broder, the keys haue we here."
> (*Adam Bell* st. 66)

Each time a character expresses one of these "stereotyped" assertions of identity or appropriations of false identity, the poet is able to draw upon the centrality and potency of such assertions in the tradition as a whole. By the end of the tale, of course, all false roles have been relinquished, and the audience is impressed with the harmony that results when everyone maintains his proper place. Traditional and formulaic narratives, as Susan Wittig points out, reinforce important social messages by reflecting "the culture's ideal world—imbalances ideally balanced, riddles resolved, perfection attained through prescribed language and prescribed action" ("Formulaic Style" 133).[18] Such an approach to the language of these poems should make us reconsider not only the New

[18]See also Wittig (*Structures* 41-46).

Critically-inspired condemnation of repetition in these works but also the accusation of "thinness of texture."

While my discussion of metonymy here is limited to its relation to formulaic language, it may well be that grasping the metonymic quality of medieval narrative art will help to answer other fundamental questions about the crafting of the romances. In their work with epic, Foley and Renoir apply the principle to larger elements such as repeated scenes or the creation of character in traditional works. Derek Brewer has argued that metonymy rather than metaphor is Chaucer's favored linguistic axis, and that this fact has created a problem for modern criticism, which "only acknowledges metaphoric structures in poetry" ("Metonymic Relationships" 37). A. C. Spearing makes a similar suggestion in regard to the narrative style of *King Horn,* pointing out ways in which the metonymic rather than metaphoric art of early English narrative puts it out of harmony with many of our modern critical and aesthetic assumptions (*Readings* 24-55). We need to study more closely the applicability to Middle English literature of Foley's link between metonymy and proximity to orality. Taken together, these observations suggest ways of making our critical methods and categories more responsive to the contextual differences between medieval and modern literature.

The second element proposed here for a new poetics moves into territory less well charted by scholars of oral tradition. I am intrigued by the frequency with which medieval narrative makes use of a technique that one might call "resinging" in works very close to their oral ancestry and "renarration" in more thoroughly textualized works.[19] Often in Middle English romance, an event is first reported as action by the narrator and then recast as speech from a narrating character and then sometimes narrated again by another character, occasionally to a very striking effect. One thinks immediately of similar examples in orally derived epic in which the reported action is altered in interesting ways when renarrated from the point of view of the hero. For example,

[19] I take the term "resinging" from Chickering (353). While all oral-traditional singing is in a sense "resinging," I follow Chickering in using this term to refer to a retelling of the same events within a single narrative. "Renarration" I adopt from Spearing, "Marie de France and her Middle English Adapters" (120), where he notes subtle uses of renarration in Marie's work. If indeed Marie wrote down her own versions of oral songs as she claimed, she provides another example of a literate putting an oral effect to new, textualized purposes, playing Virgil to the Breton *lai*'s Homer.

Beowulf's account to Hygelac of the events at Heorot (1999-2151b) diverges in interesting ways from the poet's account of the same events.[20] Significantly, the new details that he introduces are attested elsewhere in Germanic folk tale, suggesting that Beowulf's account may be a direct legacy from the narrative's oral past: a fresh combination of traditional elements. Odysseus's revisionist, or at least selective, account of his stay with Kalypso in Book VII of the *Odyssey* is another example: while the poet earlier reported that Kalypso had eventually ceased to please Odysseus (V.153)—implying that she once had—Odysseus's own account to Arete naturally omits any reference to initial pleasure with Kalypso and speaks of his stay only as a period of captivity.[21] Here, resinging (in the poem's original oral context) or renarration (in the textualized version that survives to us) gives us an insight into Odysseus's character, as do the many false retellings of the events of his journey that he gives upon returning to Ithaka in disguise. This technique of recasting the action from different perspectives belongs both to oral and to literary technique, but its effect will necessarily be quite different in each, since a textual tradition (whether written or memorial) offers a clearer distinction between the original account and subsequent, variant ones, while a multiform oral tradition is all variants, all versions.

It is not surprising that oral traditions would make ample use of resinging since it is a reflection in small of the overall technique of composition: the Homeric poet sings to his audience and Odysseus sings to the Phaiaikians, revisiting some of the same narrative ground. And it is not surprising that even a highly literary work like the *Aeneid* would make its own textualized uses of a technique so prevalent in its orally derived Homeric models. Similarly, the writers of Middle English romance would have ample precedent for the technique in their own orally transmitted models. The skillful uses of renarration in the examples that follow show the composers of English romance adapting a technique prevalent in oral poetry to their mixed milieu of memorial and written transmission.

To begin with an example of renarration that in some ways resembles resinging or traditional variation, I turn to a quite spectacular example in *Havelok the Dane*, where an important account of the hero's adventures is narrated three times in a row, first in 153 lines by the nar-

[20] I refer to Klaeber's line numbers here.
[21] I cite Allen's edition of the *Odyssey* throughout.

rator (1767-1920), and then in 53 lines by one of the participants in the fight in question (1955-2008), and finally in 16 lines by a group of bystanders (2021-37).[22] The most obvious effect of this renarration is, of course, emphasis. The renarrated incident involves a rough and tumble battle in which Havelok, armed with the bar to the door, helps his host to fend off a large band of intruders. After he acquits himself heroically in this unequal battle, Havelok is knighted and ultimately recognized as the legitimate heir to the Danish throne. The renarration signals in the simplest way possible the fight's importance to the tale.

More interestingly, the three accounts show what we would call traditional variation in an oral work and what are often called anomalies or inconsistencies in written ones. In the first account, by the narrator, Havelok and his companions are at table when the intruders arrive (1766). In contrast, the renarration by the host, Bernard Brun, mentions that Havelok and his men "lay by the wall" (1963-64), suggesting that they were asleep at the time, a possibility more in keeping with the fact that they have only just returned from an enormous banquet at the Danish court. This is resinging by oral standards and inconsistency by textual ones: very likely there were versions of the Havelok-tale in which the surprise attack occurred while the hero and his host were sitting down to a late supper and versions in which it came when the hero and his men were asleep. In reading a work more thoroughly acclimated to literate ways, we would assume either that the author "nodded" when he had the defenders of the household first eating and then sleeping at the time of the attack, or else that he was deliberately undercutting our confidence in the reliability of the narrator. Such "anomalies" can be distressing to readers accustomed to fixed texts and have been the occasion for elaborate theories of interpolation in earlier studies of the Bible, the Homeric poems, and *Beowulf*. It is interesting that the *Havelok*-poet, textual as his orientation is in some other ways, shows himself in this example to be entirely comfortable with traditional variation. He also uses renarration to achieve a nicely cumulative effect by having the motives and identities of the violent intruders entirely unspecified in the first and most suspenseful narration, then identified by the host in his version as thieves come to rob and murder his household, and finally identified by the bystanders as the

[22]I cite Smithers's edition of *Havelok* throughout. The poem survives in one nearly complete manuscript version, Laud Misc. 108, Bodleian Library. Some fragments are found in Cambridge University Library MS Add. 4407.

band led by the apparently infamous Griffin Gale. Other marks of individuality also distinguish the accounts: for example, the narrator is preoccupied with the numerous makeshift weapons used by the defenders of the household, while the host is more interested in the wide variety of wounds sustained by the hero.

A more delicate example of renarration comes from *Sir Orfeo*, a medievalized version of the myth of Orpheus and Eurydice. In the Middle English version, Orfeo's queen falls asleep under a tree and has a dream, the contents of which are not at first disclosed. Its terrifying effect on her is presented as narrated action:

Ac, as sone as she gan awake,
Sche crid, & loþli bere gan make:
Sche froted hir honden & hir fet,
& crached hir visage—it bled wete;
Hir riche robe hye al to-rett,
& was reueyed out of hir witt.
(77-82)[23]

Her attendants bring her husband, who renarrates the physical effect of the dream upon the queen:

O lef liif, what is te,
Þat ever ȝete hast ben so stille,
& now gredest wonder schille?
Þi bodi, þat was so white y-core,
Wiþ þine nailes is al to-tore.
Allas! þy rode, þat was so red,
Is all wan, as þou were ded;
& al-so þine fingres smale
Beþ al blodi & al pale.
Allas! þi louesom eyȝen to
Lokeþ so man doþ on his fo!
(102-12)

The narrator's account is vivid enough, but the contrast with Orfeo's renarration is striking. The latter begins with the same physical details: her shrieking and the tearing of her flesh with her nails. But, unlike the narrator, the husband characterizes each physical detail as a shocking

[23]I cite Bliss's edition of the Auchinleck version. Two other manuscript versions survive: Bodleian Library MS Ashmole 61 and British Library MS Harley 3810.

change from her familiar state: she is habitually quiet and now is shrieking; her skin is usually exquisitely white, but now is torn. The new details that Orfeo introduces all take this same form: her ordinarily rosy cheeks are now wan; her slender fingers are bloody and pale; as he stands before her, her formerly "louesom" eyes now look as though they are confronting an enemy. The last detail is most telling, I think: the renarration serves not to convey the surface facts of the queen's appearance, already well established, but rather to capture the perspective of a loving husband who beholds his wife in such a state. This is brought home by the repeated contrasts to her habitual appearance and by the greatly increased intimacy of his account, contemplating her body, her fingers, and the expression in her eyes in a way that the narrator never presumes to do. Orfeo's speech is the more poignant for being addressed directly to her, "O lef liif," with repeated use of "þi" and "þou."

Although this renarration is more textual than the example from *Havelok* because it involves the audience's perceiving meaningful variation from a fixed original version, it does not mean that *Sir Orfeo* was necessarily designed for private reading. As Jabbour points out, a primarily memorial tradition "entertains roughly the same attitude toward 'the text' found in lettered tradition, for it endeavors to preserve a work in detail as well as in main outline" (181). The renarrations I have observed in Middle English romance generally follow immediately upon the first account, and their significant variations seem to me well enough marked to be accessible to audiences accustomed to taking in similar tales by ear. In this example from *Sir Orfeo*, the husband stresses the contrast between the queen's familiar state and her altered one in every single feature he mentions: five times we find what she was contrasted with what she is now. This is a heavier marking than would be necessary to ensure that a reading audience noticed the meaningful difference between the narrator's and the husband's descriptions. Short as it is, *Sir Orfeo* contains a surprising number of effectively used renarrations: the poet has our rapt attention when the queen herself begins yet another narration of what happened under the tree, this time from the point of view of the only person who can tell us firsthand the contents of her terrifying dream.

The English version of the well-known story of *Amis and Amiloun* illustrates another important function for renarration, the shifting of perspective for purposes of moral commentary. As we wait at the end of the tale for the recognition of the unfortunate Amiloun by his sworn brother Amis, dramatic tension builds. Hideously afflicted by the leprosy he has contracted as a result of his loyalty to Amis, Amiloun lies begging in a cart at the gate of Amis' castle, accompanied by his nephew, a handsome and compassionate youth who has refused to desert Amiloun in his misery. One of Amis' retainers spots the pair and is struck by the boy's shining nobility and his master's grotesque deformity. He offers the youth a desirable position in Amis' retinue, which is courteously refused:

> . . . he answerd wiþ mild mode
> & swore bi him þat dyed on rode
> Whiles he miȝt walk & wake,
> For to winne al þis warldes gode,
> His hende lord, þat bi him stode,
> Schuld he neuer forsake.
>
> (1939-44)[24]

This youth, Amoraunt, is essentially an idealized version of the two loyal but flawed heroes, his own loyalty uncontaminated by the indirect perjury of which the heroes are guilty. His exemplary character is well established by the author, who assigns to him the full complement of aristocratic virtuous attributes: "curtays," "hende," "fre," "wiþ-outen wrong," "gentil," and "fair." He and his unfortunate master have suffered from cold, poverty, hunger, and exhaustion, finally falling together into the muddy road, with no change in the boy's "milde mod" or his loyalty. Thus the retainer's offer to Amoraunt of a lucrative position with a new master is from the audience's perspective morally obtuse. It is made more so by the audience's knowledge that this well-heeled retainer is himself dependent on the terrible sacrifice made by Amiloun so that the retainer's master, Amis, might prosper. The retainer's reaction to Amoraunt's rejection is to assume that the youth is mad or a buffoon or, as a last possibility, that his foul-featured lord is of much higher worldly station than his circumstances suggest (1945-50). Uncompensated loyalty does not occur to him as a possibility.

As in the case of so many renarrations, the entire scene of the knight's offer to Amoraunt is immediately repeated in speech, in this case by the retainer to his master, Amis. He begins by offering to tell

[24] I cite Leach's edition of the Auchinleck version of *Amis*. For the argument that *Amis and Amiloun* is "a good story by oral standards," see Hume (40).

his lord the best joke that he has heard since he was born, that is, Amoraunt's seeming folly in turning down his offer (1954-56). He repeats all the circumstances we have just heard: the ugliness of the leper in the cart, the fairness of Amoraunt, the retainer's offer, Amoraunt's refusal. Limited by his own moral vision and in stark contrast to the narrator's assessment, the retainer's report again labels Amoraunt a great fool and a madman. His master, of wider vision, suggests a new range of possibilities for the action being renarrated, this time drawn from the most fundamental moral obligations of secular society:

"... þei his lord be lorn,
Par auentour, þe gode man haþ biforn
Holpen him at his nede,
Oþer þe child is of his blod yborn,
Oþer he haþ him oþes sworn
His liif wiþ him to lede.
Wheþer he be fremd or of his blod,
Þe child," he seyd, "is trewe & gode,
Also God me spede.
Ȝif ichim speke er he wende,
For þat he is so trewe & kende,
Y schal quite him his mede!"
(1993-2004)

Thus Amoraunt's action is first presented by the poet, then recapitulated from the unsympathetic perspective of a knight lacking in moral vision, then reinterpreted more perceptively by one of the heroes. It is not hard to see why the poet lavishes so much attention on this scene. It reenacts the fundamental issue of the whole romance: how loyalty responds to various pressures. Far from inept or mechanically repetitive, this sort of renarration is clearly a mark of skill, and foreshadows the many manipulations of point of view that will come to characterize the modern novel.

My third and final suggestion for an element in a new poetics for the English romances involves recognizing the way in which the best-told narratives isolate and emphasize the emotional core of a received story. This phenomenon has been noted in connection with the ballad and the folktale, and it may also help to explain the power of some of the best romances.[25] For example, the widely appreciated re-

[25]For the term "emotional core" applied to the traditional ballad, see Coffin (246-56).

alism of *Havelok the Dane* appeals powerfully to modern literates raised on the novel, but *Havelok*'s realism is not that of Flaubert or Tolstoy. The fullness and intensity of the *Havelok*-poet's verbal realization varies greatly, and his alternation between fairly simple summary and the richly imagined, detailed creation of scene articulates the tale's emotional core. Psychologists and folklorists who incline toward psychological explanations argue that a Cinderella-like, rags-to-riches plot such as that of *Havelok* dramatizes the feeling that children experience of being mistreated and unloved, their superior merits unrecognized (Bettelheim; Wilson; Dundes 219-28). In *Havelok,* the pathos of the mistreated child—perceived in physical terms of ragged clothing, cold, and lack of food—alternates with and is ultimately succeeded by contrasting scenes of warmth, light, "brand-new" clothing, and plentiful food, accompanied by love and acceptance. This contrast is the imaginative center of the story for the *Havelok*-poet, and thus it is such scenes that receive the fullest, most "realistic" treatment, even when that "realism" creates what modern critics have identified as serious anomalies in the narrative.[26]

This same sort of concentration of emotional impact helps to lift *King Horn* and *Sir Orfeo* above the general run of Middle English romance. *King Horn* is in essence a return song, and the emotional core of this story pattern often centers on recognition, in traditional works a non-naturalistically slow and tortuous process (Thompson III: 370). One thinks of another return song, the *Odyssey*, where Penelope has had numerous indications that her husband is alive and nearby; she has even had an extended interview with him in disguise. Still she engineers the test of the bow, and even after Odysseus passes, she remains skeptical about his identity. Her reluctance to recognize him may seem excessive to us, as it does to Telemachus, but not to Odysseus, who silences his son's protests with "Hush, let your mother test me here in our hall" (XXIII.113-14). Recognition in *King Horn* also calls for more evidence than seems necessary in naturalistic terms. Horn is disguised as a pilgrim and engages in a protracted conversation with his intended bride, who has been desperately awaiting his return. She does not recognize Horn, but her heart "chills" when she sees him. He reminds her of a prophetic dream she had about their separation, alludes to the length of his absence, puns on the word "horn," and gives her back a ring that she gave to him. Like Penelope, she is agitated but does not recognize her

[26]I argue for this point in "The Traditional Origins of *Havelok the Dane*."

long absent lover, and when the disguised Horn tells her openly that her lover is dead—despite all the evidence to the contrary—she believes him, and, like Penelope, she wants to die. When he is finally ready, Horn wipes the dirt off his face, announces his identity, and is received by his bride with open arms. The delay and the emotional intensity that surround recognition might seem out of proportion in the ordinarily pared-down style of *Horn*, unless one sees that recognition of the hero as a fully initiated adult is the core of the story. Thus this part of the tale is both fully detailed and emotionally fraught. Significantly, Horn's return and the process of recognition make up the whole of the traditional ballad "Hind Horn" (Child #17), a descendent of the medieval versions of the Horn story, and an example of the tale's further compression toward the emotional core that gives *King Horn* an intensity lacking in many romances whose traditional roots have been left further behind.

In short, postwar aesthetic judgments of the romances have been strongly influenced by New Critical canons of value that obscure rather than illuminate the artistry of these narratives. These canons based entirely on highly literate modes of thought and expression must inevitably give way to ones that can encompass the vibrant interaction of writing, oral performance from memory, and limited improvisation. A new poetics might recognize the evocative use of formulaic language to create a density of associations in the minds of the audience, the skillful use of "renarration," and the successful amplification of passages central to a tale's emotional core.

Department of English
Smith College

Works Cited

Allen, Thomas W. *Odyssey*. Oxford: Clarendon, 1917.

Andersen, Flemming G. *Commonplace and Creativity: The Role of Formulaic Diction in Anglo-Scottish Traditional Balladry*. Odense: Odense UP, 1985.

Barnicle, Mary Elizabeth, ed. *The* Seege *or* Batayle of Troye. EETS os 172. London: Oxford UP, 1927.

Baugh, Albert C. "The Authorship of the Middle English Romances." *Annual Bulletin of the Modern Humanities Research Association* 22 (1950): 13-28.

—. "Improvisation in the Middle English Romance." *Proceedings of the American Philosophical Society* 103 (1959): 418-54.

—. "The Middle English Romance: Some Questions of Creation, Presentation, and Preservation." *Speculum* 42 (1967): 1-31.

Bettelheim, Bruno. *The Uses of Enchantment*. New York: Knopf, 1977.

Bliss, A.J., ed. *Sir Orfeo*. 2nd ed. Oxford: Clarendon, 1966.

Bradbury, Nancy Mason. "The Traditional Origins of *Havelok the Dane*." *Studies in Philology* 90 (1993), 115-42.

Brewer, Derek. "Medieval Literature, Folk Tale and Traditional Literature." *Dutch Quarterly Review of Anglo-American Letters* 11 (1981): 243-56.

—. "Some Metonymic Relationships in Chaucer's Poetry." *Chaucer: The Poet as Storyteller*. London: Macmillan, 1984. 37-53.

Burrow, John A. *Ricardian Poetry*. London: Routledge, 1971.

—. "*Sir Thopas* in the Sixteenth Century." *Middle English Studies Presented to Norman Davis*. Ed. Douglas Gray and E.G. Stanley. Oxford: Clarendon, 1983. 69-91.

Carruthers, Mary. *The Book of Memory: A Study of Memory in Medieval Culture*. Cambridge: Cambridge UP, 1990.

Chaytor, H.J. *From Script to Print*. Cambridge: Heffer, 1945.

Chestnutt, Michael. "Minstrel Reciters and the Enigma of the Middle English Romance." *Culture and History* 2 (1987): 48-67.

Chickering, Howell D., Jr., ed. Beowulf: *A Dual-Language Edition.* Garden City: Doubleday, 1977.

Child, Francis J., ed. *The English and Scottish Popular Ballads.* Cambridge Edition. Ed. G.L. Kittredge and H.C. Sargent. Boston: Houghton, 1904 and 1932.

Coffin, Tristram P. "Mary Hamilton and the Anglo-American Ballad as Art Form." *The Critics and the Ballads.* Ed. MacEdward Leach and Tristram P. Coffin. Carbondale: Southern Illinois UP, 1961. 245-56.

Coleman, Janet. *Ancient and Medieval Memories.* Cambridge: Cambridge UP, 1992.

Duggan, Hoyt N. "The Role of Formulas in the Dissemination of a Middle English Alliterative Romance." *Studies in Bibliography* 28 (1976): 265-88.

Dundes, Alan. Cinderella: *A Casebook.* New York: Wildman, 1983.

Eagleton, Terry. *Literary Theory.* Minneapolis: U of Minnesota P, 1983.

Edwards, A.S.G. "Middle English Romance: The Limits of Editing, the Limits of Criticism." *Medieval Literature: Texts and Interpretation.* Ed. Tim William Machan. Binghamton: State U of New York P, 1991. 91-104.

Fewster, Carol. *Traditionality and Genre in Middle English Romance.* Cambridge: Brewer, 1987.

Foley, John Miles. *Immanent Art: From Structure to Meaning in Traditional Oral Epic.* Bloomington: Indiana UP, 1991.

Frye, Northrop. *Anatomy of Criticism.* Princeton: Princeton UP, 1957.

Furnivall, F.J., ed. The Story of England *by Robert Mannyng of Brunne.* Rerum Britannicarum Medii Aevi Scriptores, 1887. Vol 1.

Galvin, Ruth Mehrtens. "Speak, Memory." *Harvard Magazine* 90 (1988): 42-46.

Greene, Richard L. *The Early English Carols.* 2nd ed. Oxford: Clarendon, 1977.

Greenfield, Stanley B. "The Formulaic Expression of the Theme of 'Exile' in Anglo-Saxon Poetry." *Speculum* 30 (1955): 200-06.

Guddat-Figge, Gisela. *Catalogue of Manuscripts Containing Middle English Romances.* Munich: Verlag, 1976.

Hall, Joseph, ed. *King Horn*. Oxford: Clarendon, 1901.
Hardman, Phillipa. "Fit Divisions in Middle English Romances." *Yearbook of English Studies* 22 (1992): 63-80.
Hirsh, John C. "*Havelok* 2933: A Problem in Medieval Literary History." *Neuphilologische Mitteilungen* 78 (1977): 339-49.
Hofstrand, G. The Seege of Troye: *A Study in the Intertextual Relations of the Middle English Romance*. Lund Studies in English 4. Lund: Gleerups, 1936.
Holland, William. "Formulaic Diction and the Descent of a Middle English Romance." *Speculum* 48 (1973): 89-109.
Hume, Kathryn. "*Amis and Amiloun* and the Aesthetics of Middle English Romance." *Studies in Philology* 70 (1973): 19-41.
Jabbour, Alan. "Memorial Transmission in Old English Poetry." *Chaucer Review* 3 (1969): 174-90.
Jakobson, Roman. "Two Aspects of Language and Two Types of Aphasic Disturbances." *Fundamentals of Language*. Roman Jakobson and Morris Halle. The Hague: Mouton, 1956. 69-96.
—. "Closing Statement: Linguistics and Poetics." *Style in Language*. Ed. Thomas A. Sebeok. Cambridge, MA: Harvard UP, 1960. 350-77.
Jauss, Hans Robert. "The Alterity and Modernity of Medieval Literature." *New Literary History* 10 (1979): 181-227.
Kane, George, ed. Piers Plowman: *The A Version*. London: Athlone, 1960.
—, and E. Talbot Donaldson, eds. Piers Plowman: *The B Version*. London: Athlone, 1975.
Klaeber, Friederich, ed. Beowulf *and the* Fight at Finnsburh. 3rd ed. Lexington: Heath, 1950.
Knight, S.T. "The Oral Transmission of *Sir Launfal*." *Medium Ævum* 38 (1969): 164-70.
Kölbing, Eugen, ed. *Sir Beues of Hamptoun*. EETS es 46, 48, 68. London: Oxford UP, 1885, 1886, 1895.
—. *Ipomedon in drei englischen Bearbeitungen*. Breslau: Koebner, 1889.
Krishna, Valerie. "Parataxis, Formulaic Density, and Thrift in the Alliterative *Morte Arthure*." *Speculum* 57 (1982): 63-83.
Leach, MacEdward, ed. *Amis and Amiloun*. EETS os 203. London: Oxford UP, 1937.

Lodge, David. *The Modes of Modern Writing: Metaphor, Metonymy, and the Typology of Modern Literature*. Ithaca: Cornell UP, 1977.

Loomis, Laura Hibbard. "The Auchinleck Manuscript and a Possible London Bookshop of 1330-40." *PMLA* 57 (1942): 595-627.

Lord, Albert. *The Singer of Tales*. Cambridge, MA: Harvard UP, 1960.

—. "Memory, Fixity, and Genre in Oral Traditional Poetries." *Oral Traditional Literature*. Ed. John Miles Foley. Columbus: Slavica, 1981. 451-61.

—. "Perspectives on Recent Work on the Oral Traditional Formula." *Oral Tradition* 1 (1986): 467-503.

McGillivray, Murray. *Memorization in the Transmission of the Middle English Romances*. New York: Garland, 1990.

Mehl, Dieter. *The Middle English Romances of the Thirteenth and Fourteenth Centuries*. London: Routledge, 1969.

Ong, Walter J. *Orality and Literacy*. London: Methuen, 1982.

Parks, Ward. "The Oral-Formulaic Theory in Middle English Studies." *Oral Tradition* 1 (1986): 636-94.

—. *Verbal Dueling in Heroic Narrative*. Princeton: Princeton UP, 1990.

Pearsall, Derek. "The Development of Middle English Romance." *Mediaeval Studies* 27 (1965): 91-116.

—. "The *Troilus* Frontispiece and Chaucer's Audience." *Yearbook of English Studies* 7 (1977): 68-74.

—. *Old English and Middle English Poetry*. The Routledge History of English Poetry 1. London: Routledge, 1977.

Quinn, William A. and Audley S. Hall. *Jongleur: A Modified Theory of Oral Improvisation and Its Effects on the Performance and Transmission of Middle English Romance*. Washington, DC: UP of America, 1982.

Reichl, Karl. "The Middle English Popular Romance: Minstrel Versus Hack Writer." *The Ballad and Oral Literature*. Ed. Joseph Harris. Cambridge, MA: Harvard UP, 1991. 243-68.

Renoir, Alain. "Oral-Formulaic Rhetoric: An Approach to Image and Message in Medieval Poetry." *Medieval Texts and Contemporary Readers*. Ed. Laurie Finke and Martin Shichtman. Ithaca: Cornell UP, 1987. 234-53.

—. *A Key to Old Poems: The Oral-Formulaic Approach to the Interpretation of West-Germanic Verse*. University Park: Pennsylvania State UP, 1988.

Severs, J. Burke. *A Manual of the Writings in Middle English*. I: Romances. New Haven: Connecticut Academy of Arts and Sciences, 1967.

Skeat, W.W., ed. *The Tale of Gamelyn*. Oxford: Clarendon, 1884.

Smithers, G.V., ed. *Kyng Alisaunder*. EETS os 227, 237. London: Oxford UP, 1952, 1957.

—, ed. *Havelok*. Oxford: Clarendon, 1987.

Spearing, A.C. *Readings in Medieval Poetry*. Cambridge: Cambridge UP, 1987.

—. "Marie de France and her Middle English Adapters." *Studies in the Age of Chaucer* 12 (1990): 117-56.

Stock, Brian. *The Implications of Literacy: Written Language and Models of Interpretation in the Eleventh and Twelfth Centuries*. Princeton: Princeton UP, 1983.

—. *Listening for the Text*. Baltimore: Johns Hopkins UP, 1990.

Strohm, Paul. "Storie, Spelle, Geste, Romaunce, and Tragedie." *Speculum* 46 (1971): 348-59.

—. "The Origin and Meaning of Middle English *Romaunce*." *Genre* 10 (1977): 1-28.

Taylor, Andrew. "Fragmentation, Corruption, and Minstrel Narration: the Question of the Middle English Romances." *Yearbook of English Studies* 22 (1992): 38-62.

Thompson, Stith. *Motif-Index of Folk Literature*. Rev. and enl. ed. 6 vols. Bloomington: Indiana UP, 1955-58.

Vinaver, Eugene. "Principles of Textual Emendation." *Studies in French Language and Mediaeval Literature presented to Professor Mildred K. Pope*. Manchester: Manchester UP, 1939. 351-69.

Vitz, Evelyn Birge. "Rethinking Old French Literature: The Orality of the Octosyllabic Couplet." *Romanic Review* 77 (1986): 307-21.

Wilson, Anne. *Traditional Romance and Tale*. Ipswich: Brewer, 1976.

Wittig, Susan. "Formulaic Style and the Problem of Redundancy." *Centrum* 1 (1973): 123-36.

—. *Stylistic and Narrative Structures in the Middle English Romances*. Austin: U of Texas P, 1978.

Zumthor, Paul. *Essai de poétique médiévale*. Paris: Éd. Seuil, 1972.

—. *Introduction à la poésie orale*. Paris: Éd. Seuil, 1983. Trans. Kathryn Murphy-Judy. Minneapolis: U of Minnesota P, 1990.

Oral Tradition in the Middle English Romance: The Case of *Robert of Cisyle*

Alexandra Hennessey Olsen

Robert of Cisyle is the story of a king, the brother of the Pope and the Emperor, who hears the *Magnificat* sung in church and rebels against God, assuming that no one can remove him from his high position. In punishment, God sends an angel to take Robert's place as king while Robert is made the court fool. After some years and the failure of his brothers to recognize him, Robert repents and is restored to his royal honors by the angel, who returns to Heaven leaving Robert a better and wiser king for the duration of his reign. *Robert of Cisyle* is found in ten extant manuscripts, which can be dated between 1375 and 1500.[1] One

[1]According to Hornstein ("A New Manuscript" 453-54), the versions are as follows: Trinity College Oxford D57 (c. 1375; 440 lines); Bodleian 3938 (c. 1390; 444 lines); BM Additional 22283 (c. 1400; 454 lines); BM Additional 34801 (c. 1400; a fragment of 46 lines); BM Harley 1701 (c. 1425-1450; 486 lines); Cambridge University Library I.4.9 (c. 1450; 374 lines); BM Harley 525 (c. 1450-75; 472 lines); Trinity College Dublin 432B (c. 1458-61; an abridgement of 79 lines); Cambridge University Library Ff.2.38 (c. 1475-1500; 516 lines); Caius Cambridge 174 (c. 1475-1500; 470 lines). Since Bodleian 3938 is usually known as the "Vernon manuscript," I have used the notation "Vernon" to refer thereto in the text. Hazlitt believes that *Robert* "was formerly to be found in a printed shape," a "*ballett*" from "1569-70" (269). Even if the ballad was not identical to any of our extant manuscript versions, its existence attests to the continuing popularity of the legend in the sixteenth century. The edition

is a fragment of 46 lines and one an abridgement of 72 lines; the other eight vary in length from 374 lines to 516 lines. The language is probably that of the late fourteenth-century southeast midlands, and the versions are in four-stress couplets (Hornstein, "A New Manuscript" 453). Modern critics have viewed the poem with disfavor partly because it is one of the works we *call* romances which do not fit into neat generic pigeonholes, but instead inhabit the murky borderland between romance proper and hagiographic narrative. Lillian Herlands Hornstein classifies it among works she calls "legendary romances of didactic intent" which are "excellent vehicle[s] for instruction, for teaching and enforcing a lesson" ("Miscellaneous Romances" 167). In the Vernon version,[2] the poem has a heading that points the moral before the story begins: "Her is of Kyng Robert of Cicyle, Hou pride dude him begyle" (French and Hale p. 933). Many who study romances are uncomfortable with *Robert*; because it is a pious *fiction*, it is ignored by most who study hagiography. One of the few good literary studies of *Robert* can be found in Hanspeter Schelp's *Exemplarische Romanzen in Mittelenglischen*; other scholars study the folkloristic elements in the romance (Olsen) or matters like theatricality (Walsh).

The dearth of scholarship on *Robert of Cisyle* coupled with the wealth of manuscript versions, however, make it a logical candidate for study. The lack of criticism means that readers can come to the poem unprejudiced by interpretations which have acquired more canonical validity than the work itself. The wealth of manuscript versions, almost unparalleled for such a work, makes a comparative study of the versions possible. Such a comparative study enables us to trace the development of a popular romance over 175 years and will be of immense help to studies of oral tradition during the Middle English period. One

---

of the Vernon manuscript used is that of French and Hale; that of Cambridge Ff.2.38 that of Hazlitt; and that of Trinity Dublin 432B that of Brotanek.

[2]The Vernon version is the closest to a modern received text of the poem; it is the best known version and the evidence suggests "the genetic primacy of the Vernon tradition" (Hornstein, "A New Manuscript" 458). The Vernon version is an early version, probably copied in 1390. Trinity College Oxford D57 is somewhat earlier (1375) and somewhat shorter (440 lines as opposed to 444), but it obviously derives from the same original as does Vernon. The shortest full-length version (Cambridge University Library I.4.9, 374 lines) is from the mid-fifteenth century and is therefore less likely than Vernon to preserve the original text. The two manuscripts dated before 1400 suggest what the original version of the romance may have been like, and it is therefore logical to compare the other versions to Vernon.

problem with studying *Robert of Cisyle* is that not all the manuscripts have been edited and those which have been are not available in good modern editions. As a result, it is sometimes difficult to perform careful comparative study of the versions. Comparison of those versions which have been edited helps us to determine whether differences between versions may be scribal or whether they may represent oral improvisation. Scribes would often emend the text in accordance with their ideas of aesthetics; oral improvisors, on the other hand, usually substituted words when they forgot the exact wording of a line but remembered the sense of it. The probable original orality of *Robert* is seen in the description of the angel/king in Rome: "Þe steede was feir þer he ȝede" (French and Hale 256). As Walter Hoyt French and Charles Brockway Hale point out in their edition, one manuscript "has *place* for *steede*" (940), a substitution that does not change the *content* of the passage and therefore suggests oral improvisation.

At one point, the Vernon poet says, "For þat name i hedde pride: / And angels þat gonne from ioye glyde, / And in twynklyng of an eiȝe / God binom heore maystrie" (French and Hale 341-44); French and Hale remark, "the construction is faulty, the sense clear" (943). In Cambridge Ff.2.38, in contrast, the grammar is appropriate because Cambridge's use of "As" (Hazlitt 385) makes the sentence grammatical:

> And thorow that worde y felle in pryde,
> As the augelle that can of hevyn glyde,
> And with the tywnklyng of an eye
> God for-dud alle that maystrye.
>
> (Hazlitt 384-87)

The rhyme elements in Cambridge are the same as in Vernon, indicating a common source. French and Hale, in fact, observe that one editor, Nuck, "read *As in*" in line 385 of Vernon (943); Nuck assumed a written provenance for the romance and read the manuscript to accord with the grammar of the sentence. The lines in Vernon, which make good sense even though the grammar is erratic, suggest the original orality of the poem: an oral improvisor would have had no time to revise an infelicitous line once he had stated the connective.

A major problem in the study of oral tradition in Middle English has always been that we are dependent on written texts to help us understand the nature of oral poetry during the Middle Ages. As Ward

Parks states the matter, "the object of our search, orality and oral tradition, becomes accessible to us only when it ceases to be oral" (673). It is especially difficult to deal with romances because many of them have precise *written* sources.[3] C. Stephen Jaeger observes that "in the sociology of literary life at court we can distinguish two basic types of narrative poet: the professional singer of tales, and the cleric in possession of the deeds of the ancients preserved by written record," the latter of whom claimed that his work "brought useful moral instruction" rather than merely "foolish lies" (228-29). It is therefore tempting to believe that all versions of a romance represent manuscript transmission, especially in the case of *Robert of Cisyle*, which provides "useful moral instruction." In articles composed in 1959 and 1967, however, Albert C. Baugh made some insightful remarks about oral tradition in Middle English, arguing that variation between different manuscript versions often occurs at such a level as to make untenable the theory that scribal corruption was responsible for all differences. He points out that the manuscripts include "deliberate changes" which "involve not just the substitution of a better word, but the rephrasing of a line or several lines" and often the substitution of "banalities, clichés, and rime-tags" ("Middle English Romance" 29). Baugh hypothesizes that there must have been an original version of a poem (possibly composed in writing) which minstrels recited from memory, introducing changes into the text in accordance with principles of oral-formulaic improvisation when memory failed.[4] Then the revised text was recorded in another manuscript. *Robert of Cisyle*, whose eight complete versions differ by 142 lines and exist in manuscripts copied over a span of 125 years and whose abridged version is less than one-seventh the length of the longest version, provides a useful text to study the oral transmission of Middle English poetry.

With the exception of the abridgement, Trinity College Dublin Manuscript 432, the manuscript versions of *Robert of Cisyle* fall into groups of related texts (Hornstein, "A New Manuscript" 457-58). According to Hornstein, the modern authority on *Robert of Cisyle*, this text

[3]For example, the Middle English *Ywain and Gawain* is a translation and adaptation of *Yvain* by Chrétien de Troyes.

[4]In a major recent study, McGillivray argues that oral transmission of romances can be seen when verses in different versions of a romance like *Sir Orfeo* appear in different parts of the text; he suggests that the text was memorized and performed but that memorial transmission was not completely eidetic.

is "not derived from any extant manuscript" ("Miscellaneous Romances" 171). It is, however, usually assumed that the abridgement was made by a scribe from an "Urhandschrift" (Brotanek 46).

A stanza in rhyme royal spoken by a "Doctor" (Brotanek p. 36) introduces the abridgement:

> This riall kyng Robert of cesile lond
> To þe churche went, on a seynt Jones nyght,
> As a prynce pereles to here his evyn song
> With a prowde hert, a ioly and a light.
> But the goode lord that is ful of myght
> ffrom þat pride put hym into pouerte lowe,
> Ensaumple to all men hem self for to knowe.
> (1-7)

This stanza in a highly literate verse form must have been added to the poem by a scribe to point the moral that God "ffrom þat pride put hym into pouerte lowe" before the story begins. The stanza is analogous to the couplet at the head of the Vernon version, but the seven lines permit the poet to introduce the story as well as to emphasize the moral. The word "Rex" 'king' repeated twice "in roten Buchstaben" (Brotanek 36) separates the stanza from the body of the poem, another indication that the stanza was added to an existing poem.

In Trinity Dublin, the story itself begins *in medias res*, when Robert hears the choir sing, "Deposuit potentes" 'He has put down the mighty' (Brotanek 8). The abridgement, composed in four-stress lines and rhymed couplets like the full versions, undoubtedly represents a version *reconstructed* by a poet trained in the techniques of oral-formulaic composition who had heard the poem read or performed and then composed his own version. William A. Quinn and Audley S. Hall have argued that the key to oral improvisation in Middle English lay in rhyming pairs so that each oral poet could use his associated rhyming pairs to cover lapses in memory during recitation. If an oral poet forgot the exact phrasing of the work during recitation, he would "select a semantically suitable word from the appropriate, preestablished rhyming vocabulary . . . in order to avoid any awkward hesitation during his public performance" (7-8). We can see this process at work when we compare the Trinity Dublin version of *Robert of Cisyle* to the version in the Vernon manuscript. The Trinity Dublin poet preserves the storyline but focuses more closely on King Robert than the full-length versions like Vernon do. In the interests of succinctness, he omits some dramatic lines found in Vernon, including the angel's comment before departure, "I am an angel, þou art kyng" (French and Hale 414). In addition, he omits much of the moralizing that has given the poem a reputation as a boring didactic piece.

Many lines in the Trinity Dublin version, including the most dramatic couplet of the poem, are found in a form little changed from that of Vernon. In the pivotal couplet, the angel tells the repentant Robert, "I am an angel of renoun, / Isent to kepe þi regioun" (French and Hale 405-06); according to Trinity Dublin, he says, "I am an aungel of gret renovne, / Sent from hevyn to kepe þi regiovne" (Brotanek 68-69). The presence of "gret" in the Trinity Dublin version is of no importance narratively, although it is interesting that the later version (ca. 1458-1461) adds an additional unstressed word to the four-stress line. Often, however, because the story in Trinity Dublin is abridged, the poet either substitutes new rhyming couplets or preserves one rhyming word found in the standard text. When the angel leaves the court of Sicily, according to Vernon, "He went in twynklyng of an eȝe; / No more of him þer nas seȝe" (French and Hale 415-16). The Trinity Dublin poet preserves the memorable phrase "twynklyng of an eȝe," but although "yie" is still in the rhyming position, it is the second element of the couplet: "Robert felle on kneis, and mercy gan to crye; / Þe augel voydeþ with twynkeling of an yie" (Brotanek 70-71). In their statistical study of rhyme elements in *King Horn*,[5] Quinn and Hall show that a common rhyme element is *-eie*, and two members of the group including it are "Seye" and "eye" (380). In the dialect of *King Horn*, "crye" does not rhyme with "eye," but in the dialect of the Trinity Dublin poet, it does rhyme with "yie." It is therefore reasonable to assume that the words formed part of what Quinn and Hall have called the poet's "preestablished rhyming vocabulary" (8).

In one of the most dramatic episodes in *Robert of Cisyle*, Robert falls asleep in the church and an angel takes his place. The Vernon poet uses eight lines to describe the episode:

> And in his þouht a sleep him tok
> In his pulput, as seiþ þe bok.
> Whon þat euensong was al don,
> A kyng ilyk him out gan gon,

[5]*Jongleur* by Quinn and Hall is the only statistical study of the rhyming elements in Middle English poetry; it provides a useful methodology which can be applied to a romance like *Robert of Cisyle* as well.

And alle men wiþ him gan wende;
Kyng Robert lafte out of mynde.
Þe newe kyng was, as i ou telle,
Godes angel, his pruide to felle.
(French and Hale 59-66)

The important rhyming words are "tok" (59) and "bok" (60) when Robert falls asleep and "telle" (65) and "felle" (66) when the poet speaks about the angel. The Trinity Dublin version abridges the eight-line passage to a single couplet, one line about Robert and one about the angel: "In that grete pride þe kyng a slepe fell; / God of his goodenes sent an aungell" (Brotanek 12-13). "Tell," "fell," and "aungell" are members of a group where the rhyme element is *-ell* or *-elle* (Quinn and Hall 333). The Trinity Dublin poet has used the second element of the couplet found in Vernon —"fell"—as the first element of another couplet. His use of "þe kyng a slepe fell" enables him both to abridge the passage and to eliminate the necessity of using a couplet where "a slepe him tok" (French and Hale 59) rhymes with the empty tag-line "as seiþ þe bok" (French and Hale 60). French and Hale comment that "the book is unknown" (935), implying that they assume that the Vernon poet had a written source. In contrast, I would suggest that the phrase is a "tag" line whose only purpose is to provide the poet with a rhyming word and therefore indicates oral transmission. Although romances are part of "the shift from reliance on oral transmission to reliance on the written word" (Jaeger 230), I would argue that the author of *Robert of Cisyle* pays only lip service to the written tradition while working within the conventions of oral improvisation.

Because a longer passage shows the poet's processes more clearly than the brief ones do, I turn now to compare a twenty-two line passage from the Vernon version in which the king hears the choir singing the psalms and rebels against God with the analogous passage from the opening of the Trinity Dublin version. Vernon describes King Robert's pride and obduracy when he hears the *Magnificat* sung at Vespers:

He made a clerk hit him rehers
In langage of his owne tonge;
In Latyn he nuste what heo songe.
Þe vers was þis, I telle þe;
"Deposuit potentes de sede,
Et exaltauit humiles."

Þis was þe vers, wiþouten les.
Þe clerk seide anon riht,
"Sire, such is Godes miht
Þat he may make heyȝe lowe,
And lowe heiȝe, in luytel þrowe;
God may do, wiþoute lyȝe,
His wil, in twynklyng of an eiȝe."
Þe Kyng seide, wiþ herte vnstable,
"Al ȝor song is fals and fable;
What mon haþ such pouwer
Me to bringe lowe in daunger?
I am flour of chiualrye;
Myn enemys i may distruye;
No mon lyueþ in no londe
Þat me may wiþstonde
Þen is þis a song of nouht!"

(French and Hale 36-57)

The poet has woven the Latin text into his English poem, using the last word of each half-verse of Luke 1:46 as the element of a rhyming couplet. The poet clearly considered it important to preserve the Latin: to rhyme with "sede" 'seat' (40) he uses the empty tag "I telle þe" (39). He repeats the first half of the line, "Þe vers was þis" (39) three lines later, "Þis was þe vers" (42), just before another empty tag, "wiþouten les" (42), which rhymes with the Latin "humiles" 'humble' (41).[6]

The rhymes which make it possible to interweave Latin and English seem to be more important than the narrative sense of the passage, producing the repetitions and tag-lines. The "clerk" (43) then explains the passage to both Robert and the audience in six lines, and the king becomes angered and calls the psalm "fals and fable" (50). The poet expands on Robert's anger and pride for an additional seven lines. Clerical authors "argue against the *fabulae*" of oral traditional poetry

[6]The Cambridge version replicates the lines in Vernon:

The vers was thys, as y telle the,
Deposuit potentes de sede,
Et exaltavit humiles.
Thys was the verse withowten lees.

(Hazlitt 39-42)

Except for dialectal variations and the inclusion of extra syllables in some lines ("as" added to "y telle the" [Hazlitt 39] and "a" to "lytylle throwe" [Hazlitt 46]), the lines are basically identical. The extra syllables suggest oral improvisation, as in lines discussed in the body of the essay.

"and commend the salutary effects of their own 'truthful' historical material" (Jaeger 229) derived from written tradition. Part of the irony of the poem derives from the fact that Robert labels material derived from written tradition (and specifically from Scripture) as fabulous. When he repents, Robert realizes that "Holy Writ i hedde in dispyt; / For þat is reued my delyt" (353-54). His repentance involves acknowledging the validity and truthfulness of the written tradition. Since Trinity Dublin is an abridgement, the poet simply says, "and Robert is fully repentid in þe same while" (Brotanek 57). Because the poet omits the scene of Robert's repentance, he omits as well Robert's realization that he has rebelled against written tradition.

In Trinity Dublin, it is the Doctor who praises Robert as a "riall kyng" (Brotanek 1) and "a prynce pereles" (Brotanek 3) rather than the poet putting the praise in Robert's own mouth. He criticizes him as having a "prowde hert" (Brotanek 4) rather than having him condemn himself by a display of pride. When Robert is condemned by his own language and behavior, it is clear that he deserves his punishment. What Trinity Dublin loses in dramatic intensity by the elimination of this episode, however, it gains in narrative succinctness. The passage describing Robert's rebellion takes four lines rather than twenty-two:

> "Deposuit potentes," þey in þe quere songe;
> Þe kyng wex wroþe and seid it was wronge
> Worship to be put downe in ony maner wise,
> And pouerte to worship by ony mene to rise.
> (Brotanek 8-11)

The version shortens the Latin to the first two words of the *Magnificat*[7] and has Robert himself explain the meaning to us rather than an extraneous clerk. Like Vernon, in which "in Latyn he [Robert] nuste what heo songe" (French and Hale 38), most versions represent Robert as ignorant of the meaning of the Latin. Jaeger shows, however, that medieval noblemen were "highly learned, highly articulate" (263) even when illiterate. Robert's knowledge of Latin in Trinity Dublin is there-

[7]Latin texts are habitually identified by their first two words, as is the *Pater noster* 'Our father' or the *Ave Maria* 'Hail Mary,' and occasionally by one words as the Creed is: *Credo* 'I believe.' Therefore, the Trinity Dublin poet could assume that "Deposuit potentes" would remind his audience of the entire text from Luke.

fore appropriate for a king in a fifteenth-century poem. In addition, since the poet does not include any Latin words in a rhyming position, he does not need to use "tag" rhymes as the Vernon poet does in lines 39 and 42. In the Vernon version, the choir is singing, and the poet uses "songe" (French and Hale 38) to rhyme with "tonge" 'language' (French and Hale 37). The Trinity Dublin poet preserves the singing and the use of "songe" in a rhyming position, but as the first element of his couplet. The Vernon poet rhymes "songe" with "tonge" to introduce the clerk's explanation and paraphrase in English; the Trinity Dublin poet rhymes "songe" (Brotanek 8) with "wronge" (Brotanek 9) in his description of the king's anger. Quinn and Hall show that in *King Horn*, "songe," "tonge," and "wronge" are part of a group whose rhyme element is *-onge* (400). The Trinity Dublin poet seems to have substituted one member of such a group for another to further his own narrative.

Study of the rhymes in the Vernon and Trinity Dublin versions of *Robert of Cisyle* suggests that Trinity Dublin is not a scribal abridgement because a scribal abridgement would presumably resemble one of the full-length versions more closely than Trinity Dublin does. Instead, it is an abridgement and revision by an oral improvisor which found its way later into manuscript form, and a learned scribe is undoubtedly responsible for the introductory rhyme royal stanza.

A similar comparison can be made of the other versions as well to demonstrate the original orality thereof. One intriguing variant is the longest version, that found in Cambridge University Library Manuscript Ff.2.38, which is one of the two latest versions, composed between 1475 and 1500. There is some reorganization of episodes in Cambridge, most noteworthy that Robert's repentance in Vernon takes place *before* the brothers leave Rome, although he receives his pardon in Sicily. In Cambridge, however, he repents in Sicily and is immediately pardoned, a more dramatic arrangement of the material. Trinity Dublin has the same arrangement as Cambridge:

> Whan þe aungel come home agayne into Cesile,
> and Robert is fully repentid in þe same while,
> And neuer desireþ he to be grettyr lorde.
> But loweþ his hert with his aray to corde.
> (Brotanek 56-59)

The Trinity Dublin manuscript dates from the mid-fifteenth century (1458-61), and if Vernon preserves the original version of the story, it is possible that a late poet introduced the more dramatic version of the repentance story into the poem and that that version is retained in several late versions.

Cambridge has a number of brief passages not found in Vernon and three long ones, fourteen, sixteen, and eighteen lines long (Hazlitt 192-205, 470-85, and 490-507). One brief passage occurs when the porter refuses to acknowledge that Robert is his king. In Vernon, Robert merely calls the porter a "foule gadelyng" (French and Hale 81), but in Cambridge, he rages at him at greater length, although he does call him a "false gadlynge" (Hazlitt 106). Robert threatens the porter in a passage which casts a negative light upon Robert's reign and presents him as a tyrannical ruler as well as a rebel against God and therefore suggests to the audience that his punishment is just. Cambridge adds a couplet wherein Robert says, "I schalle yow teche me for to knawe, / And brynge yow fro yowre lyfe dawe" (Hazlitt 103-04), and the longer version makes the point more fully than that in Vernon does. Another addition occurs in Rome, when Robert appeals to his brothers to help him. According to Vernon, "Þe Pope ne þe Emperour nouþer / Þe ffol ne kneuȝ not for heor broþer" (French and Hale 287-88). Given that he is shaven and "cloþed in lodly garnement, / Wiþ ffoxes tayles mony aboute" (French and Hale 248-49), their lack of recognition is reasonable. Cambridge adds, "God put hym in odur lyknes / For hys grete unbuxumnes" (Hazlitt 322-23), making the failure of recognition part of the divine retribution. This passage is not found in Trinity Dublin although it and Cambridge present the same order of events; in it, brevity is more important than the didactic message and it says merely, "Robert disgised as a fole renneth by" (Brotanek 37).

Generally, both the short and long passages add explicit moralizing to the story, making the didactic message even clearer than in Vernon. When Robert refuses to eat with the hounds and almost starves, the Cambridge version says, "Bettur he were, to yow sey y, / So to do, then for hunger dye" (Hazlitt 218-19). After Robert has been clothed as a fool, the Cambridge version says, "At lowar degré, he myght not bee, / Then become a fole, as thynkyth me" (Hazlitt 192-93) and "Lo, how soone, be Goddys myght / He was lowe, and that was ryght!" (Hazlitt 196-97). Likewise, near the end of the poem, the poet reiterates the point:

> For he wende he myght not be
> Thorow Godes myȝt at lowar degré.

He was made lowe in a lytylle throwe,
And that was kyd and fulle welle knowe.
(Hazlitt 470-73)

Part of Robert's repentance involves self-condemnation in a brief passage not found in Vernon wherein Robert excoriates himself as "wrech of wrechys" (Hazlitt 397) and "fole of alle folys" (Hazlitt 398). In the last passage added to the text, the poet reinforces the theme of pride in the form of a sermon by the Pope:

The pope of Rome hereof can preche,
And the pepulle he can teche,
That ther pryde they schulde forsake
And to gode vertues they schule them take.
(Hazlitt 496-99)

The major omission from Cambridge is the prayer to the Virgin found in Vernon in Robert's speech of repentance:

Blisful Marie, to þe i crie,
As þou art ful of cortesye;
Preye þi Sone, þat dyed for me;
On me, his fol, þow haue pité.
Blisful Marie, ful of graas,
To þe i knowe my trespas;
Preye þi Sone, for loue of þe,
On me, his fool, he haue pité!
(French and Hale 365-72)

The omission of a passage that emphasizes that Robert is a "fol" (368) guilty of "trespas" (370) is surprising in a long version which consistently underscores the poem's moral message. The omission may, of course, be influenced by the manuscript's late date of composition, but it may also represent a capricious omission by the poet such as is to be found in orally improvised poetry.

One of the most striking differences between the Vernon and Cambridge versions involves the number of syllables in each line. Each version uses four-stress lines, but the lines in Vernon are regularly octosyllabic, whereas those in Cambridge tend to be longer (up to thirteen syllables in length). The beginning of the poem mentions Robert's brothers. According to Vernon, "His broþer was mad emperour; / His oþer broþer, Godes vikere" (French and Hale 16-17). According to Cambridge, "And hys odur brodur was emperowre. / Hys oon brodur in ȝorthe Godes generalle vykere" (Hazlitt 16-17). Although line 17 is longer in Cambridge than in Vernon, the phrase "in ȝorthe" and the adjective "generalle" do not add information that is necessary to the poem; instead, they suggest that the improvisor of the Cambridge version included the phrases while he was recounting the poem.

Quinn and Hall argue that an oral improvisor "was committed during performance to preserve" the "established form" (7) of the work he was reciting. They suggest that the "established form" was the couplets, or at least the rhyme elements thereof. The versions of the couplet forming lines 16-17 are virtually identical in Vernon and Cambridge, despite the inclusion of the extra syllables in Cambridge and the inversion of lines 16 and 17 so that "odur" is in line 16 of Cambridge. The rhyme elements are preserved even when there are dialectal differences. When the emperor sends messengers to Robert, the angel welcomes them and gives them gifts. According to Vernon, "Þe angel welcomede þe messagers / And ȝaf hem cloþes riche of pers" (French and Hale 233-34). According to Cambridge, "The augelle welcomyd the messengerys, / And clad them alle in clothys of pryse" (Hazlitt 264-65). Because of the differences in dialect, the word rhyming with "messagers" (French and Hale 233) is "pers" 'sky-blue material' (French and Hale 234) whereas that rhyming with "messengerys" (Hazlitt 264) is "pryse" 'value' (Hazlitt 265). Nevertheless, the sense of the two passages is the same. Like Trinity Dublin, Cambridge preserves the sense of lines and the rhyming elements. Vernon says, "Lord, i leeued not on þe. / On þi fool þou haue pité" (French and Hale 351-52), and Cambridge, "And that ys ryght that y so bee, / For, Lorde, y leevyd not on the" (Hazlitt 391-92). The line about Robert's disbelief has been transposed in the couplet, but the rhyme element remains the same.

Lines 49-50 provide an example of a passage in which Vernon and Cambridge share rhyming *elements*, presumably replicating those of the original text, but have different phraseology. According to Quinn and Hall, the performer would "improvise the exact phrasing of the lines themselves" (8) as long as he preserved the rhyme. Such freedom would explain the difference between "herte" (French and Hale 49) in Vernon and "thoȝt" (Hazlitt 49) in Cambridge, both of which express the essential idea of the king's mind or soul. Quinn and Hall observe that a performer "was apparently permitted much stress variance" (8) as he improvised lines, and we see this process at work in *Robert of Cisyle*. In Vernon, lines 49 and 50 are both octosyllabic; in Cambridge, line 49 has nine syllables and line 50, twelve. Vernon, which dates from around 1390, is one of the three earliest manuscripts; Cambridge, which dates from between 1450 and 1500, is one of the latest. In the process of oral improvisation, the couplets must have lost their regular octosyllabic form but preserved their formulaic rhyming words.

Despite such differences, the Vernon and Cambridge versions are remarkably similar, even down to details of phraseology and rhyming words. Many lines in Cambridge are almost identical to those in Vernon. As was noted earlier, in the pivotal couplet, the angel tells the repentant Robert, "I am an angel of renoun, / Isent to kepe þi regioun" (French and Hale 405-06); according to Cambridge, "I am an aungelle of renowne, / Sente to kepe thy regyowne" (Hazlitt 444-45). It is likely that the drama of these lines meant that they were unforgettable and the lines therefore survived with little change. When the lines themselves differ in content, the rhyming words tend to be unchanged, and the changes are those which suggest oral improvisation. When Robert falls asleep, for example, Vernon says, "a sleep him tok / In his pulput, as seiþ þe bok" (French and Hale 59-60), whereas Cambridge substitutes "closet" (Hazlitt 60) for "pulput." Likewise, in the passage describing the king's anger Vernon says, "Þe Kyng seide, wiþ herte vnstable, / 'Al ȝor song is fals and fable'" (French and Hale 49-50). In the corresponding passage in Cambridge, "The kyng seyde than with thoȝt unstabulle: / Ye synge thys ofte, and alle hys a fabulle" (Hazlitt 49-50). The point of the lines is identical in the two versions and is underscored by the rhyming words: the king is angered and accuses the choir of singing falsehoods.

The variation between Vernon and Cambridge that most clearly suggests oral transmission of *Robert of Cisyle* is found in a passage in which Cambridge replaces a couplet with three rhyming lines. The passage occurs after Robert has awakened alone in the church and returns, indignant, to his palace. According to Vernon, "Þe porter com to þe ȝate, / And him he called, in to late" (French and Hale 121-22). Cambridge says, "The portar came unto the ȝate, / And calde hym swythe yn ther-ate, / And he began for to debate" (Hazlitt 123-25). The improvisor must have been searching for a rhyme for "ȝate" and forgot that the word in his exemplar was "late." He used two words from his pool of rhymes to make both the rhyme *and* the sense of the passage work. Quinn and Hall speak of the "substitution of one (i.e., *systematic*) rhyme word for another" accompanied by "the same couplet-defining rhyme element" and modification of "the idea expressed in the individual line containing the substitute rhyme" (86)—in the case of *Robert of Sicily*, two lines containing substitute rhymes. I would argue that it is unlikely that a scribe, however incompetent or erratic, would make such a substitution but that it is, instead, a sign of oral improvisation.

This comparative study of the versions of *Robert of Sicily* shows that we can apply the tools of oral-formulaic criticism to neglected poems and develop an appreciation of the oral elements of Middle English poetry. Although romance is a genre that developed with rising literacy (especially that of the laity [Jaeger 228-31]), there was a need to recount the stories found therein in a form accessible to the illiterate. The techniques were those of oral improvisation, which survived long after the introduction of widespread literacy.

Department of English
University of Denver

Works Cited

Baugh, Albert C. "Improvisation in the Middle English Romance." *Proceedings of the American Philosophical Society* 103 (1959): 418-54.

—. "The Middle English Romance: Some Questions of Creation, Presentation, and Preservation." *Speculum* 42 (1967): 1-31.

Brotanek, Rudolf, ed. "A Story of King Robert of Cesyle." *Mittelenglishe Dichtungen aus der Handschrift 432 des Trinity College in Dublin.* Halle/Saale: Verlag, 1940. 36-47.

French, Walter Hoyt and Charles Brockway Hale, eds. *Robert of Sicily. Middle English Metrical Romances.* New York: Russell, 1964. 933-46.

Hazlitt, W. Carew, ed. *Kynge Robert of Cysille. Remains of the Early Popular Poetry of England.* 1864. New York: AMS,1966. 264-88.

Hornstein, Lillian Herlands. "*King Robert of Sicily*: A New Manuscript." *PMLA* 78 (1963): 453-58.

—. "*King Robert of Sicily*: Analogues and Origins." *PMLA* 79 (1964): 13-21.

—. "Miscellaneous Romances." *A Manual of the Writings in Middle English.* Ed. J. Burke Severs. New Haven: Connecticut Academy of the Arts and Sciences, 1967. 144-72 and 325-32.

Jaeger, C. Stephen. *The Origins of Courtliness: Civilizing Trends and the Formation of Courtly Ideals, 939-1210.* Philadelphia: U of Pennsylvania P, 1985.

McGillivray, Murray. *Memorization in the Transmission of the Middle English Romances.* New York: Garland, 1990.

Olsen, Alexandra Hennessey. "The Return of the King: A Reconsideration of *Robert of Sicily*." *Folklore* 93 (1982): 216-19.

Parks, Ward. "The Oral-Formulaic Theory in Middle English Studies." *Oral Tradition* 1 (1986): 636-94.

Quinn, William A. and Audley S. Hall. *Jongleur: A Modified Theory of Oral Improvisation and Its Effects on the Performance and Transmission of Middle English Romance*. Washington, DC: UP of America, 1982.

Schelp, Hanspeter. *Exemplarische Romanzen in Mittelenglischen*. Palaestra 246. Göttingen: Vanderhoeck and Ruprecht, 1967.

Walsh, Martin W. "Looking in on a Lost Drama: The Case of *King Robert of Sicily*." *Fifteenth-Century Studies* 14 (1988): 191-201.

Tradition and Heroism in the Middle English Romances

Dave Henderson

Transitional texts have been a problem of considerable interest in studies in oral tradition. Such texts stand on the borderline between orality and literacy, employing oral traditional forms, exemplified by the well-known concepts of formula and theme, in the milieu of a written literary tradition. In the context of Old and Middle English studies, for example, transitional texts comprise a considerable proportion of the body of works that remain to us. Even a work such as *Beowulf*, which was clearly composed using oral-formulaic techniques, cannot be declared to be of unambiguously oral provenance. Unlike the "unambiguously oral texts" of the South Slavic guslari collected by Milman Parry and Albert B. Lord in the first half of this century, the finest distinction we can draw, according to John Miles Foley, is that of declaring *Beowulf* (as well as its companions in the Old English corpus) to be "oral-derived" (*Traditional Oral Epic* 5-10). Clearly, the Middle English romances' reliance on oral traditional techniques identifies them as oral-derived, and the complex transition from orality to literacy can be understood in part by considering the changes in the ways such techniques create meaning in these texts.

The Middle English romances provide a striking example of the range of transitional texts.[1] As they have come down to us, the ro-

[1]Reichl makes many useful observations on the transitional nature of Middle English romance, and Lord's viewpoints ("Merging of Two Worlds") on oral

mances are the products of literate authors as well as scribes. The scribes worked in modes that may have included both transcription of oral—or, more probably, "memorized"—performances[2] and intentional modification of texts during the copying process.[3] Conjectures regarding performance modes and the use of oral-traditional techniques have been explored by numerous authors,[4] and comparison of multiple versions of the same or similar romances shows a variety analogous, though certainly not in all respects identical, to that exhibited by multiple performances of an orally-composed work. In both cases, couplets may be inverted or displaced, rhymes and verse form may vary from version to version, and the story itself may be truncated, expanded, or reshaped from one version to the next.[5] In the context of the editing of the Middle English romances, Jennifer Fellows has suggested that, in view of the nature of their composition, the reconstruction of "Ur-texts" is "inappropriate" and that "the archetypal text, even if it were possible to establish its readings with more certainty than can be achieved on the basis of the extant evidence, would be of less interest than the relationships between the redactions we have" (10).

Since all the extant Middle English romances use, to some degree, traditional techniques like minstrel tags, formulae, and other devices of spoken or sung performance, it is actually more correct to

---

tradition in general are indispensable. See Stock and Clanchy for general surveys of the transition from orality to literacy, and for additional theoretical and practical considerations see the articles in Doane and Pasternack.

[2]Reichl writes that it is "clear that those minstrels who performed narrative texts orally must have memorized their texts, the formulaic style of the poems 'easing' their memory as well as providing a technique for rapid telling, or in the event that memory failed" (261). Such performances must have given rise to the same kind of textual variations evidenced in the manuscripts.

[3]Allen claims that "scribes did rework romances, and produced quite different versions with extensive additions or deletions" (18), and Fellows has argued that "the scribes themselves have authorial status" (7). Interesting results can be obtained by adopting this point of view in examining the way Middle English verse translations of romances modify their source texts.

[4]Reichl discusses the Middle English romances in the context of both oral-traditional techniques and performance. See Crosby, Baugh ("Middle English Romance), and Ramsey (*Chivalric Romances* 18-22) for general examinations of performance. See Parks ("Oral-Formulaic Theory") and the accompanying citations, as well as Camargo, Fewster, and McGillivray in regard to oral-traditional techniques. For an interesting treatment of performance and transmission in regard to a single text, *Sir Launfal*, see Knight.

[5]See Hurt; Baugh ("Improvisation"); Reichl; and Fewster (50-81).

speak in terms of more traditional versus less traditional texts rather than of works composed in the manner of the South Slavic guslari versus works written down by literate authors.[6] More traditional romances are typified by works like *King Horn* and *Havelok the Dane*, which are characterized by extremely heavy dependence on formulaic tags and other performative techniques. Although less traditional romances, such as *Sir Gawain and the Green Knight*, also rely on performative techniques, such usage is distinctly less marked and repetitious. More importantly, the more traditional romances create meanings and characterizations quite different from those of works generally agreed to be of authorial rather than minstrel provenance, such as *Sir Gawain*.[7] The romances mentioned above admittedly (and intentionally) represent extreme cases of the phenomena I hope to illustrate; hence, at the end of this essay I will consider *Amis and Amiloun* as an illustration of a romance whose degree of traditionality falls somewhere between the extremes described above.

As we trace the spectrum from romances that are closer to a hypothetical oral provenance to less traditional ones, we can observe a steadily increasing degree of ambiguity in the characterization of the protagonists. The strongly didactic nature of *Horn* and *Havelok*, on the one hand, with their casts of perfectly good and perfectly bad characters, contrasted with the universally agreed-upon ambiguities of *Sir Gawain*, on the other, implies a complex relationship between the degree of traditionality of a given text and the degree of difficulty encountered in explicating it.[8] One of the most striking features of *Sir Gawain*,

[6]See Foley (*Immanent Art* 1-37).

[7]A caveat is in order here, since the fact that *Horn* and *Havelok* are both dated earlier than *Sir Gawain* may suggest that what I am describing is an evolutionary process. In view of the difficulty of dating the majority of Middle English romances, I would suggest that a better way of looking at the romances and their traditional nature is as a spectrum of modes of meaning only secondarily affected by the progress of time. (For a cogent discussion of romance as a mode, see Gradon [212-72].) There is no reason to suppose that both more and less traditional works could not have been in production at the same point in time.

[8]The question of the explicability of texts far removed from us in terms of both time and culture is an important one. I would not deny that all criticism must, by virtue of its element of subjectivity, "adjust" reality to bring one age into focus for another, but what I am referring to here as ambiguity could just as easily be described as moral complexity. Texts that seem inexplicable to us were no doubt complex and difficult for medieval audiences as well, who had a demon-

for instance, is its problematization of ideals that are taken for granted in more traditional romances like *Horn* and *Havelok*.

In order to place what I am saying about meaning and reception in a more theoretical context, it is instructive to consider the nature of the hero in oral traditional texts. Foley has detailed the metonymic contract, emphasizing that the audience's reception in a traditional context is manipulated with the use of story patterns, characterizations, and phraseology that are part of their culture's knowledge held in common. These devices bear extraordinary significative weight in their most traditional contexts (*Immanent Art* 1-37). Stocks of such traditional techniques collect around various heroes as they become part of their particular tradition (*Immanent Art* 99-100; 195-210).

While there is little more explicit evidence of a Horn-tradition than there is of a Beowulf-tradition, both belong to the tradition of heroic character in general, and English heroic character in particular. Thus, while we may not have as much textual evidence with which to construct a detailed character portrait of Horn as we do in the case of, say, the South Slavic hero Kraljevic Marko, we can draw conclusions about the type of figure Horn is and what sort of behavior an audience would naturally expect of him. While the audience's expectations may be quite complex, violation of these expectations in the form of unanticipated behavior on the part of the protagonist obviously leads to interpretive difficulties. The meanings that arise are, in a traditional context, deeply ambiguous.

The very traditional nature of *Horn* and *Havelok* is emphasized by their continuity with the English tradition that precedes them,[9] a continuity validated by these romances' modification of their source materials for the purpose of stressing subjects and themes that have

---

strated taste for conundra and other literary puzzles. The tribulations of a Gawain or a Lancelot embroiled their original audiences in the shifting tug of motivations just as strongly as they do audiences today.

[9]The justification for suggesting a continuity from *Beowulf* and other Anglo-Saxon verse to *Horn* and *Havelok* lies in the fact that I am limiting my comparison to a consideration of the hero's characterization and the resultant impact on meaning in each poem. I emphasize only common icons and conventions, not generic continuities. Foley outlines a program for textual comparison that transcends the limitations of genre (*Traditional Oral Epic* 5-10). See Amodio for a consideration of oral traditional continuities between the Old and Middle English periods, and Cable, who considers analogous continuities in the context of Old and Middle English prosody.

generally been identified as the Matter of England.[10] The social structure commonly called the "comitatus," along with the workings of its various configurations, informs much of the thematic and dramatic content of Old English poetry, and analogous concerns clearly motivate both *Horn* and *Havelok*.[11] In both romances the give and take between lord and vassal becomes very explicit in the endings, when the respective kings' tried and true retainers, the analogue to the *Beowulf*ian "duguð," are rewarded for their assistance in assuring their sovereign's ascent to the throne. Both Horn and Havelok, like Beowulf, are embodiments of the very best qualities of men and rulers, a fact that I will emphasize and explain below.

Besides their continuity with Anglo-Saxon tradition, both *Horn* and *Havelok* reach beyond their immediate milieu to the larger field of modes and techniques exemplified in oral-traditional compositions. Both poems utilize, in modified form, the story-pattern that Lord has identified as the Return Song ("Theme of the Withdrawn Hero").[12] The elements of the Return Song are Absence, Devastation, Return, Retribution, and Wedding. For instance, during Horn's enforced absence from his home in Suddenne, Saracens devastate his kingdom. Upon his return, he avenges himself upon these enemies, shortly afterward marrying Rymenhild.

Arthur G. Brodeur defines the formal poetic device of variation, another fundamental characteristic of traditional composition,[13] as

[10]See Barron (63-88); and, indirectly, Field.

[11]Ramsey (*Chivalric Romances*) evokes the "comitatus" in his description of Horn's father, King Murry: "His virtues are conventional ones, all relating to one thing, his ability to keep the ravages of war away from the kingdom and to assure his subjects that they need not fight to maintain their safety" (30). He notes additionally that "since the very fabric of feudal government depended on the making and keeping of oaths, the existence of men who would solemnly vow to do one thing and then do something else not only threatened continual trouble but also promised to destroy the social system itself" (33).

[12]I am presently preparing an essay on the Return Song in Middle English romance. Barron identifies *Horn* as "a folk-tale of the exile-and-return type" (65), although he does not elaborate on the notion in great detail. For a comparison of the Return Song in another Middle English romance, *Sir Orfeo*, with those in two South Slavic poems and the *Odyssey*, see Parks ("Return Song"). For comparative purposes see also Foley (*Traditional Oral Epic* 359-87) on the Return Song in South Slavic epic.

[13]Ong has emphasized the "additive rather than subordinative" nature of oral composition (37-38). Greenfield writes that variation "is probably the most dis-

"a double or multiple statement of the same concept or idea in different words, with a more or less perceptible shift in stress" (40). Also important is the distinction that "one member of a variation may state the thought either more generally or more specifically than the other; or the second member, while restating essentially the same concept or idea, may do so in a manner which emphasizes a somewhat different aspect" (idem). The use of variation, which, as Fred C. Robinson notes, is chiefly distinguished by its paratactic nature (3), establishes another thread of continuity between the Middle English romances and the Old English tradition, in which variation is crucially instrumental in shaping characterization and meaning.

The very paratactic nature of *King Horn* is emphasized by its use of what Rosamund Allen has identified as the "ship-voyage" theme (84-85).[14] The use of this theme to mark paratactic units should not be underestimated. For instance, when Horn is exiled from his homeland of Suddenne by the Saracens in the poem's first episode, he is set adrift in a ship with his companions. The ship-voyage ends when Horn and company land in Westernesse, where the second episode takes place. Likewise, Horn's first round of adventures in Westernesse conclude when he is again forced to take ship, this time to Ireland. The sea-voyage is a principal structuring device in marking off the poem's various episodes and it comprises, along with its accompanying changes of locale, a very powerful enforcement of parataxis.[15]

A marking device easily recognized by *Horn*'s audience, the sea-voyage theme has its precedent in many Old and Middle English poems, from *Beowulf* to *Havelok*. Having recognized the theme and its implications and function, the listening audience would doubtless have started drawing parallels between the various incidents in the respective episodes, guided by their knowledge of the code of ethics and conduct that shapes Horn's behavior. The set of parallels embodied by Horn's relative degree of maturity at the time of each departure is particularly

---

tinctive as well as pervasive stylistic feature in Old English poetry" (60). His discussion (60-83) of the technique is largely theoretical in nature, however, and goes beyond the implications of variation in Old English poetry alone. See also Robinson for a discussion of variation in Old English poetry, and Bauman on theoretical aspects of performance.

[14]See Ramsey ("Sea Voyages") and Foley (*Traditional Oral Epic* 336-44).

[15]Barron writes that "[l]ike someone engaged in a ritual, Horn goes through six moves, crossing water between each of them and in each enacting variations on the same theme" (65-66).

telling. When the Saracens set him adrift at the end of the poem's first episode, Horn is a child recognized mainly for his physical beauty, which is what saves him. When Horn departs from Westernesse, it is as a young man caught in a love intrigue with King Aylmar's daughter, Rymenhild. He sails to Ireland, and, later, hearing of King Modi's plans to marry Rymenhild, returns to Westernesse at the head of an army. Having rescued Rymenhild, he sails back to Suddenne, now equipped with sufficient maturity and wisdom to take back his rightful kingdom. This set of parallels describes a kind of *bildungsroman*, or tale of moral and psychological maturation, of the sort encountered in, among other places, *Beowulf* and *Havelok*. This story pattern describes the growth from innocence to maturity of an ideal ruler, the central figure in the "comitatus." In all circumstances Horn's behavior is exemplary, beyond reproach, from his insistence on being chaperoned on his visits to Rymenhild to his perfect deportment at court, which instantly wins him advancement.

It is interesting to note, in still another pair of parallel elements, the elevation of Horn to a status more than exemplary; as such, he joins the ranks of oral traditional characters described as "heavy"—what literate readers might call "flat"—by Walter J. Ong (69-71). In the poem's first episode, King Murry, Horn's father, is attacked by Saracens whom he sees weighing anchor on the shores of Suddenne while on his morning ride with two companions. Murry, though a perfectly exemplary character himself,[16] is unable to resist the Saracens' onslaught:

> þe king hadde al-to fewe
> Toȝenes * vele schrewe:
> So fele miȝten [eþe]
> Bringe hem þre to d[e]þe.
>
> (57-60)[17]

Horn, on the other hand, has better luck when, near the end of his first set of adventures in Westernesse, he is accosted while riding (alone!) in search of adventure by Saracens who, as in Murry's experience, have just landed on the beach. Again like Murry, Horn asks the Saracens what their mission is, and they again respond that they mean to conquer

[16]See note 11.
[17]I cite Allen's edition of *King Horn* throughout.

the land and kill its inhabitants. Horn attacks, and the results are a grim variation on Murry's last battle:

He sloȝ þer on haste
On Hundred bi þe laste;
Ne miȝte noman telle
þ*at* folk þ*at* he gan quelle;
Of þ*at* [þer] were a[r]iue
[Fewe he lafte] þriue.

(621-26)

Hence, blameless as King Murry may be, Horn demonstrates a puissance whose superiority is emphasized by the parallelism between the two scenes. He is truly exemplary. As the poem insists, "Nas no[man] his iliche / In none kinge-riche" (17-18).

Havelok, too, is an exemplary character. The poem minces no words in this regard:

Hauelok was a ful god gome—
He was ful god in eueri trome;
He was þe wicteste ma*n* at nede
þat þurte riden on ani stede.

(7-10)[18]

As in the case of Horn, this superior character is brought to life by the juxtaposition of paratactic units, but in *Havelok* the situation is complicated by the doubling of exemplars of good and evil. The two primary representatives of good in the poem are Havelok and his future bride, Goldeborw, who, like Horn, will emerge as national rulers. The exemplars of evil are the two usurpers, who, interestingly enough, share very similar (and ironic) names—Godrich, who steals Goldeborw's kingdom after her father, Athelwold, dies, and Godard, who commits a similar crime when King Birkabeyn dies and leaves Havelok under his aegis.[19] The two usurpations are presented paratactically at the beginning of the poem, creating, as its first priority, the contrast between blameless conduct, exemplified in these passages by Athelwold and Birkabeyn, and the reprehensible behavior of the two usurpers.

[18] I cite Smithers's edition of *Havelok* throughout.

[19] The etymons of the usurpers' names are of Old English provenance. "Godrich" is from "god ric," meaning 'virtuous power,' "Godard" from "god eard," meaning 'pleasant land.'

Like Horn's story, Havelok's is a Middle English *bildungsroman*; he passes an eventful youth in which he displays his innate nobility at every turn, advancing himself through good deeds and appropriate behavior. When he finally assumes his predestined role as king and punishes those who tried to deprive him of his birthright, the event is presented as one clearly foreseen. Indeed, the lowliness of his social status through most of the poem functions more as a way of illustrating and emphasizing the old adage that "blood will tell" than as a generator of irony. There is virtually no ambiguity reflected in the characterizations of either Havelok or Horn; both are perfect men and rulers whose nobility is innate rather than the product of their status. The didactic impulse behind both of these romances—an impulse that can be argued to be operative in some form in virtually all of the romances—is unproblematic.[20] The thematic thrust of both *Horn* and *Havelok* suggests that the man suited by nature to kingship will gain his birthright, and this assumption remains unchallenged from beginning to end. Almost all of the poems' complications arise not from thematic tensions but from dramatic ones in the form of obstructions to Horn's and Havelok's inevitable progress toward their respective thrones.

The same can hardly be said of *Sir Gawain and the Green Knight*. Martin Camargo has deftly encapsulated the poem's essential ambiguities:

> [i]ts hero undergoes a mysterious rite of passage, emerging from a naive faith in his own perfection into a mature sense of his limitations and indeed an awareness that fixed codes of conduct and human ingenuity are less than completely reliable guides through the labyrinth of experience. (121)

What we see here in miniature is a kind of character development analogous, but not identical, to that of the *bildungsroman*. Yet Gawain's character development is, in one sense at least, a reversal of what we see in *Horn* and *Havelok*. Instead of moving from a troubled childhood to mature perfection, he moves from perfection—and I agree with Camargo (121) that the sense of perfection is illusory—to a fragmented vision of whom he might be. With this brilliant stroke, the *Gawain*-poet

[20] Weiss and Staines explore the didactic nature of *Havelok*.

deeply problematizes his hero's character. Clearly, Gawain is not a hero of the same sort as Horn and Havelok; he is anything but "heavy."

Although the interaction of lord and vassal, the structuring principle of the "comitatus" as well as of the Round Table, gives rise to the oath that provides the focal point for the poem's tension, the complexity of this interaction is deepened by Gawain's vacillation. Exemplary behavior is required to make the system work. It would be pointless to deny that in a very real sense Gawain *is* an exemplary character; like Lancelot, his character raises him above lesser knights. But a distinction must be drawn between "exemplary" and the redoubtable "more than exemplary," which flattens characters. Gawain's exemplary character may be "flawed," but his very flaws lend dignity and complexity to his unquestionable nobility. The fact that Gawain's deportment does not result in his death or dishonor emphasizes the uncertain value of exemplary behavior. In this regard, *Beowulf*, with its cast of traitors at the battle with the dragon, has more in common with *Gawain* than either *Horn* or *Havelok*, although I would hasten to add that Beowulf's behavior, with its rock-solid propriety, does not give rise to the kind of ambiguity occasioned by Gawain's.

The ambiguities that the poem clearly cultivates and that are embodied by Gawain himself reverberate in our attempts at interpretation. Robert W. Hanning has written that "ambiguities multiply in direct proportion to the increasing element of [descriptive] decoration" (13). For instance, the elaborate description of the Green Knight's appearance contains elements that are evocative of both raw nature and its artful reproduction, thereby complicating the interpretation of the Green Knight as an embodiment of nature in conflict with the civilization of Arthur's court.

From a different perspective, Camargo writes in his study of the ring structure of *Sir Gawain* that "to accept all parallels as potentially significant . . . has at least one advantage: it embraces what we know to be the chief structural principle of the poem," adding that "none of the many parallels that have been discovered has been proven inconsequential" (123). In the face of the overwhelming ambiguity with which the poet confronts us, we, undoubtedly like the poem's original audience, must realize the relative uncertainty of congruence between any potential parallels. Such elements take on different meanings as they are brought into apposition with various other elements, functioning more as polysemous metaphors than as variants in a paratactic design. Even a single pair of elements may take on different significations when seen in the context of Gawain's protean behavior.

Consider, for example, the Green Knight's challenge to King Arthur's court at the beginning of the poem in conjunction with the resolution of the challenge at the end. The Green Knight is particularly threatening in the opening scene, when his outlandish appearance is described and he challenges the court in his markedly discourteous way. However, he hardly compares with the extraordinarily "heavy" villains of *Havelok*, both cold-blooded child-killers. The Green Knight is, in fact, a correspondingly less traditional "heavy" villain, and we cannot even call him "villain" at all times. In the resolution scene at the Green Chapel, his wry humor may even endear him to audiences, creating a rather diffuse resonance between this scene and the challenge episode.

If we agree that the meanings of the romances we have discussed are focused through the protagonist (or protagonists) in each case, it is clear that the degree to which the protagonist conforms to traditional codes of conduct and patterns of behavior—in other words, the degree to which he is himself traditional—stands in direct proportion to the degree of ambiguity invested in the poem's meaning and implications. Traditional heroes like Beowulf and the saints of the hagiographic poems—and even Christ as represented in a poem like *The Dream of the Rood*—behave in conformity to codes of conduct or patterns of behavior that are inscribed in the memories of traditional audiences. When heroes fail to conform to these codes and patterns, identification on the part of the audience is stymied. In just such a fashion, even a well-versed reading audience in late medieval England might have been confused by Gawain's apparent departure from his usual randy behavior, a turn of events commented on with various emphases and explanations by various critics.[21]

Obviously, the majority of Middle English romances are neither as traditional as *Horn* and *Havelok* nor as untraditional as *Sir Gawain*. For this reason, the suggestions I have made thus far are of limited value unless they can be utilized to make valid statements about more typical romances. I will therefore present a brief discussion of *Amis and Amiloun*, a romance highly popular during the Middle Ages,

[21]Commentary on Gawain's behavior is virtually as voluminous as interpretations of the poem. For a sampling, however, see Benson's classic study (207-48); Spearing (1-40; 171-236); Burrow; the wide-ranging articles in Howard and Zacher; and Fichte.

though it has in the modern era received nothing like the attention accorded to *Sir Gawain* or even *Horn* and *Havelok*. Due to the poem's relative unfamiliarity, let me summarize it briefly.[22]

Amis and Amiloun are born of two barons in Lombardy. The two boys are, like Horn and Havelok, images of perfection, and they bear as great a physical resemblance to one another as identical twins. The Duke of Lombardy is so taken with the boys' beauty that he introduces them into his court. When Amiloun leaves the duke's service, he has two identical gold cups made and gives one to Amis.

About this time, the duke's daughter, Belisaunt, falls in love with Amis, who, like Horn, refuses the maiden's advances on account of the incompatibility of their stations. Belisaunt tells him that she is perfectly capable of enriching him, thereby making him worthy of her attentions, so he makes love with her. A jealous steward is watching, however, and informs on Amis and Belisaunt, necessitating trial by combat. Belisaunt and her mother offer their lives as pledge for Amis. Amis, realizing that the fact that he has lied to the duke will render him ineffective in combat, contacts Amiloun. Since the two are identical, they easily switch roles. Amiloun kills the steward for Amis, although on the way to the contest he is cautioned by a voice from heaven that if he undertakes the battle he will become a leper within three years.

Amiloun's wife foresees his ruin, and, indeed, Amiloun becomes a leper. He is ostracized by his wife and lords and forced into exile with only his nephew, Amoraunt, for companion. The pair winds up in Amis' dukedom. Amis is impressed by Amoraunt's loyalty to the leper, who has not been identified as Amiloun. Out of charity, he sends a draught of wine to the pair in the gold cup Amiloun gave him years before. The obvious connection is made, and Amis, counseled by a visiting angel, kills his two children in order that their blood may heal Amiloun. Miraculously, the children are later found to be alive, and Amiloun returns home. The two friends' tribulations are over, and they live happily ever after.

The provenance of *Amis and Amiloun* in its Middle English romantic form is clearly literary; it is composed in twelve-line tail-rhyme stanzas rhyming *aabaabccbddb*. The complexity of this scheme, along with its demands on the rhymer's ingenuity, differentiate it from the most traditional romances, which, like *Horn* and *Havelok*, are most

[22]I have relied on Leach's edition of *Amis and Amiloun*.

commonly written in rhyming couplets, a much easier form to manage during a performance in which lapses of memory must be overcome by improvisation. However, the *b*-lines, the tail-rhyme lines, which are usually end-stopped, lend a familiar rhythmic contour and cadence to the verse that is clearly conducive to spoken delivery.

Of course, the paratactic nature of *Amis and Amiloun* is supported by the tendency toward what Carol Fewster has called the "diptych structure" of Middle English romance (14-22). The parallels pointed up in the summary above are expanded and deepened by the consistent parallels between the experiences of the two protagonists and the oppositions drawn between their respective wives. Although MacEdward Leach's exhaustive detailing of the textual precedents and variants of *Amis and Amiloun* (ix-cii) does not necessarily establish the poem's degree of traditionality, the motif of friendship is a commonplace in both oral and literate traditions. Just as Gilgamesh had his Enkiddu, so Amis has Amiloun. "There are, however," according to Fewster,

> features of the story that set it apart from the kinds of adventures and resolution usual in romance. For example, angels intervene to set up moral dilemmas, one hero is afflicted with leprosy (regarded in some medieval theological works as punishment for sin, and in others as a period of penance before redemption), and has a long period of helpless suffering which he cannot resolve.
> (50)

Indeed, a number of critics have noted the incompatibility of the religious and secular elements of the story, as if the redactor had been unable to decide whether he wished to compose a romance or a secular hagiography.[23]

Although we cannot guarantee that the puzzlement of present-day critics necessitates similar difficulties of interpretation in the Middle Ages, one thing is clear: a medieval audience would have recognized the two visitations by angels as apposite members. Not only are the visitations absolutely unique in the context of the poem, they are

[23]See Mehl (105), for example. Ramsey claims that the romance can be interpreted "either as social propoganda favoring extended family attachments over the ties of the nuclear family, or as an allegory of self-realization" (*Chivalric Romances* 118). Richmond attempts to reconcile the tale's disparate elements, calling it "both a story of friendship and of man's relation to God" (105).

also triggered by like events. Amiloun's visitation comes when it is time for him to help his best friend, Amis' when it is time for him to help Amiloun. It is most likely that a medieval audience would have interpreted the visitations as fully functional motivational elements of the story, utilized to emphasize the extremes to which the friends are prepared to go for each other as well as to drive the story forward.

If we are content to regard *Amis and Amiloun* as a romance concerned above all with the nature of true friendship, as is generally agreed, the actions of the heroes conform to behavioral patterns that are probably as recognizable to us today as they were to medieval audiences. As Ong has written, works of oral provenance function to preserve systems of values and belief, "the ultimate concerns of existence" (74). Hence, an oral traditional work need not undertake an analysis of the pros and cons attached to moral concerns. Likewise, *Amis and Amiloun* displays limited ambiguity and no questioning of the validity of the drastic decisions made by the protagonists, decisions made with due regret over the consequences but without hesitation. Amis slits his children's throats after shedding a few appropriate tears over their sleeping forms, and explains to Amiloun that "Ih*es*u, when it is his wille, / May send me childer mo" (2336-37).

Nevertheless, Fewster's reservations are to the point. What, for instance, would a medieval audience have made of Amiloun's transformation into a leper? We may recall Cresseid's punishment for her inconstancy to Troilus in Henryson's *Testament of Cresseid*, but can we construe either of the main characters in *Amis and Amiloun* as being guilty of such a breach? It seems as if we are transported—rather suddenly—from the world of romance to that of religious allegory, and the shift casts a pall of ambiguity over what is otherwise the exemplary and easily explicable behavior of these two model friends. If Amiloun must be punished in this cryptic way for his perfectly appropriate behavior, questions must arise as to just how exemplary his behavior is in the first place. While these questions in no way fuel the kind of resonant ambiguity that characterizes *Sir Gawain*, they certainly make for more problematic results than we see in *Horn* and *Havelok*.

I would suggest, then, that *Amis and Amiloun*, although less traditional than *King Horn* and *Havelok the Dane*, is nevertheless considerably more traditional than *Sir Gawain*. Indeed, if we look at the mass of Middle English romances, it is clear that this finding will almost always be the result of our investigations, although treatment of other problematic texts, such as *Guy of Warwick* and *Ywain and Gawain*, will reinforce a sense of the great variety of the form. We must not forget, however, that behind that variety is a repertoire of techniques that shows remarkable continuity across the spectrum. It is the way in which the assumptions of tradition interact with meaning that modifies the functioning of poetic techniques and makes one romance different from another. Traditional referentiality is disrupted, meaning is dislocated from its associated expectations, and ambiguity arises. *Sir Gawain*, our example of such disruption, is truly unique for the originality and talent exhibited in its combination of traditionality and self-conscious literary artistry. We must move to later developments—Chaucer and Malory, for instance—in order to find works that rival it in terms of multivalence and complexity. But the great breadth of the spectrum of traditionality in Middle English romance should interest us more than accumulating examples of works occupying one particular niche in that spectrum. The comparison of transitional works in regard to technique and meaning can give us vital information pertaining to the gradations and characteristics of traditionality. By surveying these transformations and elaborations of tradition in transition, we can come to a new understanding of an enigmatic and endlessly fascinating body of poetic art.[24]

Department of English
University of Missouri, Columbia

[24]Thanks to Professors John Miles Foley and Martin Camargo for their astute and cheerful assistance on this project.

Works Cited

Allen, Rosamund ed. King Horn: *An Edition Based on Cambridge University Library MS Gg. 4.27 (2)*. New York: Garland, 1984.

—. "Some Sceptical Observations on the Editing of *The Awntyrs off Arthure.*" *Manuscripts and Texts: Editorial Problems in Later Middle English Literature*. Ed. Derek Pearsall. Cambridge: Brewer, 1987. 5-25.

Amodio, Mark C. "Old-English Oral-Formulaic Tradition and Middle-English Verse." *De Gustibus: Essays for Alain Renoir*. Ed. John Miles Foley. New York: Garland, 1992. 1-20.

Barron, W.R.J. *English Medieval Romance*. London: Longman, 1987.

Baugh, Albert C. "Improvisation in the Middle English Romance." *Proceedings of the American Philosophical Society* 103 (1959): 418-54.

—. "The Middle English Romance: Some Questions of Creation, Presentation, and Preservation." *Speculum* 42 (1967): 1-31.

Bauman, Richard. *Verbal Art as Performance*. Rowley, MA: Newbury, 1977.

Benson, Larry D. *Art and Tradition in* Sir Gawain and the Green Knight. New Brunswick: Rutgers UP, 1965.

Brodeur, Arthur G. *The Art of* Beowulf. Berkeley: U of California P, 1959.

Burrow, John A. *A Reading of* Sir Gawain and the Green Knight. New York: Barnes and Noble, 1966.

Cable, Thomas. *The English Alliterative Tradition*. Philadelphia: U of Pennsylvania P, 1991.

Camargo, Martin. "Oral Traditional Structure in *Sir Gawain and the Green Knight.*" *Current Research on Oral Literature: A Memorial for Milman Parry*. Ed. John Miles Foley. Columbus: Slavica, 1986. 121-37.

Clanchy, M.T. *From Memory to Written Record: England, 1066-1307.* Cambridge, MA: Harvard UP, 1979.

Crosby, Ruth. "Oral Delivery in the Middle Ages." *Speculum* 11 (1936): 88-110.

Doane, A.N. and Carol Braun Pasternack, eds. *Vox intexta: Orality and Textuality in the Middle Ages.* Madison: U of Wisconsin P, 1991.

Fellows, Jennifer. "Editing Middle English Romances." *Romance in Medieval England.* Ed. Maldwyn Mills, Jennifer Fellows, and Carol M. Meale. Cambridge: Brewer, 1991. 5-16.

Fewster, Carol. *Traditionality and Genre in Middle English Romance.* Cambridge: Brewer, 1987.

Fichte, Jörg O. "Historia and Fabula: Arthurian Traditions and Audience Expectations in 'Sir Gawain and the Green Knight.'" *Festschrift Walter Haug und Burghart Wachinger.* Ed. Johannes Janota, Paul Sappler, et al. Tübingen: Verlag, 1993. 589-602.

Field, Rosalind. "Romance as History, History as Romance." *Romance in Medieval England.* Ed. Maldwyn Mills, Jennifer Fellows, and Carol M. Meale. Cambridge: Brewer, 1991. 163-73.

Foley, John Miles. *Traditional Oral Epic: The* Odyssey, Beowulf, *and the Serbo-Croatian Return Song.* Berkeley: U of California P, 1990.

—. *Immanent Art: From Structure to Meaning in Traditional Oral Epic.* Bloomington: Indiana UP, 1991.

—. "Word-Power, Performance, and Tradition." *Journal of American Folklore* 105 (1992): 275-301.

Gradon, Pamela. *Form and Style in Early English Literature.* London: Methuen, 1971.

Greenfield, Stanley B. *The Interpretation of Old English Poems.* London: Routledge, 1972.

Hanning, Robert W. "Sir Gawain and the Red Herring: The Perils of Interpretation." *Acts of Interpretation: The Text in Its Contexts 700-1600: Essays in Medieval and Renaissance Literature in Honor of E. Talbot Donaldson.* Ed. Mary J. Carruthers and Elizabeth D. Kirk. Norman: Pilgrim, 1982. 5-23.

Howard, Donald R. and Christian Zacher, eds. *Critical Studies of* Sir Gawain and the Green Knight. Notre Dame: U of Notre Dame P, 1968.

Hurt, James R. "The Texts of *King Horn.*" *Journal of the Folklore Institute* 7 (1970): 47-59.

Knight, S.T. "The Oral Transmission of *Sir Launfal.*" *Medium Ævum* 38 (1969): 164-70.

Leach, MacEdward, ed. *Amis and Amiloun*. EETS os 203. London: Oxford UP, 1937.

Lord, Albert B. "The Theme of the Withdrawn Hero in Serbo-Croatian Oral Epic." *Prilozi za knjizevnost, jezik, istoriju i folklor* 35 (1969): 18-30.

—. "Perspectives on Recent Work on the Oral Traditional Formula." *Oral Tradition* 1 (1986): 467-503.

—. "The Merging of Two Worlds: Oral and Written Poetry as Carriers of Ancient Values." *Oral Tradition in Literature*. Ed. John Miles Foley. Columbia: U of Missouri P, 1986. 19-64.

McGillivray, Murray. *Memorization in the Transmission of the Middle English Romances*. New York: Garland, 1990.

Mehl, Dieter. *The Middle English Romances of the Thirteenth and Fourteenth Centuries*. London: Routledge, 1969.

Ong, Walter J. *Orality and Literacy: The Technologizing of the Word.* London: Methuen, 1982.

Parks, Ward. "The Return Song and a Middle English Romance: *Sir Orfeo*, 'Cetic Osmanbey,' 'Đulic Ibrahim,' and the *Odyssey.*" *Southeastern Europe* 10 (1983): 222-41.

—. "The Oral-Formulaic Theory in Middle English Studies." *Oral Tradition* 1 (1986): 636-94.

Ramsey, Lee C. "The Sea Voyages in *Beowulf.*" *Neuphilologische Mitteilungen* 72 (1971): 51-59.

—. *Chivalric Romances: Popular Literature in Medieval England.* Bloomington: Indiana UP, 1983.

Reichl, Karl. "The Middle English Popular Romance: Minstrel versus Hack Writer." *The Ballad and Oral Tradition.* Ed. Joseph Harris. Cambridge, MA: Harvard UP, 1991. 243-68.

Richmond, Velma Bourgeois. *The Popularity of Middle English Romance*. Bowling Green: Bowling Green U Popular P, 1975.

Robinson, Fred C. Beowulf *and the Appositive Style*. Knoxville: U of Tennessee P, 1985.

Smithers, G.V., ed. *Havelok*. Oxford: Clarendon, 1987.

Spearing, A.C. *The* Gawain-*Poet*. Cambridge: Cambridge UP, 1970.

Staines, David. "*Havelok the Dane*: A Thirteenth-Century Handbook for Princes." *Speculum* 51 (1976): 602-23.

Stock, Brian. *The Implications of Literacy: Written Language and Models of Interpretation in the Eleventh and Twelfth Centuries*. Princeton: Princeton UP, 1983.

Weiss, Judith. "Structure and Characterisation in *Havelok the Dane*." *Speculum* 44 (1969): 247-57.

The Devil's Writing Lesson

John M. Ganim

Robert Mannyng of Brunne, in his *Handlyng Synne*, tells the story of a deacon who suddenly bursts out with laughter during the Mass. The priest understandably scolds him for his outburst, and is given the following excuse by the deacon:

> Þe dekene told hym why hyt fel
> þere to laghe yn hys gospel:
> "As y redde that yche tyde,
> Twey wymmen Iangled þere besyde;
> Betwyx hem to, y say a fende
> with penne and parchemen yn honde,
> And, wrote alle þat euer þey spake,
> Pryuyly be-hynde here bake.
> whan hys rolle was wryte alle ful,
> To drawe hyt oute he gan to pul;
> with hys teþe he gan to drawe,
> And harde for to tugge and gnawe,
> Þat hys rolle to-braste and rofe;
> And hys hedde aȝens the walle drofe
> So hard, and so ferly sore,
> Whan hys parchemen was no more.
> whan y say þat, y lete so gode
> Y brast on laghter þere y stode,
> Þat he so muche sorow hadde,
> As hys wrytyng was alle to-fade;
> And when he parceyued þat y wyste,

He al to-drofe hyt with hys fyste,
And went a-wey, alle for shame;
þarfore y logh and hadde gode game."
(9275-98)[1]

Two women were gossiping during the Mass, and the deacon sees a devil between them with a pen and parchment, writing down everything they say behind their back. But the women speak so quickly and say so much that the devil's parchment is soon full and in desperation he pulls at it, holding it with his teeth, until he bangs his head against the wall. It is at this point that the deacon laughs, the fiend knows he has been discovered and in fury punches the parchment with his fist and leaves. The priest is mollified and understands the mirth of his deacon. As is typical in Robert Mannyng's many stories, the rather stern moral which follows, that one should not gossip while in church, seems to conflict with the apparently multidimensional comedy of this scene. The story of the devil and his writing on parchment is one of the thirteen stories not included in Robert Mannyng's chief source, the *Manuel des Pechiez*. The motif is, however, frequent elsewhere in medieval and world literature. There are over a half-dozen versions in Middle English, including such tale collections as *An Alphabet of Tales* and the *Book of the Knight of La Tour Landry*. In hagiographic literature, the motif is widely known through an episode in the life of St. Martin of Tours which stresses laughter in the church (see Lee).

Robert Mannyng of Brunne's *Handlyng Synne* is familiar to students and to general readers largely through frequently anthologized brief excerpts of some of its remarkable, apparently popular tales, the most famous being the story of the Dancers of Colbek. It is also a key piece of evidence for the nature of oral delivery in the English Middle Ages, especially in its frequent concern with its address to its audience, and its apparent punctiliousness in distinguishing between reading aloud and reading silently. Most studies of *Handlyng Synne* have attempted to read it within one or two of these various contexts—radical of presentation, narrative collection, or religious manual. This essay seeks to argue for a dynamic relation between these contexts, suggesting that the requirement of auricular confession, the original inspiration for works such as *Handlyng Synne*'s charming stories and apparently accurate rendering of popular conversation disguise a deeper tension

[1]I cite Furnivall's edition of *Handlyng Synne* throughout.

between official and unofficial culture, and its own presentation of itself as contested medium between oral and written discourse.

The story of the Devil and his writing frenzy actually follows immediately upon the story of the Dancers of Colbek. That tale has ended with Mannyng's characteristically narrow rationale for why he has told us these stories. In this case it has been to keep us from caroling in the church or in the church yard, especially if the priest has asked us not to. The story of the Devil and his recording of the gossips in the church is introduced by means of a transition from this previous tale: "Ianglyng longeþ to sacrylage; /. . . / Alle þat we do Iangle, the fend doþe wryte" (9253-56). What sounds like a proverb is expanded into a literal narrative. The devil does literally try to write down everything the women say. As is the case with Robert Mannyng's transitions and summaries, the address is to a much more childlike interlocutor than his stories might suggest. The deacon, who is taken to be a fool by the priest for his laughter, is in fact recognized as holy. He has seen this happen many times, he says, but never has the devil been frustrated. If we speak to God in prayer (9314), says the narrator, the fiend will not hear us. Robert Mannyng's frame for each incident typically tries to limit the anarchic interpretative possibilities of his tales. In so doing, he moralizes the energies of tales such as this one, extolling the virtue of controlled over uncontrolled speech.

Throughout *Handlyng Synne*, the spoken word is accorded a considerable power, almost magical in its potential, and therefore requiring control and constraint. The chief strategy of this containment of potentially anarchic everyday urges, besides the condemnation of obviously flagrant activities, is the proscription of uncontrolled and malicious speech, a proscription formerly associated with highly regulated religious life, but now applied more generally to everyday lay existence. In fact, many of Robert Mannyng's most colorful strictures on language occur in tales describing religious figures. Even the earliest stories in *Handlyng Synne* repeatedly stress the power of the spoken word, but a power conditioned by its circumstances. In illustration of the first commandment, Robert Mannyng tells a typically surrealistic story of a witch who concocts a magic bag that sucks the milk from cows under its own power, something like a cross between modern milking equipment and an old-fashioned vacuum cleaner. The image of the large leather pouch lurching through the landscape is striking and even comical, probably laden with antifeminist associations that even

Robert Mannyng does not underline. His stress is on the scene after she is caught. Upon inquisition, she reveals the magic charm that causes the bag to operate, and the inquiring bishop "made a clerk þan wryte / Al that she seyd" (528). After his clerk writes it down, the bishop then attempts the experiment himself, reciting the charm, to see if it is true. When it fails to work, the witch explains that one has to believe in the charm for it to be effective. Interestingly, it is the witch herself who points out that "ȝe beleue nat as y do" (544). One must believe in it in order for the charm to work. It's not what you say but how you say it. While the written record of the orally transmitted charm is itself a significant detail, as if writing could neutralize the power of magic, Robert Mannyng's stress is on the consciousness of the speaker, his or her awareness of the efficacy of the spoken word. Similarly, in a story which is supposed to illustrate the fourth commandment (1255-1306), a woman enters her bath and orders her daughter to have her clothes ready. When the daughter does not respond, the women curses and summons the devil, who is of course ready, scaring the woman out of her wits. And in a story that resembles a combination of Agamemnon and Iphigenia and Abraham and Isaac, a soldier is given victory in battle after promising to sacrifice the first things he sees upon returning home, which unfortunately turns out to be his daughter (2845-2902).

Handlyng Synne, perhaps because of its dual address to both pastor and flock, offers some remarkable comments on the nature of authority and these are invariably linked to the power of the spoken voice. "Ianglyng" turns out to be both dangerous and protective. The caroling in the story of the Dancers of Colbek turns out to be both transgressive and holy. Conversely, the voice of authority is rendered conditional, not always aware of the impact of what it commands. The priest who reprimands the deacon becomes aware of a higher truth; the priest in the Dancers of Colbek learns a tragic, almost Old Testament lesson by uttering his curse, and further, by seeking to spare his daughter its consequences by ordering her to be pulled from the magic dancing circle.

In keeping with a late medieval legal tendency to accord felonious status to hostile speech, *Handlyng Synne* is deeply concerned with slander and backbiting. The tale of a slanderous nun who is found after her death with her mouth cut in half and one side of her body burned illustrates this concern (1515-25). Apparently virtuous in other respects, her slanderous speech condemns half of her to brutally symbolic punishment, consistent with Robert Mannyng's assertion that slander equals murder. Similarly, a backbiting monk reappears as a ghost who bites his own burning tongue as he returns to warn his fellow monks against his shortcoming (3566-3620). These narratives are reinforced by recurrent commentary throughout the work on the dangers of uncensored speech. Backbiting is particularly singled out (4170-85), but the power of lecherous speech to lead to illicit actions is also underscored (8289-96). Robert Mannyng limits his explicit censure of secular song and secular speech to such speech in inappropriate settings, especially in church settings and particularly during services. However, in the world of *Handlyng Synne,* uncensored speech is generally a danger to Christian community and civil society as well as the individual soul.

Unconsciously vicious statements turn out to have literal power in other stories. In his fulminations against swearing (which contains the interesting conjunction especially not to use Christ's name in oaths that refer to "any menbre of hys manhede / Byneþyn the gyrdyl" [683-84]), Robert Mannyng makes the orthodox point that swearing is an attack on the body of Christ. But he illustrates the point (690 ff.) in the startling image of a woman appearing to a rich blasphemer (the rich being notorious for their swearing) holding in her arms a bloodied and wounded child.

Beyond its connections to the ambiguous place of the spoken in *Handlyng Synne*, the scene of the devil writing also sets up another complex set of dichotomies. The comic image of the women's gossip frustrating the devil pulls in several directions. It fits traditional antifeminist stereotypes at the same time that it accords a certain power to spoken gossip, here bracketed virtually as a female cultural activity, as potent in its way as writing. It is the female voice here which thwarts the clerical devil. In the representation of the devil as writing and the women as speaking, a representation complicated by the reading of the deacon, the drama of the scene is itself gendered. The paternal warning of the priest is deflected by the astonishing vision of the deacon, and even the infraction of the two women is partially mitigated by the frustrating effect it has on the devil. The scene presents the devil (whom we must assume to be a minor devil, like the one in Chaucer's *Summoner's Tale*) as the parodic representative of official culture, and the gossiping women as the emblems of unofficial culture. The scene, despite its drift towards orthodoxy, predicts the tensions of the *Wife of Bath's Prologue*, with its opposition between clerical male textual authority and female performance, largely executed in speech. The scene represents writing not as a mysterious skill, but as a technology, and, in this case, a technology in danger of breaking down in the face of the pre-technological, significantly gendered as feminine. This gendered opposition is based on a larger underlying dichotomy between popular and official culture, to borrow by now familiar Bakhtinian terms.

These tensions are not necessarily class-bound or even historicized in the text. Official culture is not the culture of the aristocracy, in the sense of an elite culture. Nor is the dichotomy reducible to an easy division between writing as the medium of official culture and spoken language as the medium of popular culture. The typical voice of authority in many of Mannyng's most memorable moments is that of the priest, and more often than not that voice is too stern, and is corrected, comically or pathetically, by the workings of the story. *Handlyng Synne* offers a complex negotiation between popular and official culture, coopting the anarchic urges of popular culture to the moral guardianship of official culture, at the same time that the excesses of official culture are moderated by the festive laughter of popular culture. In the story of the devil and his manuscript, the disruptive laughter of the deacon and the disruptive chatter of the gossips end up ironically in the service of the "holy" priest's values, without his knowing it. The image of the fiend furiously writing on his inadequate parchment, finally punching it in fury, becomes a parodic image not only of clerical and monastic textuality, but also of the legal and financial figures associated with the repressive power of the technology of writing.

Despite the concern with curbing the excesses of popular belief in *Handlyng Synne*, the fact is that the power of many of Robert Mannyng's stories depend on folkloric plots and devices and he frequently calls upon magical images to drive home his points.[2] The practice of confession on the part of his sinful characters inevitably results in the release of a "blak"—a black cloud or figure—from the person. The miracles and supernatural acts typical of a saint's life pepper the most dramatic stories he tells (some of which are extracts of saint's lives), from the yearlong dizzying dance of the Dancers of Colbek and the arm of "Eva," the daughter of the priest who curses them, which refuses to be buried, to the rich man and his wife who take sanctuary on church grounds only to be stuck together like dogs when they attempt

[2]What seems to be original in Robert Mannyng's fascination with witchcraft and popular superstition, warns Robertson, is in fact traditional ("Certain Theological Conventions").

to have sex, freed only by the determined singing of the monks in the abbey. No sinful character dies without accompaniment of fiends to torture his body before death as well as his soul afterwards. Other characters are redeemed or assist the souls of the dead by the frequent appearances of ghosts who wake them from their sleep. Mysterious doings in graveyards and tombs are followed by exhumations in which bodies are discovered to be split down the middle or gnawed or deformed in ways symbolic of their transgressions. A dead knight appears to his brother in arms (2221-60) and grabs his arm, at which point afterwards the living knight's bones show through. For Robert Mannyng and his readers, sin is palpable and material and the violation of the spirit is translated by equivalent violation of the body. Conversely, Christ's body is dramatized in literal ways. A skeptical man sees an angel carve up the body of a child and in the chalice he sees real blood and bits of flesh. The materiality and sensory validation of popular cultural belief are appropriated in order to correct the errors attendant to that way of knowing.

But in *Handlyng Synne*, oral discourse acquires a special importance and a special complexity because of the work's origins in confessional literature. The genre to which it belongs is not literary fiction. It stands in the tradition of manuals concerning confession and the responsibilities of parish priests necessitated by the reforms of the Fourth Lateran Council of 1215. The Fourth Lateran Council had promulgated the minimal requirement of annual aural confession, and in its wake a large number of tracts detailing the procedures of confession were produced.[3] In England, under an interdict when the first impact of the Fourth Lateran Council was being felt, these reforms were slightly later, but also carried out with extreme diligence, and the various parts of *Handlyng Synne* can be explained by the requirement that clergy be conversant with and be able to themselves explain the Seven Deadly Sins, the sacraments, the ten commandments, and how to prepare for and what to expect from shrift. Originally intended for the clergy, by the late thirteenth and early fourteenth century, similar tracts are being produced for the laity. *Handlyng Synne*, in its concern with the points of "shryfte" retains this concern, particularly in its reminder that confession must be oral, not written (11765-84), a theologically consistent but nevertheless interesting qualification given the broader audience of its advice.

[3]See Robertson ("Cultural Tradition"; "English Episcopal Degree"). The most recent full treatment of *Handlyng Synne* is found in Kemmler.

Although nearly all of *Handlyng Synne*'s stories have written sources, the work is significant for its frequent meditations upon the relation of oral and written discourse, as well as for its use of tales that have folkloric analogues and oral qualities. At various points it presents itself as if it were orally presented. Although the work is not a sermon manual, as a collection of exempla and anatomy of sins, it strongly resembles manuals designed to assist in the preparation of orally delivered sermons. The work's place in its larger genre as a collection of religious tales designed for eventual oral dissemination and its own mode of reception and distribution attempt to negotiate the poles of written and oral discourse. Its chief purpose, the delineation of sins and the encouragement of orthodox piety and regular confession and communion, itself requires an alternation of pastoral encouragement and doctrinal definition, which expresses itself formally as an alternation of practical experience embodied in spoken language and authority as recorded in the written word, an opposition which, whether or not it has any natural or actual basis, is familiar enough as a topic in medieval literature.

At various points *Handlyng Synne* presents itself as if it were orally presented, suggesting its own adaptation to reading aloud to a small group. Indeed, it makes an explicit distinction between a "lerned" and a "lewed" audience, but is capable of addressing both as if orally, rather than addressing one audience as if in writing and the other as if in speech. It is possible that this dual address might be explained locally, in terms of the specific conditions of Robert Mannyng's Gilbertine order at Sempringham.[4] The Gilbertines, the order to which he belonged, was the only indigenous English order. Gilbert himself had headed a group of nuns and lay brothers, and originally sought Cistercian membership. When this was not forthcoming, he devised a practical, and somewhat eclectic organization of his own, with a largely Cistercian model for the nuns and a largely Augustinian model for his priests. There was, however, a clear distinction between training for canons and for lay brothers. Lay brothers were not to be taught to read nor allowed to have books. Their instruction, from a master of novices, would have been oral. Ruth Crosby suggests that in this light Mannyng's oral style and his use of popular imagery may not have been an attempt to reach a broad, lay audience, nor even to distinguish between readers and hear-

[4]On the local conditions in general, see Platts; on the political context of Robert Mannyng's writings, see Turville-Petre's important article.

ers, but may have been addressed to this dual audience at Sempringham:

> in "ȝe lewed men" Mannyng refers here to the lay brothers who can neither read nor write and for whom his poem is chiefly intended; and in "þese clerkys" to those novices who are now being taught their letters and undergoing the long probation before they can become canons . . . . Mannyng, himself a canon, is writing with two groups of hearers in mind: the "lewed men" or lay brothers, for whom he adopts a simple, friendly manner that he may not awe them with his learning; and the novices who will one day be canons and in whom he wishes to instil the duties of the priesthood.
>
> (27)

Crosby argues here against Frederick Furnivall's assumption that because of the respect for priests evinced in the work, Mannyng himself may have been a lay brother. Still, the evidence for either position is hypothetical. What it does suggest for our purposes is that the possible original audience for *Handlyng Synne* encapsulated the segmentation of a larger public.

Confession and the control of individual conscience was only one part of the agenda of the Fourth Lateran Council's decree, which was no less than the regulation of village life through the influence of the parish church and the reform and revitalization of the clergy. In the wake of the Albigensian crusade, the Council was also deeply concerned with combating heresy and encouraging orthodoxy. While heresy may have been a relatively abstract consideration for Robert Mannyng despite the bursts of heterodox doctrine flaring on the continent, the structural basis of the genre he works in links confession to control. The role of the parish priest becomes one of surveillance and containment, alert to the backsliding potential of everyday life and faulty human judgment, and the eagerness of the fiend to take shape in the rhythms of everyday life. Hence, the realism of *Handlyng Synne* expressed in its folkloric narratives and colloquial discourse, is in fact a highly charged style, at the center of which is the relation of speech to belief.

Beneath its generally benign and avuncular voice, *Handlyng Synne* reveals the program of social control that followed upon the reforms of the early thirteenth century. The work has been mined frequently by historians, perhaps more than by literary critics, for information about popular beliefs and customs. Yet it is important to stress that the images of popular culture and belief and activity are represented in *Handlyng Synne* frequently in order to constrain them. At one point, Robert Mannyng tells a story from Bede and points out that in Bede's time some parts of England remained pagan and different kingdoms espoused different creeds, leading to warfare. But Robert Mannyng describes his present-day social world as incompletely or insufficiently christianized. Pathetic attempts at witchcraft and wild superstitions abound. We should worry about making children stare at their reflection in the blade of a sword or a basin. If you meet someone going into town and your business does not work out while you are in town, do not curse that person, who had no intention of wishing bad luck upon you. In a passage and story about the responsibilities of midwives, the midwife is instructed to very carefully recite the articles of baptism when an infant seems not about to survive, and he tells the story of a priest who scolds a careless midwife who fails to say the right word, the result of which is that the soul of both the baby and the midwife are lost. The episode is an interesting reflection of the ways in which female and male authority conflict in *Handlyng Synne*, almost always (except in the case of nuns) as laywomen in relation to priests, friars, and holy men, rather than between laymen and laywomen.

The cultural impact of regular confession was complex. The most obvious development was an increased awareness of the role of the individual, specifically in terms of his or her relation to intent and conduct. This development was already underway, indeed it was central, to the Renaissance and the new spirituality of the Twelfth Century. But the regulation of spiritual life envisioned by the Fourth Lateran Council was intended to operate at every level of civil and religious life, not just with elites or in highly developed population centers. So, paradoxically, the stress on confession and the institutionalization of conscience turned the development of individualism against itself, subsuming the quasi-romantic quest (obvious in both narrative form and the new theology and history) to social and liturgical control.[5] One way of interpreting this change is as a reaction, to see the thirteenth century as a conservative retreat from the energies of the twelfth century.[6] But

[5]On the relation of the new practice of confession to pious romances, see Crane (*Insular Romance*).

[6]See Hanning:

another way, perhaps grimmer and less faithful to the ideals of humanism, is to see the structuring of the self in the later Middle Ages as intimately bound up with its observance, analysis, scrutiny, and limitation. Confession can be seen as a form of control which shapes a certain awareness of the self as limited, bounded, and in constant danger of its own excess. The power of this control comes only partly from the threat of tortures and mutilations so colorfully described in *Handlyng Synne*;

> Ecclesiastical justice became a smoothly functioning system, while the Lateran Council of 1215 imposed new, binding order on a range of theological concepts and disciplinary practices—order which the papacy and curia now had the authority and power to enforce. The codification of confessional practice, and especially the priest's role in interrogating the penitent systematically concerning the latter's sins, tipped the balance of Christian repentance away from the contritionism of the twelfth century, which had laid stress on the moment of inner openness to God's love that individualized the penitent's experience.
>
> (235)

But why should characters and their articulation in works like *Handlyng Synne* be so memorable even if only partially developed? Braswell offers an existential answer. The sinner must finally surrender his or her activity to the process of confession:

> But until the confession is ended, until the priest has issued his order that the penitent go and sin no more, the sinner stands alone. Isolated from his environment, his will at odds with the Divine Will, he is an individual indeed. And his personality is composed of those *particular* sins which he has committed in his own inimitable way. While he remains sinful, he is possessed of a special kind of *engin* and is able both to affect the fates of others and to manipulate literary plots. And because a knowledge of sin necessitates an inner awareness, his internal nature is as important as his external one. He is a lively, rounded character, unacceptable to the Church but attractive both to modern readers and to those sinners in the medieval audience who were able to view him in a special way.
>
> (13)

See also McNeil and Gamer on earlier Celtic penitentials: "Beyond the theological considerations, we see in the detailed prescriptions the objective of an inward moral change, the setting up of a process of character reconstruction which involves the correction of special personal defects and the reintegration of personality" (46).

it also comes from the internalization of the policing mechanism activated by the awareness of sin, and the ritual release offered by the practice of confession. The development of character in the centuries preceding the Renaissance may not be the story of Burckhardtian individualism triumphing over liturgical surveillance; it may be that the self is the result of that surveillance. In *Handlyng Synne*, the sinful individual character struggles constantly with the homogenizing effect of contrition. *Handlyng Synne*'s Foucauldian premises conflict constantly with its Bakhtinian operations.

The scene of the devil's "writing lesson" acquires a special importance, exorcising the tensions of *Handlyng Synne*'s agenda, at the same time that it exposes these tensions. The scene parodically reverses one of the key motive forces for the work itself. The devil here is writing down the women's speech. But the function of *Handlyng Synne*, at least in its address to clergy, is to assist with confession. What we see here is a parody of the confession scene. The devil is presented as a monkish scribe, stretching his inadequate parchment to cover the text. In a peculiar way, however, he represents not only the scribal transmitter, but the author himself, whose own relation to popular culture and to his sources is as dependent as the devil's.

The devil's "writing lesson" here serves as a commentary on the most famous "Writing Lesson" of our own epoch. In *Tristes Tropiques*, Claude Lévi-Strauss describes what the Nambikwara Indians of Brazil, and the anthropologist himself, learned from "The Writing Lesson."[7] He had distributed pencils and paper, the tools of the anthropologist in the field who writes down what the observed do, to the Indians themselves. He is then distressed when their leader pretends toward written communication with the western observer, as if to appropriate traces of the power of civilization with which to elevate his own status and extend his control. For Lévi-Strauss, writing operates here as it does in the process of civilization in general, allowing, even engendering, hierarchization and domination, besides which the intellectual and memorial liberation afforded by writing are entirely secondary.[8] But by

[7]"The Writing Lesson" has become an occasion for important discussions of medieval discourse recently; see Bloch (1-29); Lerer (1-29); Crane ("Writing Lesson"); see also Mileur's excellent discussion (156-201).

[8]It is, after all, precisely Lévi-Strauss's interpretation of his own evidence that generates one of the key demarcations between structuralist and post-structuralist thought (Derrida 101-140). Derrida uncovers the lapsarian myth behind Lévi-Strauss's thinking, as well as its continuation of the "logocentric" bias of

representing literacy and orality as equally powerful in their potential, and more conditioned by their uses and the intent of their users than by their essential nature, *Handlyng Synne* complicates any neatly evolutionary or binary assumptions about their relation.

Department of English
University of California, Riverside

Western philosophy and linguistics. Domination and hierarchy, replies Derrida, do not require writing and do not proceed from its introduction. Writing, says Derrida, can be more than alphabetical inscription, and there are forms of "arche-writing" that even pre-literate societies manifest. Indeed, we may consider the various forms of symbolic discourse that inhabit *Handlyng Synne* as "arche-writing," not only its representation of writing, but its variously authorized acts of speech, its signifying bodies, and even the laughter of the deacon in the church at the frustration of the Devil's own writing lesson.

Works Cited

Bakhtin, M.M. *Rabelais and His World.* Trans. Hélène Iswolsky. Bloomington: Indiana UP, 1984.

Bloch, R. Howard. *Etymologies and Genealogies: A Literary Anthropology of the French Middle Ages.* Chicago: U of Chicago P, 1983.

Braswell, Mary Flowers. *The Medieval Sinner: Characterization and Confession in the Literature of the English Middle Ages.* Rutherford: Farleigh-Dickinson UP, 1983.

Crane, Susan. *Insular Romance.* Berkeley: U of California P, 1986.

—. "The Writing Lesson of 1381." *Chaucer's England: Literature in Historical Context.* Ed. Barbara Hanawalt. Minneapolis: U of Minnesota P, 1992.

Crosby, Ruth. "Robert Mannyng of Brunne: A New Biography." *PMLA* 57 (1942): 15-28.

Derrida, Jacques. *Of Grammatology.* Trans. Gayatri Chakaravorty Spivak. Baltimore: Johns Hopkins UP, 1976.

Furnivall, Frederick J., ed. *Robert of Brunne's* Handlyng Synne *and Its French Original.* EETS os 119, 123. 1901, 1903. New York: Kraus, 1981.

Hanning, Robert W. *The Individual in Twelfth-Century Romance.* New Haven: Yale UP, 1977.

Kemmler, Fritz. *"Exempla" in Context: A Historical and Critical Study of Robert Mannyng of Brunne's* Handlyng Synne. Studies and Texts in English 6. Tübingen: Narr, 1984.

Lee, Brian. "'This Is No Fable': Historical Residues in Two Medieval Exempla." *Speculum* 56 (1981): 728-60.

Lerer, Seth. *Literacy and Power in Anglo-Saxon Literature.* Lincoln: U of Nebraska P, 1991.

Lévi-Strauss, Claude. *Tristes Tropiques.* Trans. John Russell. New York: Atheneum, 1964.

McNeill, John T. and Helena Gamer. *Medieval Handbooks of Penance.* New York: Columbia UP, 1938.

Mileur, Jean-Pierre. *The Critical Romance: The Critic as Reader, Writer, Hero.* Madison: U of Wisconsin P, 1990.

Platts, Graham. "Robert Mannyng of Bourne's 'Handlyng Synne' and South Lincolnshire Society." *Lincolnshire History and Archeology* 14 (1979): 23-29.

Robertson, D.W. "Certain Theological Conventions in Mannyng's Treatment of the Commandments." *Modern Language Notes* 61 (1946): 505-14.

—. "The Cultural Tradition of *Handlyng Synne*." *Speculum* 22 (1947): 162-85.

—. "*The Manual des Peches* and an English Episcopal Degree." *Modern Language Notes* 60 (1945): 439-47.

Turville-Petre, Thorlac. "Politics and Poetry in the Early Fourteenth Century: The Case of Robert Mannyng's Chronicle." *Review of English Studies* ns 39 (1988): 1-28.

Dorigen's Promise and Scholars' Premise: The Orality of the Speech Act in the *Franklin's Tale*

Leslie K. Arnovick

The promises spoken in the *Franklin's Tale* have long fascinated readers. By now, three generations of scholars have argued over whether Dorigen's words to Aurelius constitute a promise. Looking only at the words she says in lines 997-98, "Thanne wol I love yow best of any man; / Have heer my trouthe," we might well be tempted to interpret them as a pledge.[1] A pragmatic, or contextual, analysis of the larger discourse, however, reveals a different speech act and, at once, the source of the confusion scholars have sought to clarify.[2] In fact, what might look like confusion is no more—but no less—than a rich multivalency of oral threads which gives the *Tale* its engaging texture. As soon as one element forces us to believe that a promise has been made, another element causes us to doubt our certainty. A series of embedded contradictions within and among competing oral contexts creates a provocative tension. We can use a mathematical model to envision how such competing strains combine, following linguist Jennifer Coats who borrows the notion of the fuzzy set to illustrate the overlap of semantic realms within modal auxiliaries. Orality in the *Franklin's Tale* forms

[1]I cite Benson's edition of the *Franklin's Tale* throughout.
[2]I have tried to offer the broadest possible definition of pragmatic study. Readers interested in pursuing the realm of "context" and linguistic methodologies used to analyze it should consult Levinson.

similar fuzzy sets. In one set we find social practices associated with a legal tradition. In another we find philosophical assumptions governing the linguistic tradition. In yet a third we find folkloric structures resulting from a formulaic tradition.

A.C. Spearing's discussion of the oral formula in *Sir Gawain and the Green Knight* can be extended to treat the discourse of Dorigen and Aurelius; although it extends beyond the formula, the oral here nevertheless consists of a "lexical," "semantic," and, I would add, pragmatic "nexus" (21). Before we can investigate this nexus, however, we must briefly address relevant terminology and its methodological implications. As Alain Renoir succinctly remarked, "the term *oral-formulaic* is . . . slippery" (316). When we broaden both the term and its use to "orality," the problem of sense is compounded. At least one generation of scholars has attempted to extend the theory proposed by Milman Parry and refined by Albert B. Lord, defining orality and oral literature. Thus they have discovered metrical formulae, type-scenes, folkloric structure, thematic context, and aesthetic imagery, among other symptomatically oral features and have tried to isolate their distinctly oral, versus written, manifestations. After observing their efforts, John Miles Foley has questioned the desirability of assigning to orality merely one discrete meaning. Indeed, as Foley has demonstrated, there may be as many aspects to orality as there are levels of oral influence in written texts.

The recent application of this rich and multi-dimensional theory to Middle English literature is particularly productive.[3] Referring to types of orality and their respective frequencies in a text, Ward Parks has called the combination of oral and literary processes in Middle English texts a "labyrinthine tangle" (659). In Chaucer's works we find a variety of oral elements, only recently and partially addressed in the critical literature.[4] A few scholars have concentrated on the question of oral derivation or whether the poet's oral delivery to an actual listening audience might affect theme and structure in his poetry (see Fisher and Rowland). Others have applied insights from folklore studies to Chaucerian verse (see Lindahl and Brewer). Lamenting the dearth of additional criticism, Parks has challenged medievalists to adapt to Chaucer methodologies that have proved productive with other works

[3]See Parks ("Oral-Formulaic Theory") for a detailed review of the literature up to 1986.

[4]See esp. Parks ("Oral Tradition").

(679). Parks echoes the more general call to arms made by Foley, who argues that future work on oral literature requires interdisciplinary, "methodological synthesis" (*Oral-Formulaic Theory and Research* 3). By their nature synthetic, language studies have much to contribute to the debate about the orality of Chaucer's work.

The oral nature of conversation, elucidated by such scholarship, plays a crucial role in informing the meaning of Dorigen's promise. An exploration of the orality of her utterance and its grounding in speech must therefore precede an analysis of its interpretive challenges. If writing entails language without voice, as Paul Zumthor claims (227-28), perhaps dialogue—the written representation of voice—restores voice to writing. Indeed, Richard Martin argues that the literary representation of speech retains the essential orality of that speech; almost by definition, then, dialogue offers readers direct access to orality in a written text (10). Nowhere is orality more transparent, furthermore, than in speech which constitutes performative action.

Utterances that mandate action, performative speech acts provide us clear revelation of orality in literary texts. Because the connection between illocution and orality is not obvious, we should pause a moment to explicate their linkage. We begin by noting a fact which will be discussed below: the utterance of a performative embodies its speaker's intention. For example, promises are intentional, as are rejections and insincere promises (acts whose relevance will be demonstrated). Performative acts such as these do more than express intention, however; through them a speaker exercises agency. The utterance of a performative actually initiates a change in reality: if successful, it will cause the world to be changed to reflect the speaker's words. For Martin, this particular power of articulating, of mandating a course of action, *is* nothing less than the power of the poet. As it exercises "expressive creativity," speech echoes the poetic act. One purpose of Martin's *The Language of Heroes* is thus "to draw the analogy between this everyday linguistic phenomenon and Homer's 'formulaic' art" (32-33). Yet oral means of composition constitute only one aspect of orality and pursuing it can neglect others deserving recognition. The speaker's use of power in performing intentional speech acts, power which resembles closely that used by the poet, is itself significant. Observing this power, in turn, reminds us that orality is not a static artifact within a written text. Rather it forms a creative and vital force whose literary effect warrants exposition.

To reiterate, because written dialogue belongs to an oral genre, it composes one aspect of orality in a literary text. Entailing the creative rather than merely expressive functions of language, speech acts such as promises preserve orality or voice even when they are written down. Martin's argument makes sense from a linguistic standpoint too. After all, "the formal similarities between natural narrative and literary narrative derive from the fact that at some level of analysis they are utterances of the same type," explains Mary Louise Pratt (69). Dorigen's promise retains its orality even in writing precisely because it is a speech act.

Thus we locate a major nexus of orality in the dialogue between Dorigen and Aurelius and observe its concentration in the promise she seems to make him. From another point of view, we can say that the orality of Dorigen's speech act is essentially illocutionary or linguistic in the largest sense that it is 'of language.' Pushing a definition, we observe that the particular language system underlying this orality is pragmatic. Because the ability to perform and to interpret is reciprocal, one way to describe the pragmatic core is from the perspective of its readers. By identifying the pragmatic knowledge the audience must possess in order to understand Dorigen's promise, we reveal the substance of orality. As Pratt reminds us, the cooperative principle of conversation extends to literary discourse: assuming that meaning is intended, readers will try to decode a text according to their competence with the language (125-32). The pragmatic or contextual competence necessary for the interpretation of a speech act is broadly based. Readers of the *Franklin's Tale* utilize an awareness of at least three pragmatic realms as they place Dorigen's promise in its linguistic, legal, and folk contexts.

The mathematic metaphor of the set helps us envision the inter-relatedness of these contexts. Each one of the three pragmatic realms enumerated can be said to form a set. Altogether aspects of the larger entity we call the orality of the speech act, the three sets form a larger grouping. As they join together, the sets invariably intersect. Extending the analogy, we can say that the overlap looks fuzzy. Zumthor evokes another figure to describe the amorphous combining of oral elements:

> [i]n concrete terms, there is no orality in itself; rather there are middle structures of simultaneous manifestations, structures that, each in its proper order, have arrived at

> very unequal degrees of development. Their common substratum . . . [,] always perceptible[,] . . . results from the linguistic specificity of all vocal communication.
> (21)

Thus, where overlap occurs, distinctions among individual sets blur and new meanings arise. Undoubtedly each set of pragmatic features resounds within the larger individual tradition of which it is a part, and contexts yet to be observed participate in the larger "meaning" of the *Tale*. Both this resonance and an exhaustive accounting of oral features working in the text lie beyond the scope of this essay. My purpose here is to delineate pragmatic overlap and to point to the resultant tension as linguistic, legal, and folkloric contexts inform the orality of Dorigen's promise.

A formal linguistic analysis of the discourse between Dorigen and Aurelius begins to illuminate and explain some of the tensions among oral elements in this tale; for, to extend Stanley Fish's comments about the value of speech-act explication in understanding *Coriolanus*, the *Franklin's Tale* is a speech-act poem which, like the play, "is about speech acts" (1024):

> it is about what the theory is "about," the conditions for the successful performance of certain conventional acts and the commitments one enters into or avoids by performing or refusing to perform these acts.
> (1002)

Indeed, linguistically-based theory can be most productive in interpreting medieval thought and literature. As Judith Ferster notes, "[s]ince most of the modern 'methods' have something to do with language . . . the case can be made that 'they' [i.e. medieval people] did indeed think like that" (149).[5] Let us therefore allow a philosopher of language—a philosopher of the mind—to atone for the role of the "Briton" scholar and shed some light on the oral entrapment Dorigen suffers.

In *Speech Acts*, philosopher John Searle presents what he calls a "complicated way" of promising (57-63). Elaborating on the work of John Austin, he demonstrates that in order for an utterance to be interpreted as a successful linguistic act such as a promise, vow, or pledge,

[5]Schlieben-Lange considers the theoretical implications of viewing speech in this way, i.e. as a genre with its own pragmatic historiography.

certain conditions must be satisfied.[6] Reaching beyond native-speaker intention, Searle's technical observations demand a brief but specialized review. A short digression from Chaucer's text should enable us to return to it with a powerful tool for interpretation in hand; for just as Dorigen's utterance eludes intuitive judgment, it requires a more formal means of analysis. The relevance of philosophical insights about promises will become clearer when we move through the dialogue between Dorigen and Aurelieus, but I will try to seed my argument as we proceed.

Before we consider Searle's complete typology for promises we need to acknowledge two general conditions requisite to the successful completion of *any* speech act. First of all, there can be no "impediments" which prevent communication between speaker and hearer. A "general condition of meaningfulness" must hold (Lyons 735). The speaker must intend "to produce a certain illocutionary effect by means of getting the hearer to recognize his intention to produce that effect" by the use of an utterance conventionally associated with that act (Searle 60-61). On close inspection we shall see that this general condition fails to hold for Dorigen's utterances even while the conventionalized form of her "pledge" in lines 997-98 makes it look like a promise.

When these general conditions are established, the utterance of a sentence can constitute the performance of a specific illocutionary act. The nature of the act, however, results from the presence of additional and specific conditions. Propositional content rules apply first. In promises, the proposition must "predicate a future act" of the speaker (Searle 57-58). The propositional content of lines 997-98 certainly predicates Dorigen's future act, but other factors ultimately preclude such a proposition. In addition to requirements for propositional content, "various felicity conditions" must be met if an "illocutionary act . . . is to be successful and non-defective" (Lyons 733). Compliance with preparatory conditions, sincerity conditions, and essential conditions is necessary in order for an act to be "happy" (Searle 57-63).

Two prerequisite preparatory conditions must be established before the speech act of promising can be performed. A promise can be made only if the speaker believes that the hearer would prefer the speaker do (rather than not do) this future act and if, in fact, the hearer would prefer this course of action. It follows, then, that a promise can

[6]The following discussion of the conditions underlying promises is based on the more detailed treatment of promises in Arnovick (91-98).

be made only if it is "not obvious" to both speaker and hearer that the speaker will perform this future action "in the normal course of events" (Searle 57-59). Aurelius makes his impossible preference known to Dorigen quite plainly. More interesting, as we shall discover, is the way in which his resulting expectations for what he hears affect those of the reader.

Preparatory conditions logically lead into certain sincerity conditions for promises. The sincerity condition represents the psychological state or attitude the speaker must possess in order to perform the speech act sincerely (Searle 60); for a promise to be felicitous the speaker must *intend* to do the proposed action. The making of a promise, furthermore, constitutes "an expression of that psychological state" of intention (Searle 65). Insincere promises are also possible. They follow all the rules of sincere promises except this one regarding psychological state. While the insincere speaker may not have the intention to fulfill the promise at the time he or she utters it, the speaker must nevertheless assume the "responsibility for having the intention" in order for the utterance to have the illocutionary force of a promise (Searle 62).

In addition to the condition of sincerity, Searle notes the need for an essential rule: when the speaker utters a promise he or she assumes the obligation to do the future action (60). And the utterance of the promise itself finally "counts as the undertaking of an obligation" to do that action (Searle 60). It seems clear, to return to Chaucer's promise, that Dorigen has assumed an obligation to the squire. Yet the question of Dorigen's sincerity—or insincerity—remains and forms the crux of our problem with her promise. We will consider shortly not only the responsibility she assumes but Dorigen's psychological state.

Because of the moral agency required for promissory expressions in general we should also consider the ways in which a speaker's necessity-based attitude can be encoded grammatically. Another perspective (slightly different from but complementary to Searle's) can be brought to bear on our determination of illocutionary force. Following R.M. Hare, we may identify three grammatical components in promises.[7] Altogether they will reflect and reveal within an utterance a present-time imposition of obligation or speaker will for a future event. The first component to delineate is the phrastic. It contains the propositional content of an utterance and thus will vary greatly from one utter-

[7]Lyons offers a cogent outline of Hare's tripartite system (749-50).

ance to another. The tropic, a second component, qualifies the phrastic and correlates with the type of speech act that the sentence is characteristically used to perform, while a third component, the neustic, "expresses the speaker's commitment to the factuality, desirability, etc." of the proposition (Lyons 749-50). It is the combination of the tropic and neustic that gives each utterance its illocutionary force. Utterances such as promises have an "I say so" element in their neustics as well as a "so be it" component in their tropics. The force of promises is therefore doubly purposeful; the desiderative and instrumental functions of language provide the basis of promissory utterances. Complicated as it may seem, this tripartite analysis will reveal one reason why Dorigen's words have inspired mutually exclusive readings: internal contradictions confuse their illocutionary force.

Indeed, readers receive quite a mixed message as individual features of Dorigen's speech, normally in accord within successful speech acts, compete. We need only to look closer at this speech to appreciate the intricacy of the pragmatic tension which results. With our brief exploration of speech act theory as a background, we turn now to assess Dorigen's utterance and to see whether the requisite propositional and felicity conditions obtain. To what extent has Dorigen expressed her intent to obligate herself to a future course of action? The answer to this question does not lie within any single line of text. Scholars trying to pin down any one phrase continually discover others that qualify or contradict the first. Because a promise inhabits the pragmatic realm of discourse, as does any other speech act, we can only understand what illocutionary act has occurred by studying the whole of the discourse in which it is embedded. For the same reason, it is important to limit attention to the discourse once it has been demarcated.

Let us look, then, at the words actually exchanged between Dorigen and Aurelius as "they fille in speche" (964) in the garden on that infamous sixth of May. In lines 967-78, Aurelius addresses his complaint to Dorigen and exposes the love he has kept hidden. The lady responds with a direct question: "is this youre wyl?" (980). Even more plainly she continues, "and sey ye thus?" (980). After inviting him to retract inappropriate confessions, which he does not, she confronts his desire, concluding, "I knowe youre entente" (982). We can be sure, just as he is, that she has understood him correctly. In turn, all she can do is discourage him:

By thilke God that yaf me soule and lyf,

Ne shal I nevere been untrewe wif
In word ne werk, as fer as I have wit;
I wol been his to whom that I am knyt.
Taak this for fynal answere as of me.
(983-87)

Knowledge of Middle English usage aids our interpretation here. The modal auxiliaries appearing above play a precise role in Dorigen's declarations. Two constructions bear scrutiny: "I *wol* been" and "Ne *shal* I nevere been" (emphasis mine). As I have shown elsewhere, in the first person "will" generally communicates the volition of the speaker, conveying either intention or desire; in the first person "shall" usually expresses obligation or necessity. Because she has stated her intentions so straightforwardly, we are given evidence of her state of mind. Explicitly and unequivocally, she has made her intentions clear: she intends to be faithful to her husband.

But given the dangers that inhere in investigating the "mind" of a literary construct, we must proceed cautiously in reaching this conclusion about Dorigen's psychological state. Although Gerald Morgan may be correct in arguing that Chaucer's interest lay in exploring moral rather than psychological truths, he nevertheless dismisses the psychological a bit too readily (see "Defense"). Wisely, Morgan warns against attributing to Dorigen feelings and motivations "drawn from our own experience of emotional distress" ("Defense" 80) when there exists a definite literary model for the speeches she makes. In other words, he cautions against reading into the text a mental state not represented there. We do not risk committing such a sin when examining Dorigen's first dialogue with Aurelius because a certain transparency is provided us. Limiting ourselves to what the text explicitly sets forth, we can interpret direct statements of her intention as reflections of the psychological state of intention. Recognition of this psychological truth, moreover, provides a valuable insight into moral truths in the *Franklin's Tale*.

What emerges as we listen to their exchange in the garden is a speech act different from the one we sought. Instead of a promise, her utterance in lines 980-87 (and, I would argue, the discourse in its entirety [980-1005]) constitutes a rejection. More plainly, we can call it an assertion of her intention *not* to love him.

This other speech act, the rejection, proves illocutionarily successful: Dorigen's utterance meets all the general and felicity conditions required of assertions. Even further evidence of her words' force as a rejection can be seen in her hearer's response to her speech. Indeed, the result of her utterance, its perlocutionary effect, is as expected: Aurelius feels the rejection intended. Comprehending her rebuff, he moans, "Is ther noon oother grace in yow?" (999). As this careful dialogue reveals, the two achieve "perfect understanding" (Ferster 154-55).

Up to this point in their conversation, Dorigen's psychological state correlates with the form of her utterance. In fact, each character has effectively revealed and expressed his or her heart's truth. Each has acknowledged the other's "entent." What follows in the discourse demands a careful analysis if we wish to reconcile this speech act of rejection with the one more frequently attributed to her. Malcolm Golding and David Seaman, to name only two of the scholars specifically concerned with the courtly dialogue, as well as many others addressing the tale as a whole, regard Dorigen's words in lines 989-98 as a promise. At most, however, these lines represent a secondary speech act embedded within the first. As the first frames the second, it compromises it.

The second act proves flawed even as it begins, because Dorigen offers her commitment "In pleye" (988). We do not even need this comment by the Franklin to reveal her stance, however. What she says both before and after her speech in lines 989-98 provides a clear enough context, while what Aurelius says in lines 1009-10 confirms the narrator's interpretation. Within this larger discourse Dorigen and Aurelius actually engage in a meta-dialogue about her "pledge"; they recognize its simultaneous sincerity as a rejection and its insincerity as a promise.

The speech act typology sketched above affords us insight into the logical assumptions and structures which give her words this twofold nature. Before we scrutinize the passage in question further, however, we must remember that an illocutionary act will often take several individual sentences to perform. We must, therefore, look beyond the commonly quoted declaration, "Thanne wol I love yow best of any man; / Have heer my trouthe" (997-98), to find all the elements composing the utterance. Applying Hare's tripartite analysis to Dorigen's larger speech reveals the irreparable flaw preventing the utterance in lines 997-98 from constituting a true promise. The phrastic, or proposition, at the center of Dorigen's "pledge" contains a future action, namely her loving of Aurelius. Recall that the tropic qualifies the phrastic and correlates with the type of speech act performed. Most obviously, Dorigen does say "so be it" when she exclaims "Have heer my trouthe" (998): her words take the conventional form associated with promises. The word "trouthe," in fact, appears so customarily in promises that, while originally a variant form of "truth," meaning "faithfulness, good faith, loyalty" or "honesty," it becomes synonymous with "pledge." Thus the *Oxford English Dictionary* records its use as "one's faith as pledged or plighted in a solemn agreement or undertaking; one's plighted word; the act of pledging one's faith, a promise, covenant" (s.v. "troth"). She could not have chosen a more formal promissory expression. Although the requisite emphasis of the proposition occurs, Dorigen's words do not commit her to either the desirability or the possibility of what she proposes because when she states flatly "wel I *woot* that it shal never bityde" (1001; emphasis mine), she contradicts the "I say so" neustic belonging to promises. Without a neustic in accord with the tropic, the utterance loses its illocutionary force. To put this another way, despite the form of her words in lines 997-98, the utterance simply does not add up to a promise.

The application of Searle's constitutive rules for promises shows even more precisely how Dorigen violates her "pledge" when we consider whether the general conditions for communication—preliminary to any speech act—hold during the conversation between Aurelius and his would-be lover. If we assume that they have not been interrupted since they began speaking (there is no interruption of dialogue by the narrator) then there appear to be no impediments to their communication. Because they continue to question each other about the meaning of their words, they continue to understand each other perfectly. Does a general condition of meaningfulness thus hold? If we ask whether the woman intends to produce a promise by means of getting her hearer to recognize her intention to produce that effect, the answer is "no": "She wende nevere han come in swich a trappe" (1341). She reveals later that she did not mean the promise:

> "Allas," quod she, "that evere this sholde happe!
> For wende I nevere by possibilitee
> That swich a monstre of merveille myghte be!
> It is agayns the proces of nature."
> (1342-45)

Even at the time she made it, Dorigen regards her "promise" as not much of a grace (1000); at best it represents a teasingly cruel rejection.

In extending this illocutionary analysis, we discover that while the general conditions partially fail, the propositional content of Dorigen's secondary utterance completely conforms to that required for promises. She states that she will perform a specific action in the future. Although this proposition is ultimately qualified by another part of her utterance, it remains in itself valid. Linguistically sound, her proposal, however, violates what the medieval audience would have recognized as practical social constraints. As Craig McDonald explains, under medieval law the presence of certain conditions within so-called promises could render them invalid. Promises legally negate themselves "when they [are] made imprudently, without consideration of their effects; when they [are] made under stress; and when they [necessitate] an immoral course of action" (247).[8] Regardless of how well-considered her words may be, they propose sin, and Dorigen could not be held to a contract to commit adultery. This prohibition originates in Canon law, but applies in civil law as well, and as McDonald claims, we can presume that Chaucer's audience would have recognized and been intrigued by the serious defect in her promise. Legal tradition thus contradicts linguistic. Yet this teasing of expectation does more than entertain. Conflicting legal and linguistic evidence force us to ask exactly what constitutes a promise or negates it, and on what grounds.

Linguistic felicity conditions underlying the dialogue of Dorigen and Aurelius prove equally problematic when taken as a whole. The first of these, the preparatory conditions, are satisfied. Searle maintains that a promise can be made only if the speaker believes that the hearer would prefer the proposed course of action and in fact the hearer does have this preference. Dorigen has already learned the squire's desires: "Have mercy, sweete, or ye wol do me deye!" (978) he complains. Clearly, then, it is "not obvious" that she will love Aurelius in any normal course of events. Both understand quite the opposite to be true. And, as Aurelius begs for a promise of love, the audience is primed to expect one.

Sincerity conditions also illuminate the heart of this promise that is not a promise. Promises require, as stated earlier, one specific psychological condition: intention. Dorigen expresses her state of mind

[8]For a particularly lucid summary of medieval distinctions among vows, oaths, and promises, see Morgan ("Boccaccio's *Filocolo*").

just moments earlier in the conversation: she intends to remain a true wife (984-87; cited above).

Henry Ansgar Kelly believes that nothing Dorigen says in lines 997-98 necessarily speaks against this consistent intention.[9] In *Love and Marriage in the Age of Chaucer*, Kelly reports on the legal technicalities affecting nuptial contracts made with first person "wol" declarations (190-91). Like Latin "volo," Middle English "wol" possesses a subtle ambiguity as to whether it conveys the intention or the belief of the speaker. Thus vows formed with "wol" are sometimes considered suspect in questions of law. Formal wedding rites and public witness are therefore necessary, especially in the case of private (or clandestine) contracts, to solemnize the marriage. Examining the bond between Dorigen and Arveragus, Kelly argues that Dorigen's words, "I wol be youre humble trewe wif" (758), declare her present intention. He paraphrases her vow as "I will to be your wife here and now." Both their public status as husband and wife and statements Dorigen makes elsewhere reinforce this interpretation, Kelly argues. In the absence of such circumstances it would also be possible to understand the same "wol" construction as an expression of the speaker's belief. If, therefore, "its main force is future," it can be taken to mean "I will become your wife." While the former meaning can affect an indissoluble contract, the latter can only lead to "mere betrothal [which] could be easily broken" (Kelly 190-91).

Even though our concern is with a courtly promise rather than a wedding vow, Kelly's remarks stress the centrality of intention and demonstrate how linguistic and legal custom intertwine in "wol" promises. Thus, while Middle English grammars and usage surveys describe first person "wol" as generally relaying intention, court proceedings summarized by Kelly reveal contemporary medieval questioning of this force.[10] Clearly, the presence of the modal auxiliary alone proves insufficient in committing a speaker. Even though Dorigen's words in lines 997-98 follow a form typically used to convey intention, her "I wol" is therefore not enough. If a private marriage contract using the expression could be challenged legally, a private promise would share

[9]Henry Ansgar Kelly, personal communiqué.

[10]Linguists take such usage controversy as evidence of language change in progress. Indeed, the Modern English sense of "will" as a simple future probably originates in individual variations which increase in frequency over time. See Arnovick for a detailed discussion of "wol" in late Middle English usage.

the same vulnerability. Seeking other evidence of Dorigen's intention returns us to our earlier conclusions. The lady's actions—verbal and non-verbal—support an intention not to love Aurelius.

Lack of intention is not a minor qualification on promises. Even the devil in Chaucer's *Friar's Tale* requires intent to accompany spoken words in order for a promise to be binding (McDonald 246). The law actually makes provisions to nullify promissory words spoken rashly. As noted above, a promise must be well thought out, with all its effects and implications carefully considered. Because Dorigen's experience of reality discounts the possibility of magical intervention, she never expects that the rocks could disappear. Therefore, she fails even to entertain the thought of actually having to love Aurelius. Her pledge is not enforceable because it lacks not only intention but also precursory thought. Reviewing the council of moral treatises, preachers, teachers, and law-givers in the Middle Ages, Alan Gaylord reveals the unanimity of their opinion: "rash promises are not to be kept" (352). Although it originates with Cicero, this notion is elaborated by the Church Fathers who in turn pass it down into later Christian tradition (Gaylord 355). The words of Ambrose, translated and quoted by Gaylord, well represent learned authority: "It is necessary that one's condition be pure and *sincere*, so that each may proffer frank speech, maintain his vessel in sanctity, and not mislead his brother by devious words" (354; emphasis mine). On this point of "common sense," as Cicero called it, both legal and linguistic systems accord (Gaylord 355).

They diverge, however, on the issue of a philosophically-sanctioned exception, the insincere promise. The question of intent extends beyond Dorigen's regard for her proposition. Does she also intend to keep her later promise, we might ask? Are lines 989-98 an example of an insincere promise, one in which she accepts *responsibility* for having—or at least stating—an intention she does not and never did possess? The Franklin makes several claims about her feelings, describing her actions during the garden scene and throughout the *Tale*. The woman herself, however, displays her intention in all its subtleties. First of all, when Dorigen offers him hope she attaches certain conditions, claiming that she "wolde . . . graunte" Aurelius her love only if he removes "all the rokkes, stoon by stoon, / That they ne lette ship ne boot to goon— / I seye, whan ye han maad the coost so clene" (990-95). Furthermore, because she believes these conditions impossible to meet, she does not assume she will have to keep this promise. Therefore, to follow the logic to its conclusion, she does not intend it. Nor does she now intend to keep the promise: i.e., she does not accept responsibility for the pledge at this point. The elaboration she provides Aurelius when he questions her in line 999 actually confirms an intention *not* to love him. "Wel I woot that it shal never bityde," she responds (1001). Adding insult, she chides him for foolishly presuming to love a married woman in the first place (1000-05).

While Dorigen does not satisfy the first part of Searle's sincerity condition on promises, she does ultimately accept responsibility for having committed herself, however unwittingly, to a course of action. Woefully she realizes that she has in fact made a promise she will be forced to keep. "Thus have I seyd, . . . thus have I sworn" (1464) confesses wife to husband. It is this choice, whether or not to have this secondary intention and accept responsibility for the insincere promise in the end, that Morgan sees as the true test of Dorigen's moral integrity ("Boccaccio's *Filocolo*" 302). In short, the essential condition required of promises thus holds even where sincerity fails. Her words in line 997 count for her as the "undertaking of an obligation," if not at the time they were uttered, then in retrospect at least.

If Aurelius refuses to take "no" for an answer, he has at least heard it and taken it to heart. Struck by the obvious infeasability of removing rocks from a harbor, he considers his love and its chance for return hopeless. "Thanne moot I dye of sodeyn deth horrible" (1010), he announces self-pityingly. In the love sickness he subsequently suffers, he meditates as much on the pain of Dorigen's rejection as on the possibility held out by her words. Once more her words (989-98) take their perlocutionary effect. Once again, the completely felicitous speech act of rejection invalidates what Aurelius hoped to consider a promise.

An illocutionary analysis thus shows that Dorigen chooses, after her pledge is given, to accept responsibility for the expression of an intention she did not possess. What would otherwise be a rash promise becomes an insincere promise embedded within a larger rejection. Furthermore, these philosophical complications again parallel legal ones. As Robert Blanch and Julian Wasserman point out, Dorigen's verbal agreement to do something in the future should embody a covenant, a particular kind of oral contract wherein the conditions of its fulfillment are stipulated and a quid pro quo is executed (599-600). The quid here is the removal of the rocks, required in lines 993-60; "for the benefit (*pro quo*)," Dorigen incurs the debt of loving Aurelius (Blanch and

Wasserman 599). Their words look like they represent a covenant because the responsibilities of each are spelled out so clearly. Through a careful analysis of Aurelius' obligation, Gaylord determines that he never fulfills the terms of any contract: he does not himself take the rocks away, stone by stone (349). If Dorigen needed further legal grounds not to fulfill her part of the bargain, she has them here.[11] More importantly, however, there is enough disparity between semblance and reality that the opposition between legality and illegality blurs. Add to the legal opacity both the philosophical convolution outlined above and Dorigen's willingness to assume the burden of commitment, and the reader experiences enough confusion to author scores of scholarly articles about the "truth" of Dorigen's promises.

The linguistic–philosophical analysis offered above shows the self-canceling aspects of Dorigen's speech act while the legal analysis presented reveals that her ten line utterance (989-98) does not constitute a binding promise. As if these conclusions were not enough, yet another context undercuts what both modern and medieval readers have decided about her pledge. In a world beyond late fourteenth-century England, perhaps also in the parallel universe of an unfamiliar Brittany, familiar points of law (if not language) are suspended. In this world of magic and other wonders, promises made insincerely and rashly do obligate their speaker. This is the world of the folk tale.

N. Bøgholm locates a written source for the promise episode. Tracing Chaucer's story to the Sanskrit *Katha Sarit Sagara*, he finds many similar features: a) a maiden's rash promise; b) the forgiveness of husband, suitor, and a third man; and c) a question to the audience inviting them to decide which of the three is the most generous. Seeking more immediate influences, many scholars have argued that Boccac-

[11]The pledge contains so many legal and moral flaws that it seems irrelevant that certain physical activity traditionally associated with promises is missing. No third party witnesses the pledge; no handshake or exchange of tokens accompany it. For more on these legal requirements of enforceable covenants see McDonald (249). The rationale behind such non-verbal activity is explored by Stock. He discusses in more general terms the formal nature of feudal rites in which spoken words are accompanied by the gift of a concrete token and the performance of a symbolic ritual (50 ff.). Obviously, no written record of Dorigen's debt (a type of recognizance) is made, a factor which, depending on the extent of literacy in his make-believe world, could be a liability for Aurelius. For an account of English contract customs in transition from oral to written practice and the implications of practical literacy, see Clanchy.

cio's *Filocolo* offered Chaucer a literary model elaborating on these features. But, to be precise, as Germaine Dempster and J.S.P. Tatlock show, elements of the *Franklin's Tale* appear to derive from works by Boccaccio, Geoffrey of Monmouth, and St. Jerome.[12]

Despite variations on the theme, a lengthy literary tradition preserves the story of the woman's rash promise. Moreover, in all likelihood, an equally old oral tradition, i.e. one maintained by the folk, parallels this literary tradition. As Stith Thompson points out, considering the absence of contemporary medieval recordings of oral stories, written versions may be the sole evidence of a folk tradition. He urges scholars not to dismiss the written when the availability of medieval and ancient oral sources is so obviously compromised (*The Folktale* 4-5). Thus, in his *Motif Index of Folk Literature*, Thompson identifies the *Franklin's Tale* as a manifestation of oral motif M261: "Chaste woman promises herself to her lover when the rocks leave the coast" (45). The single incident of this rash promise composes a motif which belongs to a larger type, or independent tale. Antti Aarne and Thompson's *The Types of the Folktale* lists the *Tale* under type 976: "Which Was the Noblest Act?" (343). Additionally, it clearly resembles "act of truth" and "chastity test" motifs as well as "foolish bargain" types. Most generally, it allies itself with motifs and tales exploring the power of language. As Robin Lakoff observes, fairy tales frequently center on "the power of language for good or evil, the dangers of an ill-considered word, [and] the value of silence" (14). In short, the story of Dorigen's promise possesses an old and rich oral heritage.

The *Franklin's Tale* is not alone in having both oral and written antecedents; nor is their combined effect completely unique. Francis Lee Utley locates a source in folk legend for the majority of the tales in the Canterbury collection. These folktales are not only present, as Utley shows, but also play an active literary role in the *Canterbury Tales*, asserts Carl Lindahl. The presence of a legend and the folk rhetoric, behavior, and wisdom associated with it provoke a tension between popular and elite modes of literature and experience in the *Tales*. Ultimately, he argues, the folk subverts, challenging—albeit safely—elite experiences and their literary representation. Folkloric patterns "are the most earnest conceivable games, for the pilgrims use these traditional strate-

[12]Dempster and Tatlock conveniently reprint these sources and analogues of the *Franklin's Tale* along with a bibliography of scholarship about their influence on Chaucer.

gies to express their most negative and heretical thoughts—thoughts which, if given any other form, would invite frightening consequences" (Lindahl 10).

To an extent, the folk legend of the rash promise functions similarly within the *Franklin's Tale*. As Walter Ong explains, the psychodynamics of orality dictate situational rather than abstract representations (49). One constant feature of oral "literature," therefore, is its dependency on an engaging situation, especially one its audience would recognize and anticipate. The medieval audience of the *Franklin's Tale* would know its story well. They would know both the terrible bind Dorigen creates for herself and the "all's well that ends well" conclusion. They would know that she will be held unfairly to her promise, but they would also know that she will not have to keep it. Chaucer thus continues to "play" with readers' expectations by adding inherently contradictory evidence to the already conflicting legal and linguistic clues he has provided. The oral plot-formula central to the *Franklin's Tale* undercuts readers' real-world (linguistic and legal) understanding of promises. As it challenges our expectations, it allows Chaucer, within the guise of play, to question the assumptions dear to both his characters and his audience. The poet's sport is engaging. Any frustration readers might feel ultimately turns into amusement, but not before we have been forced to think seriously about the connections among words, deeds, honor, and love.

As Dorigen decides how to resolve her conflicting obligations, readers view an ethical—if not a linguistic or legal—dilemma wherein Aurelius discovers a way to keep her to the form of her promise while ignoring Dorigen's true intentions. The lady does not shirk the responsibility trapping her, however unwisely or unfairly assumed. Indeed, Golding congratulates Dorigen for realizing the significance of her commitment and then honoring her obligation so "spontaneously and with such force" (310). Her bind has offered her an ennobling lesson in the moral duties of "real" life, he argues; through this experience she learns the value of the pledged word. But psychological truth (her intention) sheds light on moral "truth" too. A cynic could object that the only reality she comes to appreciate is that of manipulation and betrayal.

If truth "is the hyeste thyng that man may kepe" (1479) is it limited to the surface form of the word? Is Chaucer celebrating the "claims of the pledged word" in this tale as J.A. Burrow, quoted by Golding (306), professes? Or, might the poet be revealing, as he does so many times elsewhere, the ambiguity of something so seemingly certain? Chaucerian poetics frequently proffer "no singular truth, only multiple values," Robert M. Jordan reminds us (49). Conflicting evidence (whether it be linguistic, legal, or folkloric) and ensuing judgments alert readers to the possibility of intended ambiguity. In fact, if we do not read too literally, but remember the context of Dorigen's words, we witness a disjunction between the form of "trouthe" and the truth underlying it. This disjunction, furthermore, pervades the text, affecting not only the words of the woman, but also the words of each major character and the Franklin himself.

Various critics have tried to assess this disjunction. Seaman exposes one aspect of it when he stresses that readers are compelled "to question what value system or systems we need to employ in order to answer" the Franklin's question (46). He demonstrates that the *Tale* supports several viable and often conflicting value systems and thereby allows various answers: "a case can be made for each of the principal characters being the one who is the most *fre*" (53). Yet Seaman fails to pursue the implications of the competing value systems, or of their plurality far enough. Like the Franklin, he assumes that each debt-holder exhibits "gentilesse."

Perhaps none is the "mooste fre" on the other hand. A niggardliness of spirit might actually accompany generous-sounding claims. As Laura Kendrick suggests, the Franklin's question itself reveals a separation between form and meaning:

> Although the Franklin's closing question imitates the *demande* or question for courteous debate (F 1621-22), it nevertheless turns a pathetic romance of accommodation centered on the predicament of a powerless heroine into a game of deciding which of three men gave up the most, who was most generous or accommodating in a more vulgar, materialistic sense of the word.
>
> (88)

Ferster addresses a similar dislocation in her hermeneutic reading of the *Franklin's Tale*. When Aurelius purposefully turns the "playful promise" into something it never was, an honorable "beheste" made before God, the *Tale* continues its preoccupation with the tension between illusion and reality (Ferster 157). Thus, Ferster argues that readers confront a false rendering of "trouthe" 'promise' into "trouthe" 'reality' (157).

These disjunctions underscore a multivalency of meaning once again. Conflicting interpretations about truth in the *Franklin's Tale*, like opposing stances about Dorigen's promise, are (and will continue to be) defensible in the end because the evidence available is at best contradictory. Perhaps, in the last analysis, the story of Dorigen's promise is about interpretation, as Ferster suggests. As Italo Calvino claims, literature is a "combinatorial game that pursues the possibilities implicit in its own material"; mythic significance is something one comes across only if one persists in playing around with narrative functions (22-23).[13] Complicating, contradicting, and compromising the insights offered by the other two, each of these three oral realms—linguistic, legal, and folk—provides a typically Chaucerian richness of meaning and implication to the text.

Department of English
University of British Columbia

[13]I am indebted to my colleagues Robert M. Jordan and J. Kieran Kealy for their insights about the multivalency of meaning in Chaucer's text. I would like to thank Michael R. Near, whose comments on the embedded obligations in the *Tale* helped focus my own thinking. I am also grateful to Mark C. Amodio and Henry Ansgar Kelly for the helpful suggestions they offered on an earlier version of this paper.

Works Cited

Aarne, Antti and Stith Thompson. *The Types of the Folktale*. Bloomington: Indiana UP, 1964.

Arnovick, Leslie K. *The Development of Future Constructions in English: The Pragmatics of Modal and Temporal Will and Shall in Middle English*. New York: Lang, 1990.

Austin, John. *How to Do Things with Words*. 2nd ed. Ed. J.O. Urmson and M. Sbisa. Cambridge, MA: Harvard UP, 1975.

Benson, Larry D., ed. *The Riverside Chaucer*. 3rd ed. Boston: Houghton, 1987.

Blanch, Robert J. and Julian N. Wasserman. "Medieval Contracts and Covenants: the Legal Coloring of *Sir Gawain and the Green Knight*." *Neophilologus* 68 (1984): 598-610.

Bøgholm, N. "A Rash Promise." *Studia Neophilologica* 15 (1942/43): 41-2.

Brewer, Derek. "Orality and Literacy in Chaucer." *Mündlichkeit und Schriftlichkeit im englischen Mittelalter*. Ed. W. Erzgräber and Sabine Volk. Tübingen: Narr, 1988. 85-119.

Bryan, William Frank and Germaine Dempster, eds. *Sources and Analogs of Chaucer's* Canterbury Tales *by Carleton Brown, Germaine Dempster, C.H. Gerould, et alia*. Chicago: U of Chicago P, 1941. New York: Humanities Press, 1958.

Calvino, Italo. *The Uses of Literature: Essays*. Trans. Patrick Creagh. San Diego: Harcourt, 1986.

Clanchy, M.T. *From Memory to Written Record*. Cambridge, MA: Harvard UP, 1979.

Coats, Jennifer. *The Semantics of the Modal Auxiliaries*. Beckenham: Croom Helm, 1983.

Ferster, Judith. "Interpretation and Imitation in Chaucer's *Franklin's Tale*." *Medieval Literature: Criticism, Ideology and History*. Ed. David Aers. Brighton: Harvester, 1986. 148-68.

Fish, Stanley E. "How to Do Things with Austin and Searle: Speech Act Theory and Literary Criticism." *Modern Language Notes* 91 (1978): 983-1025.

Fisher, John H. "Scala Chauceriensis." *Approaches to Teaching Chaucer's* Canterbury Tales. Ed. Joseph Gibaldi. New York: MLA, 1980. 39-45.

Foley, John Miles. *Oral-Formulaic Theory and Research: An Introduction and Annotated Bibliography*. New York: Garland, 1985.

—. *The Theory of Oral Composition: History and Methodology*. Bloomington: Indiana UP, 1988.

—, ed. *Oral-Formulaic Theory: A Folklore Casebook*. New York: Garland, 1990.

Gaylord, Alan T. "The Promises in *The Franklin's Tale*." *English Literary History* 31 (1964): 331-65.

Golding, Malcolm. "The Importance of Keeping 'Trouthe' in *The Franklin's Tale*." *Medium Ævum* 39 (1970): 306-12.

Hare, R.M. "Meaning and Speech Acts." *Philosophical Review* 79 (1970): 3-24.

Jordan, Robert M. *Chaucer's Poetics and the Modern Reader*. Berkeley: U of California P, 1987.

Kelly, Henry Ansgar. *Love and Marriage in the Age of Chaucer*. Ithaca: Cornell UP, 1975.

Kendrick, Laura. *Chaucerian Play: Comedy and Control in the* Canterbury Tales. Berkeley: U of California P, 1988.

Lakoff, Robin Tolmach. *Talking Power: The Politics of Language in Our Lives*. New York: Basic Books, 1990.

Levinson, Stephen C. *Pragmatics*. Cambridge: Cambridge UP, 1983.

Lindahl, Carl. *Earnest Games*. Bloomington: Indiana UP, 1987.

Lord, Albert B. *The Singer of Tales*. Cambridge, MA: Harvard UP, 1960.

Lyons, John. *Semantics*. Vol. 2. Cambridge: Cambridge UP, 1977.

McDonald, Craig. "The Perversion of Law in Robert Henryson's Fable of *The Fox, the Wolf, and the Husbandman*." *Medium Ævum* 49 (1980): 244-53.

Martin, Richard P. *The Language of Heroes: Speech and Performance in the* Iliad. Ithaca: Cornell UP, 1989.

Morgan, Gerald. "A Defense of Dorigen's Complaint." *Medium Ævum* 46 (1977): 77-97.

—. "Boccaccio's *Filocolo* and the Moral Argument of the *Franklin's Tale*." *Chaucer Review* 20 (1986): 285-306.

Ong, Walter J. *Orality and Literacy: The Technologizing of the Word*. London: Methuen, 1982.

Parks, Ward. "The Oral-Formulaic Theory in Middle English Studies." *Oral Tradition* 1 (1986): 636-94.

—. "Oral Tradition and the *Canterbury Tales*." *Oral Poetics in Middle English Poetry*. Ed. Mark C. Amodio. New York: Garland, 1994. 149-79.

Parry, Milman. *The Making of Homeric Verse: The Collected Papers of Milman Parry*. Ed. Adam Parry. Oxford: Clarendon, 1971.

Pratt, Mary Louise. *Toward a Speech Act Theory of Literary Discourse*. Bloomington: Indiana UP, 1977.

Renoir, Alain. "Oral-Formulaic Context: Implications for the Comparative Criticism of Mediaeval Texts." *Oral-Formulaic Theory: A Folklore Casebook*. Ed. John Miles Foley. New York: Garland, 1990. 313-35.

Rowland, Beryl. "Chaucer's Imagery." *A Companion to Chaucer Studies*. Ed. Beryl Rowland. Oxford: Oxford UP, 1979. 103-22.

Schlieben-Lange, Brigitte. *Traditionen des Sprechens*. Stuttgart: Kohlhammer, 1983.

Seaman, David M. "'As thynketh yow': Conflicting Evidence and the Interpretation of *The Franklin's Tale*." *Medievalia et Humanistica* ns 17 (1991): 41-58.

Searle, John. *Speech Acts: An Essay in the Philosophy of Language*. Cambridge: Cambridge UP, 1969.

Spearing, A.C. *The Gawain Poet: A Critical Study*. Cambridge: Cambridge UP, 1970.

Stock, Brian. *The Implications of Literacy: Written Language and Models of Interpretation in the Eleventh and Twelfth Centuries*. Princeton: Princeton UP, 1983.

Thompson, Stith. *Motif Index of Folk Literature*. Rev. and enl. ed. 6 vols. Bloomington: Indiana UP, 1955.

—. *The Folktale*. Berkeley: U of California P, 1977.

Utley, Francis Lee. "Some Implications of Chaucer's Folktales." *Laographia* 22 (1965): 588-99.

Zumthor, Paul. *Oral Poetry: An Introduction*. Trans. Kathryn Murphy-Judy. Minneapolis: U of Minnesota P, 1990.

Oral Tradition and the *Canterbury Tales*

Ward Parks

I

No one could deny that Chaucer was a highly literate man. As everyone knows, his work abounds with references to the literary, philosophical, theological, medical, astrological authorities of classical antiquity, learned Latin, and several contemporary vernaculars, suggesting that his comic self-portrayal as a portly bookworm without any first-hand experience in love and other fine arts may have been at any rate true on one account. Yet Chaucer's erudition does not preclude the possibility that his work registers a sensibility to the oral traditions and residual orality of his age. Indeed, his oeuvre give indication of a particularly lively engagement of just this sort.

Consider the frame in the *Canterbury Tales*. A group of pilgrims are engaged in tale-telling. None reads from a script or rehearses from verbatim memory; all compose their tales in performance, adapting their narratives, when appropriate, to the audience at hand. None seems to expect that his or her performance will be recorded for posterity, and accordingly they make themselves free to quarrel, tell dirty jokes, get drunk, and indulge in other behaviors that they would hardly have wanted to be remembered for. That the pilgrim Chaucer would choose later to write their stories down was an eventuality that they do not seem to have foreseen. At the same time, many of their tales are formulaic or incorporate formulaic elements, if I may for the moment use the term "formula" somewhat loosely. For as even a cursory review of Bryan and Dempster suggests, much of what the pilgrims heard would have seemed quite familiar. Nor do they ever see fit to object on this account: indeed, while their "hoost," hardly bashful in his aesthetic judgements, takes his performers to task on several grounds, we never hear him complain that he has heard a story before.[1] This easy acceptance of the conventional and stereotypical accords, once again, with what one would expect of an audience whose aesthetic sensibilities are largely oral. As students of oral traditions have repeatedly emphasized, typical narrative materials are well adapted to the economy of thought in contexts where an improvising raconteur and a listening audience must achieve communication under definite temporal constraints.

What I am suggesting is that the *Canterbury Tales*, by general consensus the outstanding literary production of Middle English, could be fruitfully characterized and studied as a literate author's representation of the proceedings of an oral tradition. Oral tradition is, indeed, Chaucer's explicit subject. Now it must be admitted that problems of literary "mimesis" are, in this case, particularly vexed. Obviously real-life millers and reeves in Chaucer's day did not improvise stories in rhyming couplets of iambic pentameter; further, Chaucer's actual sources were in many cases indubitably literary and not oral. Nor should we commit the anachronism of imputing to Chaucer an explicit awareness of "oral tradition" and orality–literacy issues such as obtains among scholars of the subject today. When these and other provisos have been allowed, however, the reality and pertinence of oral tradition remains. Yet this dimension of the *Canterbury Tales* has been massively neglected, despite the copiousness and richness of Chauceriana in most other respects. One wonders, indeed, whether the oral dimensions of the *Tales* might not occasion some discomfort to scholars whose own literary training has been predominantly textual and whose theoretical models hinge on terms and concepts (such as "literary allusion," close "reading," *écriture*, textuality, and intertextuality) that pre-

[1]For an excellent discussion of Harry's literary standards and preferences, see Scheps ("Tale Telling").

suppose literate modes of interpretive engagement and that implicitly disallow that poetic communication was ever intended to be oral.[2]

Of course, for more than half a century a significant sidestream of Chaucerian criticism has engaged oral issues in one way or another. While I will from time to time be tapping into this rich vein, my particular perspective grows out of the tradition of oral-formulaic scholarship, which, surprisingly enough, has seldom been brought to bear on Chaucer's poetic production.[3] While the *Tales* cannot, obviously, be characterized as "oral" in the Parry-Lord sense, they do engage, as one relevant background, the kind of literary and poetic assumptions that oral-formulaic scholarship has brought to light. If pursued non-dogmatically, this line of inquiry might indeed bring us to the recognition of aspects of Chaucer's artistry that have, to date, been largely overlooked.

II

From the outset, we must acknowledge that the relationship between Chaucer and oral tradition was probably a multidimensional one. The most significant distinction here is between *direct* and *indirect* forms of influence. That is, Chaucer might himself have been a direct witness to living oral traditions, and his observations in this capacity might have registered with the *Tales*. But in any case, he could not help but participate in the larger cultural movement from predominantly oral to predominantly literate modes of communication, in literary and other arenas. Though I intend to focus primarily on the second of these channels, the possibility that direct exposure impacted significantly on Chaucer's art is a serious one.

Of course, if we construe the term broadly, Chaucer must have encountered and participated in various "oral traditions," in the sense that anyone who has ever heard or told a joke or a story has done so.

[2]I have made this point in "Textualization of Orality." For seminal studies exploring the larger theoretical implication of orality, oral poetry, vocality, and related matters, see Ong (*Orality and Literacy*); and Zumthor.

[3]In the last decade excellent introductions and bibliographies of oral-formulaic scholarship have become available; see particularly Foley (*Oral Composition* and sources cited therein).

This kind of background may not have received the attention that it deserves precisely because it is so obvious. But if we narrow our focus further to elaborate performances common in Chaucer's own day, here too, many possible sources of influence can be identified. Carl Lindahl, in a significant reinauguration of the folkloric method in Chaucerian criticism, identifies nine dramatic and stylistic elements common to assorted medieval festivals, such as the Cour Amoreuse and the London Pui, that figure into the narrative frame of the *Tales* (*Earnest Games* 44-61).[4] The evidence he has compiled does indeed suggest that pageantry and gamesmanship of the *Tales* may very well reflect Chaucer's personal experience of such occasions. While these festivals are more ritualistically dramatic than narrative—and most of the research on "oral tradition" has indeed focused on the narrative genres—nonetheless they do translate us into a world of live speech and action that is much closer to an oral narrative performance than it is to a text.

Yet while the evidence is and probably always will be scanty, the possibility cannot be excluded that Chaucer experienced firsthand oral poetic composition in some form. The most viable candidate for an authentic oral poetic tradition in fourteenth century England would have found its home somewhere in association with the Alliterative Revival, though it is much disputed whether or not this sudden efflorescence of alliterative poetry resulted from an oral tradition continuing from Old English times.[5] In any event, such an oral tradition, if there were one, would have been remote from Chaucer both geographically and aesthetically: like his Parson, he found himself unable or unwilling to "geeste 'rum, ram, ruf,' by lettre" (the *Parson's Prologue* 43).[6] It is more probable that he encountered oral poetic composition through medieval minstrelsy. Three decades ago, Albert C. Baugh argued that minstrels practiced a limited variety of oral composition, supplementing the memorized text with oral improvisation; Baugh and others have used this hypothesis to account for variations between manuscript ver-

[4]For greater detail, see Lindahl ("Chaucer the Storyteller" 92-152).

[5]This notion has been the subject of some debate. For an advocate, see Moorman; for a critic, see Turville-Petre. One of the best-known studies that applies oral-formulaic perspectives to an alliterative work is Benson *Art and Tradition* [esp. 110-66]). For a systematic application of the "strict" Parry-Lord model to a Middle English poem see Krishna. For a survey of Middle English scholarship relevant to oral-formulaic concerns, see Parks ("Oral-Formulaic Theory").

[6]I cite Benson's edition of Chaucer's works throughout.

sions of many Middle English romances.[7] All of this is speculative, of course; we will probably never know to what degree oral poetry was practiced in Chaucer's own day and how familiar with it he was. Yet lack of evidence does not prove an absence. For it must be recalled that our evidence is perforce biased towards written poetry and against oral poetry, in the sense that oral poetry survived only if it was written down. The resurgence in our own society of oral poetic composition in the form of rap shows that such improvisational genres can indeed flourish in literate cultures. Since the *Tales* do, after all, depict poetic narrative improvisation on a large scale and at a high level of excellence, we should keep an open mind as to whether Chaucer, a well-travelled and worldly man, had met up with such activity himself.

Yet even if oral poetic tradition had no impact on Chaucer directly, its residual influence on the fourteenth-century poetic milieu would have been much harder to escape. And here the logic of oral-formulaic theory may be helpful in indicating two lines along which such inquiry can proceed. According to Milman Parry and Albert B. Lord, oral composition and a high frequency of lexical and narrative formulas—that feature of oral style that Parry and Lord give most attention to—are causally related, in that formulas serve the needs of both a performing poet and a listening audience. There are, of course, many other characteristics of oral style besides formularity; and even the notion of the formula must be carefully adapted to the tradition and genre under review.[8] Yet after making allowance for the long scholarly controversy on these subjects, the general connection between the live oral medium and high levels of redundancy remains. The introduction of writing, however, severs this link. Now the text intrudes between composer and audience, disrupting that logic that gave birth to the formulaic style in the first place.[9] Yet the formulaic style and "custom of oral delivery" are apt to survive for a time anyway as oral-derived habits whose relationship to each other is becoming more and more problematic. By adopting either practice, then, a poet would be dipping into the reservoir of inherited oral/aural experience. We need not require that an

[7]For further bibliography, see Parks ("Oral-Formulaic Theory").

[8]For a discussion of some of the complexities that must be negotiated in the comparison of oral or oral-derived texts and the principles that must be respected in this process, see Foley (*Traditional Oral Epic* [esp. 1-19]).

[9]I am using the expression "formulaic style" as a shorthand for the range of stylistic proclivities associated with oral composition. For a fuller discussion of the characteristics of oral discourse, see Ong (*Orality and Literacy*).

author employ the same specific formulas used in the parent oral tradition, or that the minstrel consciously conceive himself as an heir to the Anglo-Saxon scop or any other species of oral composer. The formulaic style and oral performance medium would in themselves link him—however strongly or tenuously, and however conditioned by other forces—with his traditional cultural past.

Now both of these topics have sponsored important lines of inquiry in Chaucerian scholarship. The subject of oral delivery was brought into prominence in 1926 by George Wilson, who situated Chaucer's work in a broad comparative and evolutionary context. A few years later Ruth Crosby treated the subject in far greater detail in a pair of articles—the first on medieval literature, the second focusing specifically on Chaucer—that remain essential reading today. Bertrand H. Bronson's "Chaucer's Art in Relation to His Audience" treats many of the same problems, though with greater attention to that poet's artistic manipulations of performer–audience interactions and narratorial self-representations.[10] Beryl Rowland has studied the art of *pronuntiatio*—the fifth branch of rhetoric—as a major tradition in the Middle Ages with important hermeneutic consequences for Chaucer's work ("*Pronuntiatio* and Its Effect").[11] Betsy Bowden adds a new twist to this scholarly tradition by recording a number of scholarly performances of Chaucerian texts and making these the basis of extended literary interpretation.[12] It will not be my purpose here to delve into this rich mine further, but merely to point out the logical diachronic relationship between oral performance and oral-formulaic tradition.

Of course, oral performance probably exerted a more determinative influence on other Middle English poets than it did on Chaucer himself. As Wilson, Crosby, Bronson, Rowland, and others acknowledge, Chaucer envisioned the dissemination of his work through both media—the oral and the written. When he writes "Go, litel bok, go, litel myn tragedye" at the end of *Troilus and Criseyde* (V.1786), he exhibits

[10]See also Bronson's later critique of the notion of the Chaucerian "persona" (*In Search of Chaucer* [esp. 25-32]).

[11]For other slants on this problem, see Rowland ("Chaucer's Speaking Voice"); Rosenberg; and Reiss.

[12]A particularly innovative feature of Bowden's book is that it comes accompanied by a cassette whose recorded performances of Chaucer's poetry Bowden's text undertakes to interpret. On the need to incorporate audio recordings into the processes of medieval scholarship and pedagogy, see Parks ("Song, Text, and Cassette").

a consciousness of the reification and permanency of *text* quite alien to oral poets. Some scholars have gone further in pointing out that the mannerisms of oral discourse could be imitated by writers and should so be "understood as a private version of the public and immediate contact of the poet and the listener" (Pearsall 295).[13] Yet one would err in assuming that the oral performance medium can on these grounds be discounted. For even if such references are merely fictive and conventional, the oral context is being imaginatively evoked, and in consequence the hermeneutical assumptions of oral discourse may well be in force. Yet there is no more reason to assume that these oral mannerisms are really literary imitations than there is to assume the opposite, that references to reading and writing are merely conventionalized and figurative.[14] On the other hand, it would be anachronistic to say, as some have, that we need concern ourselves only with literary *texts*, on the grounds that it is only the text, denuded of its extra-textual oral resonances, that descends to us.[15] Yet would we treat other backgrounds in this way? The mere fact that a condition no longer pertains to our own era cannot justify our discounting it in the interpretive process. The attitudes and presuppositions relating individuals to the *idea* of text are no more beyond time than any other historical phenomenon is. Common sense would dictate that an interaction (of one sort or another) between literary and oral receptional presuppositions is signalled by the mix of oral and written allusions in Chaucer's work. Articulating the dynamics of this interaction poses an exciting and largely unexplored problem in Chaucerian criticism.

The other channel of oral residue, consisting in the formulaic habit of expression, has been the subject of one of the oldest lines of

[13]For similar perspectives, see Mehl; and Payne.

[14]The briefest reflection will suggest many reasons why a literate poet composing for oral delivery might try fictively to suggest writer-reader communication: perhaps written discourse carries prestige among his envisioned auditors; perhaps he wishes to call attention to the premeditation that went into the making of his poem, or to its permanency beyond the mere present occasion of oral performance, or to its place in a tradition of written literature; perhaps for artistic purposes he wishes at that moment to evoke imaginatively the more private and individualized style of communication that writing and reading foster; and so forth. We must also recall that even illiterate poets make allusion to written discourse. The writing and reading of letters, for example, comprises an important motif in Serbo-Croatian oral poetry; see Lord's discussion of this oral-formulaic theme in *Singer* (82-86).

[15]For this point of view see, for example, Baum (128).

Old and Middle English scholarship. The nineteenth-century German Higher Criticism took considerable interest in formulaic matters, particularly for the light they shed on problems of authorship and date of composition. In 1923 J.S.P. Tatlock published an important study of formulaic diction in Laȝamon; a decade later, J. P. Oakden's *Alliterative Poetry in Middle English* detailed massively traditional continuities in diction and formulaic phraseology. More recently, Susan Wittig, analyzing twenty-five (non-Chaucerian) Middle English romances for formularity according to a rather strict construction of the term "formula," has found densities ranging from 10-42% ("Formulaic Style").[16] Of course, Chaucer himself relied on formulas, though not to the degree that many of his fellow-romancers seem to have done. Nonetheless, readers have long noted his "verse-tags,"[17] reminiscent of oral formulas; and in any case, he could not have failed to remark formulary tendencies in the literature that his age and tradition bequeathed to him. And more recently, other "oral" characteristics in Chaucer's style have been recognized. Particularly notable in this respect is an article by Derek Brewer ("Orality and Literacy") which studies Chaucer's distinctive integration of such oral features as set phrases, repetition and variation, sententiousness, additive style, word-play, oaths, hyperbole, kinetic imagery, historicism and essentialism, and tribal voice, with other stylistic proclivities, as towards fictionalization and self-consciousness, ambiguity, precision, the differentiation of high and low style, realism, and irony, that typify a more literate form of poetic composition.

All of this, of course, takes its place within a social history in which literacy was spreading and interacting with orality in many complex modalities.[18] It is becoming increasingly clear that the crude dichotomy of "orality versus literacy" lacks the nuance required in dealing with hybrid forms, with communities in which the degree of literacy varied enormously, and with interactions in which orality and literacy

[16]For a fuller treatment, see Wittig (*Formulaic and Narrative Structures*).

[17]See, for example, Hathaway. Crisp finds a formula in every 8.3 lines in a selection of five tales representing both the earlier and later stages in Chaucer's career.

[18]For major studies in this subject area, see Clanchy; and Stock. For a more theoretically oriented discussion, see Gellrich ("Orality, Literacy, and Crisis"). Knapp discusses the subversive role which Chaucer's discourse played with respect to social formations relating to the three estates, the Wyclif heresy, and women; it could be argued that another area of social contestation which Chaucer helps to negotiate involves orality-literacy relations.

are recycled into each other. Nonetheless, the fundamental distinction between orality and literacy cannot be done away with. In oral communication, speaker and listener are present to each other in time and space and are interacting with each other directly. In textual communication, the writing and reading acts are separated temporally and spatially; and the interaction is with a text, not a person. Of course, since both oral and written communication take place within a common world, blurrings and interdependencies arise. Yet the intrusion or non-intrusion of a text into a communication between people cannot fail to impact on how that communication is achieved. To ignore or minimalize this distinction is to open the door to anachronistic interpretations, for literary scholars are working out of an interpretative tradition that has long taken textualized communication as normative. If the norms of oral communication are not consciously studied and integrated into the interpretive process, their influence will almost certainly be undervalued.

I submit that, far more than has generally been appreciated, Chaucer's art operated with reference to a framework of aesthetic assumptions that were interperformative as much as they were intertextual. I define interperformativity as that dimension of a poem that exists in its relationship to other songs or performances.[19] In an interperformative aesthetic, the poet operates in relation to a "literary" tradition that exists only in memory and is never recuperable in the concrete, explicit, material ways that books make possible. This leads to a mode of aesthetic engagement with tradition that John M. Foley has recently termed "metonymic": that is, "textual" elements in a particular song rendering summon in the minds of an experienced audience the recollection of similar elements in other performances.[20] A traditional oral audience would be far more liable than a highly textualized readership would be to embrace a redundant or stereotypic phrase or narrative structure, since, for these oral listeners, the present performance text is always half-immersed in and enriched by a world of resonance that is generally outside the experience of readers who are not acculturated in that tradition. Now I certainly do not wish to argue that Chaucer's aesthetic principles were essentially those of an oral artist: to the contrary, writing was deeply internalized for him, and the "tradition" in which he

[19]I discuss this further in "Interperformativity and *Beowulf*"; on related matters, see Parks ("Textualization of Orality").
[20]For a fuller discussion of this, see Foley (*Immanent Art* 7-8 and passim).

operated was very largely constituted of texts, many of them Latin, French, or Italian. At the very same time, however, the *Canterbury Tales* exhibit an interest, sometimes sympathetic and sometimes critical, in a different kind of traditionality, less bookish and more community-based. It is to this dimension of his artistic accomplishment that I now attend.

III

I would now like to examine more closely the response to the formulaic style that is represented in Chaucer's parodic masterpiece, *Sir Thopas*. This poem is especially useful for my purposes since the genre that it satirizes—the English metrical romance—was more deeply rooted in orality than was the continental literary tradition out of which Chaucer's own work for the most part grows. My aim, however, will not be to enumerate or find sources for specific Chaucerian formulas. Rather, I wish to argue that one of the butts of Chaucer's satire was an *attitude* towards formulaic usage that derived ultimately from oral tradition.

Here it would be useful to recall several of Parry's insights on the relationship of formulaic units to their immediate discursive environments. It was Parry's contention that repeating noun-epithet phrases such as "dios Odysseus" 'godlike Odysseus' and "podas okys Achilleus" 'swift-footed Achilles' represent extracts from the traditional poet's formulaic inheritance and that their appearance in a given passage results from their metrical-prosodic usefulness rather than from their con-textual appropriateness.[21] This diachronic and traditional orientation helps to explain lapses and inconsistencies of various types. For example, the Homeric canon is riddled with examples of the metrical flaw known as *hiatus*, which consists in the immediate sequence of vowel sounds between words. Parry explained these occurrences as "the result of the juxtaposition of two formulae, where the end of the first is

[21]Parry did not, in fact, make this claim for all such phrases but only for those with "ornamental" rather than "particularized" epithets; on this subject see esp. "The Traditional Epithet in Homer" (1-190). For a comprehensive review of scholarship that situates Parry's contributions in the context of subsequent research, see Edwards.

not in metrical accord with the beginning of the second" (202). Similarly, infelicitous noun-epithet combinations can result from the generic use of an epithet in inappropriate circumstances (Parry [esp. 151-52]). The same idea has been applied at the narrative level also: narrative inconsistencies are often effects of the spinning out of formulaic narrative themes or type-scenes that contain elements that do not fit in with the specific narrative context.[22] The root principle in all these cases is the same: the traditional unit of discourse, on which the oral poet habitually relies, does not equally suit all discursive environments; thus the inconsistency attests to the superordination of the traditional process over the particular needs of a particular tale at a particular moment.

Now many critics of Parry and his followers have been troubled by the subordination of artistry to compositional expediency that they perceive in his view.[23] While there is certainly justice in this as a criticism of early oral-formulaic scholarship, Parry's fundamental insight does not so much deny artistry as indicate a new dimension over which it operated. The point is that, to oral poets and their audiences, traditional phraseology and other formulary materials engage diachrony in a fashion to which modern readers are unaccustomed. The phenomenology of reading automatically foregrounds what could be called the *typographic* context, by which I mean the words, sentences, narrative passages encompassing the item in question *on the written page.* Yet in an oral narrative performance, this moment in the current tale is as much environed by the evoked memories of cognate moments in prior performances as it is by what has already been told and what will be told in the story now being told, since, given the exigencies of oral communication, neither poet nor audience could very well be directing much of their conscious attention to matters of the narrative non-present while the narrative present is in the very process of unfolding. In other words, traditional diachrony *as context* is continually impinging upon the integrity of the present narrative act. Oral composition entails a dynamic interplay between memory and expression, between the di-

[22]Parry's rather preliminary remarks on this subject appear in his review of Walter Arend's *Die Typischen Scenen bei Homer* (404-07). For other work on Homer in this line, see Lord (esp. *Singer* 68-92); and Hansen.

[23]For bibliography on this debate in Homeric scholarship, see Foley (*Oral-Formulaic Theory and Research* [esp. 17-18]); and Edwards ("Homer and the Oral Tradition: The Formula, Part 1"); an especially interesting discussion is Scully. For an important reappraisal of this issue, see Foley (*Immanent Art* [esp. 1-60]).

achrony of tradition and the synchronic structures of live performance. Neither kind of context excludes the other, but the characteristic balance between them differs from that with which we as readers and writers are most familiar. Returning, then, to the subject of inconsistencies: to the traditional audience, participating in the diachronic depth to which the textualized formula is merely the barest of indicators, these small slips belong to the ephemera of performance, left behind in the flow of song almost as soon as they are enunciated. Small importance attaches to them. The real continuity transpires at a level beneath that surface that "text" has made opaque to those who are readers only.

Yet when the notion of "text" has begun to assume a major place in the process of literary transmission, these incongruities between the "formula"—of whatever type—and local narrative context pose a more serious problem. The greater leisure of authorial and readerly rumination makes textual inconsistencies—mere ephemera in the oral-performative setting—subject to repeated scrutiny. Over the course of time, as the experience of the page of text comes more and more into the foreground of the author–audience interaction, artistic attitudes towards formularity cannot help but change. It is at this stage in the movement from orality to literacy that Chaucer makes his contribution. Chaucer was by no means uniformly hostile to formularity. Yet formulary tendencies and materials have emerged in his work into a heightened artistic self-consciousness and are susceptible to irony in a way that they were not in the vernacular literature of English.[24]

This interaction between older and newer modes of aesthetic sensibility underlies much of the lexical and formulaic farce in *Sir Thopas*. Early on in the tale, for example, we learn that Thopas, that jewel of a knight, pricking his way past "stile and stoon" in search of an elf-queen whom he has suddenly decided that he loves, at last finds

[24]My present discussion is much indebted to Brewer's explorations of these and related issues in "Archaic and the Modern" and "Orality and Literacy." I would like to underscore, however, that while a historical transformation, involving orality and literacy, in poetic modes provides part of the basis for Chaucer's humor, I do not believe that it was his conscious intention to critique the oral-derived style of Middle English romance in a serious way. To the contrary, I agree with Hill that "*Sir Thopas* offers an instance of sheer play, sheer literary humor" (111). For a fuller explication of the mode of cognition involved, see Hill (16-27). Part of Chaucer's distinct individual genius lies in the simplicity of his comic delight, operating amid complex historical realities.

The contree of Fairye
So wilde;
For in that contree was ther noon
That to him durste ride or goon,
Neither wyf nor childe . . . .
(803-06)

Now in this narrative tradition it hardly stands to Thopas' credit as a hero and adventurer that women and children fear to encounter him in what rather sounds like a martial setting.[25] The joke centers on the tail-rhyme: our unhappy narrator seems to have been stuck for a word rhyming with "wilde." In fact, semantically vacuous tags of this variety are characteristic of this genre, and the three-foot lines in the tail-rhyme stanza are their most common site.[26] But Chaucer, in his capacity as pilgrim teller of this tale, has used his "wif nor childe" tag in a way that not only fails to contribute to his story but actively jars with the immediate narrative context. Thus the poetic incompetence of the storyteller brings into view what is actually a clash of attitudes towards formulaic usage. For while an infelicitous tag of this sort would contribute to the incoherence of an oral performance, its absurdities come fully into view only when it has been textualized. In this way Chaucer's irony is that of a literate author reflecting on an oral stylistic habit.

[25]This line has been suspected since it appears in only eight manuscripts; yet *The Riverside Chaucer* follows Robinson and other editors in retaining it (see note on 920). Chaucer's syntax does not specify whether "riding or going to" Sir Thopas would constitute an act of hostility. Yet certainly this possibility cannot be excluded: after all, unanticipated martial adventures are commonplace in such romances, and in the passage immediately following, Sir Thopas meets a challenge of precisely this variety in his encounter with Sir Olifaunt. Further, the collocation of the word "wilde," as well as the common designation of an act of riding through a forest by the word "priketh" (798) associates this stanza (797-806) with that in lines 754-59, in which "many a wilde best" (presumably the party responsible for Thopas' near-misfortunes [759]) turns out to refer to bucks and hares. Again, the text certainly allows for an anticlimactic reading.

[26]For an extended attempt to distinguish between "tags" (for him a pejorative term) and viable aesthetic repetition in tail-rhymes of tail-rhyme romances, see Dürmüller (esp. 71-118). Chaucer's misuse of the tail-rhyme stanzaic form has received much attention from various standpoints; see particularly Manly; Moore; Scheps ("Sir Thopas"); and Stanley. For a series of articles that deal with these and other issues in a major reassessment of the poem, see Gaylord.

To bring out the specificity of the particular stage of cultural development upon which Chaucer's humor is grounded, let us make a comparison with a well-known scene from Shakespeare. In the final act of *A Midsummer Night's Dream*, a group of semi-literate yokels put on a dramatic performance at the court of Duke Theseus. Here, as in *Sir Thopas*, the contrast involves class distinction, for while Chaucer the pilgrim is by no means the social inferior of his pilgrim colleagues, the satire that Chaucer the author directs at him and his tale grows out of an awareness of the rustic provincialism of the metrical romance genre and the style it cultivated. In fact, Shakespeare achieves much of his comic effect by assigning to Pyramus and Thisby speeches of rhyming melodrama whose infelicitously chosen clichés undermine the tragedy, and to this degree Shakespeare's practice is akin to Chaucer's. Yet Peter Quince's prologue to the play (V.i. 108-17) raises a different issue.[27] For here the humor derives from Quince's failure to render textual *punctuation* correctly in his rote-memorized delivery: by ignoring periods ("points") where they ought to be and putting them in where they ought not, Quince unwittingly converts praise of his aristocratic audience into insult. Shakespeare's satire at this juncture presupposes a higher degree of literacy since Quince has, after all, succeeded in rendering the *words* of his text accurately; but this level of literacy is not enough, in the eyes of an Elizabethan poet. In short, while for both Chaucer and Shakespeare contrasting degrees in the assimilation of literacy provide the key to their humor, Chaucer's satire attests to a greater proximity to oral tradition, while Shakespeare's registers the impact of the spread of literacy skills—even among the lower classes—in the wake of the print revolution.

The satiric principle that we have been identifying, that is, Chaucer's deployment of a formulaic phrase in an infelicitous context, manifests at the level of narrative also: thus, by using stock narrative themes without regard to what these themes might entail in terms of their larger narrative contexts, Chaucer as the pilgrim narrator of *Sir Thopas* creates a sense of narrative aimlessness. In fact, in this particular tale stock material is especially abundant, as Laura Hibbard Loomis illustrates in her chapter in *Sources and Analogues* .[28] My purpose here

[27]I cite Brooks's edition of *A Midsummer Night's Dream.*

[28]Loomis organizes her analogue material under such headings as "minstrel's comments," "the hero in arms," "the hero in combat," "the hero's vow," and so forth.

is not simply to adduce new examples, but rather to illustrate how two stock themes, the arming of the hero and the flyting or verbal contesting between Thopas and the giant Olifaunt, set up expectations that the ensuing narrative emphatically does not satisfy. And by designing his story this way, Chaucer exploits comic possibilities deriving from a literate man's perception of the formulaic narrative style. For the oral poet can rely on the narrative formula to supply its own character motivation, and this in turn is apt to project sequent action. Through this coincidence of the external and the internal—of the pattern of action and the structure of motivation—within the narrative formula, the oral poet can engage (metonymically, as Foley would say) a range of traditional cultural reference that such poets and their audiences are accustomed to bringing to bear on their oral literary productions. Since the greater significance of the narrative formula inheres in the poetic tradition, much can be assumed. To the oral poet and his auditors, the greater part of the performance is going on silently, in what the "libretto" of the poem summons to their common recollection. But to their readerly counterparts, with the very basis of this oral rhetoric receding behind a horizon of texts, the bare text of the oral performances, stripped of its extratextual resonances, is liable to seem disconnected and full of holes.

It is precisely this effect that Chaucer exploits through the narrative disorganization of *Sir Thopas*. The scenes in question, the arming of the hero and his flyting with a knightly adversary, contribute vitally in epic and romance to those formularized sequences by which heroic identity is publicly established and glory is won. In a fine article on the hero's arming, Brewer ("Arming of the Warrior") has traced the history of this stock theme in its multiforms through early Western literature, detailing its formulaic characteristics and reviewing its reappearance in *Sir Thopas* at lines 857-87. Brewer's discussion leaves the impression that Sir Thopas' arming, considered *in itself*, comprises satire of a fairly mild sort ("Arming of the Warrior" 237-38).[29] Yet my orientation here is towards the external narrative contexting of the arming theme, and from this standpoint we might observe that these scenes logically must take place *before* martial combat. Nor is this observation as trivial as it may seem, for in arming himself the hero is, so to speak, donning his heroic identity. Undoubtedly it was this symbology that gave the theme

[29]See Linn for an important earlier study of the arming theme. See also Lord's treatment of the theme in Serbo-Croatian and ancient Greek poetry in *Singer* (86-92).

the interest that it obviously had for many early and militaristically-minded cultures. Yet such preparation calls for a martial test in which the hero's excellence is demonstrated through public action. The same observation holds for heroic flyting, as I have argued at length elsewhere,[30] for such flytings are essentially contractual: even as they pit rival claims for heroic superiority, the contestants are implicitly or explicitly contracting for some kind of a trial of arms that will determine which of them should be judged the winner.[31] In the machismo ethic governing such exchanges, these flyting "contracts" can be left unfulfilled only with great loss of face. Thus both the arming and flyting themes generate the expectation of heroic combat. Traditional heroic narrative seldom inquires into the subjective states of its heroes at these moments: the establishment of heroic identity is the point in question, and the hero's motivation—his desire to prove himself—is implicit in the narrative formula. This does not mean, of course, that such martial sequences need be artistically superficial. A skilled oral artist would use these typical scenes with a sensitivity to their deeper traditional resonances, and in this way he would articulate existential paradigms of significance to oral heroic cultures. Translating these traditional associations into the syntagmatics of story, then, one would expect the arming to precede flyting, which would culminate, in turn, in combat. Reorderings are possible, of course, yet in the process these expectations would need to be responded to in some way.

Now what has become of this rather rudimentary narrative sequence in Chaucer's tale? After an opening six stanzas that describe the knight from various standpoints, the action of the poem begins with Sir Thopas equipped with lance and sword, riding forth through a dangerous forest. After a somewhat absurd interlude in which Thopas concludes from a dream of the night before that he must be in love with an elf-queen (784-96), the bold adventurer presses on until he encounters Sir Olifaunt, a three-headed giant and a "perilous man of dede" (809). The flyting follows a fairly standard pattern. In the manner of other

[30]In *Verbal Dueling*, I concentrate on Homer and Old English heroic narrative poetry but explore several other traditions as well. These "heroic" flytings, with their serious martial entailments, must be distinguished from the ludic flytings of Scottish poets such as William Dunbar and Alexander Montgomerie. On the generic criteria involved in this distinction, see *Verbal Dueling* (161-78). For a study of Scottish flyting, see Bawcutt.

[31]On the oral contract in flyting, see Parks (*Verbal Dueling* 42-48). For a contrary view, see Clover.

heroes who deem themselves in a position of superiority, Olifaunt tries to intimidate his opponent, offering him two contractual alternatives: to shrink away from the contest, or to fight (and here, ridiculously, Olifaunt threatens to kill Thopas' horse!).[32] At the same time, with an apparent prescience of Thopas' desires, the giant holds forth the tempting bait of the elf-queen who, he says, is in his possession. Thopas selects the second of these options—the fight—which he defers to the next day, when he will return in armor, and boasts that he will kill his enemy with a lance-blow through the mouth. Thopas makes his getaway—"thurgh Goddes gras" (831)—while the giant throws stones.

Though repeatedly verging on the incongruous, from the structural standpoint nothing in the flyting episode so far has gone too drastically amiss. A knight has, after all, the right to fight in armor. Indeed, Chaucer has given us a direct analogue on this point: in the *Knight's Tale*, when Arcite encountered Palamon unarmed and newly escaped from prison, he arranged to provide his adversary with weapons for a duel on the following day (I. [A] 1596-1654).[33] Yet clearly much hinges on Thopas'—or the poet's—success in seeing his way through to the fight. Will Sir Thopas manage to redeem his honor through heroic combat? With this question resonating in the background, the narrative resumes: Thopas returns home, announces his plans, and calls for his minstrels and his wine in what strikes this reader as a somewhat premature celebration.[34] Here follows the principal arming scene that occupies five stanzas, despite the fact that it must be approaching evening by this time. At this stage, the catalogue of poetic miscues and incongruities has swollen to where one cannot help but wonder if the poet is indeed keeping a handle on his story. And yet Thopas does, in the course of arming, swear to conclude his adventure successfully, "Bityde what bityde!" (874). If a combat episode were to follow in due order, the pilgrim Geoffrey would have salvaged his story in a rough structural sense, though one could hardly call it a virtuoso performance.

Yet now the breakdown becomes more serious. For with the arming type-scene the fit ends; and the next section opens with a rather

[32]On the intimidation pattern in heroic flyting, see Parks (*Verbal Dueling* 58, 100-01, and 138-39).
[33]Bloomfield discusses medieval regulation of the equivalency of armor and weaponry in the *judiceum Dei*, with particular reference to *Beowulf* and *The Battle of Maldon*.
[34]See, however, Robinson's note on lines 847 ff. in his edition of *The Works of Geoffrey Chaucer*.

desperate invocation ("Now holde youre mouth, *par charitee*" [891]), declaration of subject matter, and catalogue of knightly prototypes. It sounds, in effect, as if Chaucer were beginning the story over. We now learn that Thopas is setting out in the manner of a "knyght auntrous" (909) and travels "Til on a day—" (918): and here Chaucer's unhappy narrative venture is cut short by a host who, while objecting explicitly to the "drasty rymyng" (930), may have been infected by this same sense that the tale, at its present rate of progress, will never end.[35] What has become of Sir Olifaunt, the fairy queen, and the tale's major unconcluded adventure? Surely it would not require an indefinite term of travel for Thopas to locate that giant again whom he blundered upon with no effort on his first outing. Rationalizations on this point, like so many others in the tale, could easily have been devised: Thopas has lost his way, has become enmeshed in enchantment, cannot find the giant at his former station, is following a sportingly circuitous route, and so forth. Yet in the absence of any such, one begins seriously to wonder whether either knight or narrator remembers what the objective of the quest was supposed to have been. We start to get the impression, in fact, that the unfortunate bungler is wandering about through the chivalric landscape with no sense of purpose and no memory of what has happened the day before.

My point is that this sense of aimlessness has resulted from the storyteller's inability to order his stock materials in a coherent manner. Surely the hero's arming and flyting boasts ought to culminate in a martial display, and the songs and feasting ought to celebrate this accomplishment. Or if the narrator wishes to depart from this rather elementary scheme, his manner in doing so ought to convince us that he is following a narrative logic of some kind. But the pilgrim narrator of *Sir Thopas* seems to have relied on narrative formulas without exhibiting any concomitant sense of how to organize these into a story. Of course, no oral poet of any talent could blunder so egregiously. Yet the textualization of an originally oral form of poetic narrative has ruptured that consensus that would supply a traditional coherency overriding temporary narrative breakdowns. Now the failure of a particular storyteller begins to look like the failure of a poetic idiom. For the oral-derived formulaic style does not, to the textualized mind-set, provide an ade-

[35]Though *Sir Thopas* is not a long tale, its haphazard movement makes it seem so. In fact, the other tale which the Host sees fit to interrupt, the *Monk's Tale*, suffers similarly from the lack of a strong plot line.

quate account of human behavior and human motivation. To Chaucer and a growing class of literate brethren, formulaic repetition had become cliché.

IV

To conclude this discussion, I would like to return to a topic that was tentatively broached in the first section above: the manner in which narrators oral, literate, and Chaucerian use their traditions for the authentication of narrative discourse. This is a vast problem, of course, and can be treated here from only the most particularized of standpoints. My argument is that differences in the basic materials, the "stuff" of oral and textualized traditions, engender different characteristic modes of authorial disposition towards traditional inheritance. Chaucer's self-representations in this respect illumine and are illumined by the large-scale, continuing cultural transition in which the fourteenth century was engaged.

I will confine my observations here to the well-known and much-debated passage in the *General Prologue* in which the Chaucerian narrator rationalizes the literary representation that is to follow:

> But first I pray yow, of youre curteisye,
> That ye n'arette it nat my vileynye,
> Thogh that I pleynly speke in this mateere,
> To telle yow hir wordes and hir cheere,
> Ne thogh I speke hir wordes proprely.
> For this ye knowen al so wel as I:
> Whoso shal telle a tale after a man,
> He moot reherce as ny as evere he kan
> Everich a word, if it be in his charge,
> Al speke he never so rudeliche and large,
> Or ellis he moot telle his tale untrewe,
> Or feyne thyng, or fynde wordes newe.
> (725-36)

Ostensibly Chaucer is here providing an advance apology for offensive story material, particularly of the scurrilous sort; he reiterates similar sentiments in the *Miller's Prologue* lines 3171-86 and elsewhere. Yet an ironic reading of some kind is clearly demanded, since it is impossible to believe that the *Tales* are, literally, nothing more than a record of what Chaucer heard on the road to Canterbury. This passage, and the literary and cultural complexities that it engages, have long been central to the interpretation of the *Tales*,[36] and I do not intend to propose a global rereading. What I do wish to point out, rather, is that the tension between a more oral and a more textualized poetics comprises a significant background to this passage, and one that has, moreover, received little notice to date. In fact, Chaucer's self-characterization as a faithful scribe and reteller evinces close parallels with root narratorial self-concepts expressed in poetries growing immediately out of oral traditions. And this analogy becomes the more compelling when one recalls our observations in the first part of this essay, that it is indeed an oral tradition that Chaucer at this stage of the proceedings represents himself as recording.

Can generalizations be made concerning the self-conceptions of poetic narrators in oral or oral-derived literary traditions? Obviously vast differences divide separate traditions and authors. Yet a certain economy in the preservation of knowledge is common to all poets who operate in an oral context without the presupposition that writing will preserve their creations; and these conditions are liable to encode themselves into the narratorial function. Let us consider the case of Anglo-Saxon poetry, much of which, if not itself orally composed, probably arose in proximity to an oral tradition. Evidence for this can be found in the ubiquitous "epic" formulas "ic hyrde," "ic gefrægn," and variants, all of which mean, roughly, 'I heard.'[37] Most of these fall into what I have elsewhere called the re-presentational mode, when the narrator, having said "I heard," proceeds to recount what he heard ("Traditional Narrator and the 'I Heard' Formulas"). A famous example occurs in the proem to *Beowulf*:

Hwæt, wē Gārdena in gēardagum
þēodcyninga þrym gefrūnon,

[36]For several interesting treatments that emphasize the complexity of Chaucer's rhetorical strategies unfolding amid varying landscapes of medieval idealism, personification, multiple voicing, or intertextuality, see Reiss; Gellrich (*Idea of the Book*); and Nolan.

[37]I have treated these formulas and related matters in greater length in "Interperformativity and *Beowulf*"; "Traditional Narrator and the 'I heard' Formulas"; and "Traditional Narrator in *Beowulf* and Homer."

hū ðā æþelingas ellen fremedon!
(1-3)[38]

'Lo, we have heard of the might of the Spear-Danes, of those kings of people, in days of yore, how those noble ones did valorous deeds.'

The "I heard"—or in this instance "we heard"—expression seems to allude to one or perhaps several in a long chain of oral renderings, since the earliest feasible constructions would date the composition of *Beowulf* more than a century and a half after the incidents related therein. The narrator is thus implicitly characterizing himself as one who will tell again what has long been bruited about. We cannot infer, of course, that the *Beowulf*-narrator *in reality* does only this: the narratorial function is always and inevitably a complex one. Yet the *concept* of the narrator that this and other "I heard" expressions presuppose reflects the need of oral societies to tell and retell, for by this mechanism alone can lore, narrative and other, be sustained and transmitted.

Although Homer never uses phrases of this type, a similar idea of the narratorial function seems to underlie his invocations of the Muses.[39] Explicitly invoked once in the *Odyssey* and six times in the *Iliad,* the Muses figure not only as goddesses of the arts but as the daughters of Mnemosyne—memory.[40] This symbol is indeed apt, since it is precisely out of memory that the oral poet spins his tales. And what would be more likely to comprise the contents of memory in such matters than that which has been heard before? No doubt Homer or whoever composed these works believed in the actuality of these goddesses. Yet this characterization of the act of poesis would seem compelling to an oral poet precisely because the process of hearing, recording in the memory, and recalling for performance was the foundation of his craft.

[38]I cite Klaeber's edition of *Beowulf.* The translation is mine.

[39]For several important treatments, see Notopoulos; Minton; Havelock (97-113); and Block. I develop the comparison between the Greek and Old English concepts of narratorial self-authentication through reference to tradition in "Traditional Narrator in *Beowulf.*"

[40]See, for example, *Theogony* 915-17 or the *Homeric Hymn to Hermes* 429-30. Though Homer does not supply this bit of genealogical information, the mnemonic value of the Muses is several times suggested in the invocations, notably in *Iliad* 2.484-93.

For a third example—and one with particular bearing on the cited passage from the *General Prologue*—I would like to consider an interview between Nikola Vujnovic, Parry's interpreter and assistant, and Đemail Zogic, a Yugoslav guslar and oral poet, on the subject of a song of some 1400 lines which he had performed the night before. Đemail claimed to have learned the song by hearing a single rendering by another guslar, Suljo Makic, and further, to have performed the "same song, word for word and line for line. I didn't add a single line, and I didn't make a single mistake." Asked whether a singer, performing a song after a long interlude, would provide an identical rendering, Đemail replied, "If I were to live for twenty years, I would sing the song which I sang for you today just the same twenty years from now, word for word" (*Serbo-Croatian Heroic Songs* 241).[41] And yet, as the editor points out, comparisons of Đemail's three versions, performed at intervals of (first) four months and (later) seventeen years, together with a rendering by Đemail's source Suljo, do not even remotely bear out this claim of verbatim reproduction.[42] To accuse Đemail of prevarication would altogether miss the point. Never having created through the medium of texts, the notion of "word for word" repetition simply would not carry the same meaning for the oral poet skilled in longer narrative forms as it would for his literate counterpart. Indeed, who would even raise such a question except the learned scholar to whom the "text" is supreme? And yet, the idea of *fidelity to tradition* carries the highest prestige, because it is through adhering to this value that oral traditions stay alive. Thus it is no accident that the concept of oral poet as re-teller and re-creator has insinuated itself into these three geographically and chronologically unrelated narrative traditions. For the notion grows out of the very structure of oral transmission itself.

With these analogues in mind, let us return again to Chaucer's fiction concerning the source of the *Canterbury Tales*. On a pilgrimage to Canterbury he heard many stories, presumably wrote them down later (though he represses information on this matter), and now wishes to deliver them again, following his oral exemplars as closely as possible, indeed, reproducing "Everiche a word" (733). The source and mode of delivery that the passage indicates (through such phrases as "I speke," "I pray yow," etc.) are oral; he deviates from the model of oral

[41]For more on this issue, see Foley (*Traditional Oral Epic* 42-50).

[42]See the text to No. 24 in this volume (246-62) and the notes to Nos. 24, 25 (407-16) and 29 (424-28).

transmission only in the translation of a mnemonic "text" into a written form. I do not mean, of course, that the historical Chaucer was *consciously* mimicking the oral traditional process. Even in the fiction he depicts himself as a transcriber, not an oral poet. Yet the authenticating concept of poetic creation that Chaucer was summoning up, whether or not he perceived its source, had roots in oral aesthetics.[43] To a culture emerging from an oral past, the idea of poet as re-teller still carried force. This much at least Chaucer must have presupposed: for he would never have conceived a major work in this way had he not believed that an account of a tale-telling session of this sort would appeal to his prospective audience. And servicing this interest was a task worthy enough—so Chaucer would have us believe—for a poet of his own modest talents.

Again, this imputation of source and poetic method belongs to the fiction. Behind the fiction stands a poet who is doing far more than re-telling and knows it perfectly well. For literacy had stripped this reiterative function of its former value. Instead of an abstracted and deified Mnemosyne, or the recollection in its generic outlines of a thing heard, the literate poet was confronted with specific textual exemplars, concrete, verifiable, constant between perusals.[44] Of course, the retro-

[43]Jordan (120) has interpreted Chaucer's characterization of his poetic and scribal activity in the *General Prologue* in terms of a Chaucerian interplay between the poet and the reporter. The point that I am trying to make is that even Chaucer's act of reporting belongs to an interperformative chain of tellings and re-tellings, and that this interperformative structure derives from the context of oral culture.

[44]That is to say, a single manuscript would have these characteristics. Of course, different manuscript versions of a single work often varied enormously; yet as Baugh ("Improvisation in the Middle English Romance") has argued, this may often be due to the survival of oral-formulaic habits. Indeed, such discrepancies reflect precisely the failure of the literate mind fully to impose its authority. And as the literate mentality—aided by the new technology of print—gained an increasing hegemony over literary production in the following centuries, greater and greater uniformity between "copies" has become the rule. Oral cultures, on the other hand, live quite happily with such variations without recourse to the idea of textuality at all. Such considerations lead me to question Knight's assertion that "*The Canterbury Tales* never existed except in post-structuralist terms as a multiplicity of fragmented discourses with vestigial authorial ordering" (18). Of course, the problem that Knight is addressing involves more than just manuscript variation. At the same time, Knight's comment could apply equally well to many *transcribed* samplings from an oral tradition. Yet the post-structural critique of authority and presence presupposes a

spective orientation persisted; but what had once been oral tradition had metamorphized into scripture, text, *auctoritas*.[45] Towards such authority one owed one's veneration; yet a poet no longer had the option of simply "reproducing" it, as this activity would now be conceived by a literate creator of Chaucer's ilk. One had to amplify, comment, interpret; and such enterprises presuppose a degree of conscious differentiation of self from tradition which an oral poet, to whom tradition exists principally as memory-in-the-retelling, would not have had the same reason to interject. Yet by the later fourteenth century even this highly literate form of traditionalism was coming into question. In many phases of social and intellectual life, the inadequacies of old formulations were pressing themselves on the general cultural awareness with a greater urgency. These changes in outlook are clearly registered in the poetry of Chaucer, whose willingness to play with ideas of *auctoritas* (as in the *Wife of Bath's Prologue* or the *Nun's Priest's Tale*) is well known and has been the subject of much study.

My claim, then, is that habits of mind descending from an oral past fall within the compass of this play. Chaucer lived in an era of intense unacknowledged conflict between, on the one hand, a literate technology that had a long history in Western civilization, no doubt, but which had undergone an extraordinary development and expansion of scope in the past two to three centuries, and on the other hand, oral ways of life entrenched in many levels of culture and reluctant to cede their place. Of course, this clash dates back to Plato and before; but as Walter Ong has pointed out, "[i]n the European Middle Ages interactions between orality and literacy reached perhaps an all-time high" ("Medieval Textualization" 1). To leading literates of the time, the craft of the oral poet might have seemed rather crude and simple-minded, suited to the tastes of "lewed peple."[46] It would have been in character

---

highly advanced textuality. Discourse still largely immersed in the living, fluid world of live oral performance might *seem*, when stripped of these associations and rendered exclusively through the medium of writing, to be highly fragmentary; yet this appearance would be an effect of the fragmentary character of the evidence. As Foley (*Immanent Art*) has pointed out, the "text" of an oral performance is a kind of libretto. The text is not the poem: the performance is.

[45]The New Testament itself originated in oral discourse; thus scriptural authority is itself rooted in a prior orality. On the oral backgrounds of scriptural tradition, see Culley.

[46]Cf. the *Pardoner's Prologue* 437-38: "For lewed peple loven tales olde; / Swiche thynges kan they wel reporte and holde." As we have seen, oral po-

for Chaucer to call upon such practices as a means of denigrating himself: "My wit is short, ye may wel understonde" (*General Prologue* 746). That is not to say that he depicts himself as illiterate—not at all. Yet the concept of poetic re-presentation that he invokes, the way in which he characterizes his own creative act, is far from flattering, from the standpoint of a learned poet who numbered Dante among his teachers. Thus, wittingly or unwittingly, the orality-literacy dynamic with all its cultural resonances insinuates itself into the basic conceit on which the *Canterbury Tales* is founded.

Perhaps more than any of his predecessors or contemporaries, Chaucer epitomizes a crucial turn in the history of literacy in the English language, when the literate mind was able to cast back upon its own oral past and summon images of that past into the structure of its own comic movement. Full training in the literate traditions of the day was a prerequisite for such an accomplishment. Yet it also demanded a sympathetic attunement, an ear sensitized to the undertones of change, for the implications of the literacy revolution were not consciously understood in Chaucer's own era. On both accounts Chaucer himself was superbly equipped, and has provided us with a far more revealing record on the matter than have other illustrious poets of the Middle Ages. It is only now that we, as heirs to changes that he helped to bring about, can begin to articulate this dimension of Chaucer's artistry.

Department of English
Louisiana State University

---

ets—and presumably their audiences—like to believe in the antiquity of their material.

Works Cited

Baugh, Albert C. "Improvisation in the Middle English Romance." *Proceedings of the American Philosophical Society* 103 (1959): 418-54.

—. "The Middle English Romance: Some Questions of Creation, Presentation, and Preservation." *Speculum* 42 (1967): 1-31.

Baum, Paul F. *Chaucer: A Critical Appreciation.* Durham, NC: Duke UP, 1958.

Bawcutt, Priscilla. "The Art of Flyting." *Scottish Literary Journal* 10 (1983): 5-24 .

Benson, Larry D. *Art and Tradition in* Sir Gawain and the Green Knight. New Brunswick: Rutgers UP, 1965.

—, ed. *The Riverside Chaucer.* 3rd ed. Boston: Houghton, 1987.

Block, Elizabeth. "The Narrator Speaks: Apostrophe in Homer and Vergil." *Transactions and Proceedings of the American Philological Association* 112 (1982): 7-22.

Bloomfield, Morton. "Beowulf, Byrhtnoth, and the Judgment of God: Trial by Combat in Anglo-Saxon England." *Speculum* 44 (1969): 545-59.

Bowden, Betsy. *Chaucer Aloud: The Varieties of Textual Interpretation.* Philadelphia: U of Pennsylvania P, 1987.

Brewer, Derek. "The Arming of the Warrior in European Literature and Chaucer." *Chaucerian Problems and Perspectives: Essays Presented to Paul E. Beichner C. S. C.* Ed. Edward Vasta and Zacharias P. Thundy. Notre Dame: U of Notre Dame P, 1979. 221-43.

—. "The Archaic and the Modern." *Tradition and Innovation in Chaucer.* London: Macmillan, 1982. 1-21.

—. "Orality and Literacy in Chaucer." *Mündlichkeit und Schriftlichkeit im englischen Mittelalter.* Ed. W. Erzgräber and Sabine Volk. Tübingen: Narr, 1988. 85-119.

Bronson, Charles H. "Chaucer's Art in Relation to his Audience." *Five Studies in Literature. University of California Publications in English* 8 (1940): 1-53.

—. *In Search of Chaucer*. Toronto: U of Toronto P, 1960.

Brooks, Harold F., ed. *A Midsummer Night's Dream*. London: Methuen, 1979.

Bryan, William Frank and Germaine Dempster, eds. *Sources and Analogues of Chaucer's* Canterbury Tales *by Carleton Brown, Germaine Dempster, C.H. Gerould, et alia*. Chicago: U of Chicago P, 1941. New York: Humanities Press, 1958.

Clanchy, M. T. *From Memory to Written Record: England, 1066-1307*. Cambridge, MA: Harvard UP, 1979.

Clover, Carol. "The Germanic Context of the Unferth Episode." *Speculum* 55 (1980): 444-68.

Crisp, Delmas Swinfield. "Internal Evidence of Formulaic Diction in *The Canterbury Tales*." DAI 40 (1979): 5450A.

Crosby Ruth. "Oral Delivery in the Middle Ages." *Speculum* 11 (1936): 88-110 .

—. "Chaucer and the Custom of Oral Delivery." *Speculum* 13 (1938): 412-32.

Culley, Robert C. "Oral Tradition and Biblical Studies." *Oral Tradition* 1 (1986): 30-65.

Dürmüller, Urs. *Narrative Possibilities of the Tail-Rhyme Romance*. Bern: Francke, 1975.

Edwards, Mark W. "Homer and the Oral Tradition: The Formula, Part 1." *Oral Tradition* 1 (1986): 171-230.

—. "Homer and the Oral Tradition: The Formula, Part 2." *Oral Tradition* 3 (1988): 11-60.

Foley, John Miles. *Oral-Formulaic Theory and Research: An Introduction and Annotated Bibliography*. New York: Garland, 1985.

—. *The Theory of Oral Composition: History and Methodology*. Bloomington: Indiana UP, 1988.

—. *Traditional Oral Epic: The* Odyssey, Beowulf, *and the Serbo-Croatian Return Song*. Berkeley: U of California P, 1990.

—. *Immanent Art: From Structure to Meaning in Traditional Oral Epic*. Bloomington: Indiana UP, 1991.

Gaylord, Alan T. "Chaucer's Dainty 'Dogerel': The 'Elvyssh' Prosody of *Sir Thopas*." *Studies in the Age of Chaucer* 1 (1979): 84-104.

—. "The Moment of *Sir Thopas*: Towards a New Look at Chaucer's Language." *Chaucer Review* 16 (1982): 311-29.

—. "The 'Miracle' of *Sir Thopas*." *Studies in the Age of Chaucer* 6 (1984): 65-84.

Gellrich, Jesse M. *The Idea of the Book in the Middle Ages: Language Theory, Mythology, and Fiction*. Ithaca: Cornell UP, 1985.

—. "Orality, Literacy, and Crisis in the Later Middle Ages." *Philological Quarterly* 67 (1989): 461-473.

Hansen, William F. *The Conference Sequence: Patterned Narration and Narrative Inconsistency in the* Odyssey. University of California Classical Series. Berkeley: U of California P, 1972.

Hathaway, Charles M. "Chaucer's Verse-Tags as a Part of his Narrative Machinery." *Journal of English and Germanic Philology* 5 (1903-05): 476-84.

Havelock, Eric A. *Preface to Plato*. Cambridge, MA: Harvard UP, 1963.

Hill, John M. *Chaucerian Belief: The Poetics of Reverence and Belief*. New Haven: Yale UP, 1991.

Jordan, Robert M. *Chaucer and the Shape of Creation: The Aesthetic Possibilities of Inorganic Structure*. Cambridge, MA: Harvard UP, 1967.

Klaeber, Friederich, ed. Beowulf *and the* Fight at Finnsburg. 3rd ed. Lexington: Heath, 1950.

Knapp, Peggy. *Chaucer and the Social Contest*. New York: Routledge, 1990.

Knight, Stephen. "Chaucer and the Sociology of Literature." *Studies in the Age of Chaucer* 2 (1980): 15-51.

Krishna, Valerie. "Parataxis, Formulaic Density, and Thrift in the Alliterative *Morte Arthure*." *Speculum* 57 (1982): 63-83.

Lindahl, Carl. "Chaucer the Storyteller: Folkloric Patterns in the *Canterbury Tales*." Diss. Indiana University, 1980.

—. *Earnest Games: Folkloric Patterns in the* Canterbury Tales. Bloomington: Indiana UP, 1987.

Linn, Irving. "The Arming of Sir Thopas." *Modern Language Notes* 51 (1936): 300-11.

Loomis, Laura Hibbard. "Sir Thopas." *Sources and Analogues of Chaucer's* Canterbury Tales. Ed. W. F. Bryan and Germaine Dempster. Chicago: U of Chicago P, 1941. Atlantic Highlands, NJ: Humanities P, 1958. 486-559.

Lord, Albert B. "Homer and Huso II: Narrative Inconsistencies in Homer and Oral Poetry." *Transactions and Proceedings of the American Philological Association* 69 (1938): 439-45.

—. "Composition by Theme in Homer and Southslavic Epos." *Transactions and Proceedings of the American Philological Association* 82 (1951): 71-80.

—. *The Singer of Tales*. Cambridge, MA: Harvard UP, 1960.

Manly, John M. "The Stanza-Forms of *Sir Thopas*." *Modern Philology* 8 (1910): 141-44.

Mehl, Dieter. "The Audience of Chaucer's *Troilus and Criseyde*." *Chaucer and Middle English Studies in Honour of Rossell Hope Robbins*. Ed Beryl Rowland. London: Allen, 1974. 173-89.

—. "Chaucer's Audience." *Leeds Studies in English and Kindred Languages* 10 (1978): 58-74.

Minton, William W. "Homer's Invocations of the Muses: Traditional Patterns." *Transactions and Proceedings of the American Philological Association* 91 (1960): 292-309.

—. "Invocation and Catalogue in Hesiod and Homer." *Transactions and Proceedings of the American Philological Association* 93 (1962): 188-212.

Monro, David B. and Thomas W. Allen, eds. *Homeri Opera*. 3rd. ed. Vols. 1-2. Oxford: Clarendon, 1917-20. 5 vols.

Moore, Arthur K. "*Sir Thopas* as a Criticism of Fourteenth Century Minstrelsy." *Journal of English and Germanic Philology* 53 (1954): 532-45.

Moorman, Charles. "The Origins of the Alliterative Revival." *Southern Quarterly* 7 (1969): 345-71.

Nolan, Barbara. "'A Poet Ther Was': Chaucer's Voices in the General Prologue to *The Canterbury Tales*." *PMLA* 101 (1986): 154-69.

Notopoulos, James A. "Mnemosyne in Oral Literature." *Transactions and Proceedings of the American Philological Association* 69 (1938): 465-93.

Oakden, J. P. *Alliterative Poetry in Middle English.* 2 vols. Manchester UP, 1930 and 1935. New York: Archon, 1968.

Ong, Walter J. *Orality and Literacy: The Technologizing of the Word.* London: Methuen, 1982.

—. "Orality, Literacy, and Medieval Textualization." *New Literary History* 16 (1984): 1-13.

Parks, Ward. "The Oral-Formulaic Theory in Middle English Studies." *Oral Tradition* 1 (1986): 636-94.

—. "The Traditional Narrator and the 'I Heard' Formulas in Old English Poetry." *Anglo-Saxon England* 16 (1987): 45-66.

—. "Interperformativity and *Beowulf.*" *Narodna umjetnost* 26 (1989): 25-35.

—. *Verbal Dueling in Heroic Narrative: The Homeric and Old English Traditions.* Princeton: Princeton UP, 1990.

—. "The Textualization of Orality in Literary Criticism." *Vox intexta: Orality and Textuality in the Middle Ages.* Ed. A.N. Doane and Carol Braun Pasternack. Madison: U of Wisconsin P, 1991. 46-61.

—. "The Traditional Narrator in *Beowulf* and Homer." *De Gustibus: Essays for Alain Renoir.* Ed. John Miles Foley. New York: Garland, 1992. 456-79.

—. "Song, Text, and Cassette: Why We Need Authoritative Audio Editions of Medieval Literary Works." *Oral Tradition* 7 (1992): 102-15.

Parry, Milman. *The Making of Homeric Verse: The Collected Papers of Milman Parry.* Ed. Adam Parry. Oxford: Oxford UP, 1971.

Payne, Robert. "The Historical Criticism We Need." *Chaucer at Albany.* Ed. Rossell Hope Robbins. New York: Franklin, 1975. 179-92.

Pearsall, Derek. *The* Canterbury Tales. London: Allen, 1985.

Reiss, Edmund. "Chaucer and his Audience." *Chaucer Review* 14 (1980): 390-402.

Robinson, F.N., ed. *The Works of Geoffrey Chaucer.* 2nd ed. Boston: Houghton, 1957.

Rosenberg, Bruce A. "The Oral Performance of Chaucer's Poetry: Situation and Medium." *Folklore Forum* 13 (1980): 224-37.

Rowland, Beryl. "Chaucer's Speaking Voice and its Effect on his Listener's Perception of Criseyde." *English Studies in Canada* 7 (1981): 129-40.

—. "*Pronuntiatio* and its Effect on Chaucer's Audience." *Studies in the Age of Chaucer* 4 (1982): 33-51.

Scheps, Walter. "'Sir Thopas': The Bourgeois Knight, the Minstrel, and the Critics." *Tennessee Studies in Literature* 11 (1966): 35-43.

—. "'Up Roos Oure Hoost, and Was Oure Aller Cok': Harry Bailly's Tale-Telling Competition." *Chaucer Review* 10 (1975): 113-28.

Scully, Stephen. "The Language of Achilles: The ΟΧΘΗΣΑΣ Formulas." *Transactions of the American Philological Association* 114 (1984): 11-27.

Serbo-Croatian Heroic Songs. Vol. 1, *Novi Pazar: English Translations*. Collected by Milman Parry. Ed. and trans. Albert B. Lord. Cambridge and Belgrade: Harvard UP and the Belgrade Academy of Sciences, 1954.

Stanley, E.G. "The Use of Bob-Lines in *Sir Thopas*." *Neuphilologische Mitteilungen* 73 (1972): 417-26.

Stock, Brian. *The Implications of Literacy: Written Language and Models of Interpretation in the Eleventh and Twelfth Centuries*. Princeton: Princeton UP, 1983.

Tatlock, J.S.P. "Epic Formulas, Especially in Laȝamon." *PMLA* 38 (1923): 494-529.

Turville-Petre, Thorlac. *The Alliterative Revival*. Cambridge: Brewer, 1977.

Wilson, George P. "Chaucer and Oral Reading." *South Atlantic Quarterly* 25 (1926): 283-99.

Wittig, Susan. "Formulaic Style in the Middle English Romance." *Neuphilologische Mitteilungen* 78 (1977): 250-55.

—. *Stylistic and Narrative Structures in the Middle English Romances*. Austin: U of Texas P, 1978.

Zumthor, Paul. *Oral Poetry: An Introduction*. Trans. Kathryn Murphy-Judy. Minneapolis: U of Minnesota P, 1990.

"Now holde youre mouth": The Romance of Orality in the *Thopas–Melibee* Section of the *Canterbury Tales*

Seth Lerer

Almost from its first appearance in the manuscripts, the *Thopas–Melibee* section of the *Canterbury Tales* elicited confusion. Is this a transparent example of Chaucerian irony, a joke performance where the author tells tales guaranteed to lose the contest posed by Harry Bailly? Is this simple parody, presenting extreme versions of both popular tail-rhyme romance and learned moral prose for purposes of literary and social criticism? Is the *Thopas* to be read for a laugh, while the *Melibee* is to be seen as instruction?[1] Early scribes, much like their modern critical counterparts, had problems with the apposition. In the Northumberland Manuscript of the *Canterbury Tales,* the two tales told by one pilgrim must have hearkened back to the original "foreward" of the *General Prologue,* where each pilgrim was to tell stories both going to and returning from Canterbury. In structuring the *Tales* to fit this paradigm, the scribe-compiler of Northumberland placed Chaucer's *Thopas* first, as one of the tales told from London to the shrine, and then postponed the *Melibee* to the position of the tales told travelling back to the

[1]For the variety of critical approaches summarized here, see the studies of Burrow; Benson; Gaylord; Olson; and Patterson ("'What Man Artow'?").

Tabard.[2] For the scribe of the Helmingham Manuscript, by contrast, the *Thopas–Melibee* section posed a dilemma not of structure but of pace. Paring down the prose allegory by about a third of its original length, and excising the long digression on literary theory from the *Thopas–Melibee Link*, this scribe constructed an abbreviated performance, one to be valued less for its critical in-joking or its moral sentence than its narrative progression.[3]

The *Thopas* seems to us a parody, the *Melibee* high seriousness. Yet, for many readers of the fifteenth and sixteenth centuries, it was the tail-rhyme romance that had compelling appeal. As an example of the popular *avanture* poetry, the *Thopas* held the imaginations of an audience reared on the adventures of Guy of Warwick, Bevis of Hamptoun, and many other appealing errants. It clearly resonated with the taste for adventure and fancy in the Tudor age, and like the equally fragmentary and now critically abused *Squire's Tale,* it had an impact on Spenser's formulations of the knightly idiom.[4] But *Melibee*, too, had an effect on later generations who confronted Chaucer's work.[5] With its complex inheritance of Continental moral allegories and its massive accumulation of useful *sententiae*, the *Tale of Melibee*, much like the *Clerk's Tale*, may appear to be a bridge between the European sources Chaucer used and the English tastes controlling his fifteenth-century reception. Like the *Clerk's Tale*, the *Melibee* was frequently excerpted from the *Canterbury Tales*, appearing in anthologies of Middle English verse and prose compiled in the late fifteenth and the early sixteenth century. And like the *Clerk's Tale*, too, these excerpts sometimes ap-

[2]The Northumberland Manuscript rearranges the *Tales* to place the *Thopas* and the *Thopas–Melibee Link* preceding the *Pardoner's Tale* and the *Canon's Yeoman's Prologue and Tale*. It then presents the spurious *Tale of Beryn* before returning to the *Melibee* to complete the tales of Fragment VII. For a description of the Manuscript, see Manly and Rickert (I: 387-95). For a convincing reading of this revision as evidence for a round trip pilgrimage, see Bowers.

[3]I have made this argument in chapter 3 of *Chaucer and His Readers*, developing observations originally made in "Rewriting Chaucer."

[4]For the impact of the *Thopas* on later sixteenth-century writing, see Burrow ("*Sir Thopas* in the Sixteenth Century"). For the popularity of romances in Tudor England, and their impact on educational polemic, see the studies of Brockman.

[5]A full account of the reception of the *Tale of Melibee* remains to be written. Some gestures have been made in this direction in accounts of manuscript transmission (Silvia), generic impact (Patterson, "'What Man Artow'?"), and social context (Lerer, *Chaucer and His Readers*).

pear without title and attribution, as if the *Tale of Melibee* had become a free-standing lesson for a preceptory public.

To these many medieval, Renaissance, and modern paradigms of understanding Chaucer's brace of tales, I would like to add one more. My purpose will be to approach this section of the *Canterbury Tales* as one which raises problems with the fictionality of both oral performance and textual self-definition. It is a commonplace of Chaucer criticism that the *Tales* present a written work whose "fiction" is that it is told. Donald R. Howard classified the phenomenon as the difference between "voiceness" and "bookness" (63-67), a difference turned to *différance* in H. Marshall Leicester, Jr.'s equation of voiceness with presence and bookness with absence (8-13). Leicester's plan is to preserve the voiced quality of Chaucer's *Tales* while at the same time preserving their status as texts. "In maintaining that the *Canterbury Tales* is a collection of individually voiced texts," he writes, "I want . . . to begin with the fact of their textuality, to insist that there is nobody there, that there is only the text" (9). But, he affirms, there may be texts that "actively engage the phenomenon of voice, exploit it, make it the center of their discourse—in fact, make it their content. This sort of text is *about* its speaker . . ." (10). For Leicester, this is a phenomenon not so much of Howard's idea of "unimpersonated artistry," but rather of what he calls "impersonated artistry because [the *Tales*] concentrate not on the way preexisting persons create language but on the way language creates people" (10).

Chaucer's *Tale of Sir Thopas* is the supreme moment in the *Canterbury Tales* that actively engages the phenomenon of voice. More than any other tale it is about its speaker, not just in that its performance augments our appreciation of the Chaucerian persona, but in that its performance is the subject of its telling. The occasion of *Sir Thopas* dramatizes the pitfalls of orality in literary presentation. Together with the following *Thopas–Melibee Link*, it represents the Chaucerian narrator as the real hero of the piece and illustrates what I will take to be the poet's critique of presence in literary making. By contrast, the *Melibee* is (perhaps second only to the *Parson's Tale*) a text that actively *dis*engages the phenomenon of voice. This sort of text is about other texts. Its announcement in the *Thopas–Melibee Link* places it within the ambience of scriptural inheritance and scholarly translation rather than in a dynamic of oral transmission or collegial communication. Its presentation illustrates the retreat of the narrator into the absence that controls the written. Its overarching fiction is that it in fact is no telling at all, but rather a piece of writing, a "treatise" as the poet calls it, meant not to be heard but read.

It is important to distinguish at the outset that I do not mean to appose the oral and the written in the *Thopas–Melibee* section as social phenomena.[6] I do not claim that the *Tale of Sir Thopas* was performed by Chaucer or his later audiences (though this habit could not be ruled out); nor do I claim that *Melibee* was apprehended exclusively as a document to be perused in silence or in solitude (though this, too, may have happened). Instead, my primary concern is with the ways in which each of these *Tales* thematizes their respective modes of transmission, and furthermore, with how the drama of reception constructs what I call a "romance" of orality. The telling is a kind of quest, the teller beset by the giants of mistaking critics and aberrant audiences. The telling also is a form of education, a growth from the childish fascinations with the mouth and ear to the adult appreciations of the eye and mind. Throughout, orality is associated with disturbing action, violent challenge, and unthinking personal response. It is associated, too, with childishness: with the temptations of romance or with the babble of baby-talk. By contrast, textuality is to be linked to sober understanding, rational discussion, and reflective civic duty. It signals an adult appreciation of the world and a generic interest in the forms of pedagogy shaped by literate understanding. The idea of the oral in this paper, therefore, should be

[6]Though I am indebted to a range of recent studies on the tensions between orality and literacy in medieval narrative, I eschew discussion of the historicity of such tensions in Chaucer's work or in the romances. For purposes of clarity, however, let me affirm here certain presuppositions: that the persona of the oral narrator does not necessitate the historical condition of oral composition or transmission; and, furthermore, that within literate contexts of reception, orality remains a narrative pose. Traditional arguments for the oral delivery of medieval literature were made by Crosby and affirmed by Baugh (though Baugh's claim is that the pose of the oral narrator in obviously literate or learned romances may be a remnant of the original, oral context for romance performance and a testimony to the ongoing transmission of works through recitation, regardless of their status as written works). For arguments that oral presentation is wholly a fiction of the writer, see Turville-Petre on the alliterative romances and, more generally, Bäuml on the construction of the persona in medieval narrative. The *Tale of Sir Thopas* has long been associated with the habits of minstrelsy (Burrow, *Ricardian Poetry* 12-46), and thus has been read as Chaucer's critique of what may have become by the late fourteenth century a declassé tradition, at least at court (Patterson, "'What Man Artow'?" 124-25).

seen as both a method and a metaphor—an idea with resonances both to late medieval literary practice and Augustinian educational allegory—and in closing, I will try to suggest ways of framing the concern with mouths and speech in the broad structures of Fragment VII of the *Canterbury Tales* as a whole.

I

Beyond the plot devices and suspensions of the hero's confrontations, the *Tale of Sir Thopas* is above all a poem about its teller's presence. From his initial appeal for the audience to listen to his final injunction to "holde youre mouth" (VII 891), the poem's narrator intrudes his speaking self into the story.[7] His bothersome announcements to "telle yow" in various forms (713, 728, 749, 758, 835, 897), together with his seemingly self-conscious set of tag lines, fillers, and clichés (e.g., the "it is no nay" of 766, the "*par ma fay*" of 820, and the "*par charitee*" of 891) make the narrator appear nearly as often as his hero. More than the dead time of the minstrel idiom, these phrases redirect the audience's attention away from Sir Thopas' struggle with giants and toward the narrator's struggle with his own line. His stanzas, by the end of the Second Fit, take on an almost mimetic feel, reproducing both the amblings of Thopas' horse and the circumnavigations of the story's plot.[8] Errancy is as much a narrative device as it is a performative strategy, most notably in the last stanza of the Second Fit:[9]

His spere was of fyn ciprees,
That bodeth were, and nothyng pees,
The heed ful sharpe ygrounde;
His steede was al dappull gray,
It gooth an ambil in the way
Ful softely and rounde
In londe.
Loo, lordes myne, heere is a fit!

[7]I cite Benson's edition of Chaucer's works throughout.
[8]This feature has been noticed and described at length in Gaylord ("Chaucer's Dainty 'Dogerel'" and "The 'Miracle' of *Sir Thopas*").
[9]See Patterson ("'What Man Artow'?" 126-27) who associates the phenomenon with Chaucer's governing interest in patterns of incompletion, circularity, and self-revision.

If ye wol any moore of it,
To telle it wol I fonde.
(881-90)

The wanderings of Thopas' horse mirror the amblings of these lines, its trips and circles imitated in the metrical break in the stanza's middle. Shifting his focus from the quest of his hero, the narrator makes the structure of his verse itself the subject of his lines—"heere is a fit!"—as if the mere completion of the second portion of his poem was a veritable conquest over insurmountable obstacles. The poem is the object of this narrator errant, an object of discovery or "finding," thematized within the mock performance of the poet: "If ye wol any moore of it, / To tell it wol I fonde." If you desire any more of the story, he says, he will try to tell it. But read both more literally and more theoretically, "fonde" here signals the discovery of both a topic of performance and the object of a quest. "Finding" throughout the English Middle Ages is the vernacular translation of *inventio*, the rhetorical discovery of topics as well as the narrative discovery of objects.[10]

Chaucer would have been familiar with the rhetorical traditions of *inventio*. A close reader of Geoffrey of Vinsauf, a citer of Cicero, an appropriator of a host of tropes and theoretical positions, he would have been sensitive to the various resonances of the Latin term and its English equivalent.[11] The famous passage at the close of Book I of *Troilus and Criseyde*, for example, rephrases Geoffrey of Vinsauf's

[10]This is not the place to review the history of *inventio* in medieval rhetorical theory or in English practice. Murphy's *History* provides the broad contours for research. It may suffice to say, however, that as early as the *Owl and the Nightingale*, the verb "finde" appears in specifically disputative contexts to refer to processes of topical discovery and *inventio*. See, for example, the characterization of the two birds' search for proper answers as processes of finding (470, 665), and the remarks on the poem's appropriation of rhetorical techniques in Murphy ("Rhetoric and Dialectic in the *Owl and the Nightingale*"). I had offered a critique of Murphy's reading, and a more detailed account of the relations between Middle English "finde" and *inventio*, in my unpublished Ph.D. dissertation (101-46). For Chaucer's and Gower's uses of *inventio*, see the stimulating discussion of Copeland (179-220), especially her observations on the *Prologue to the Legend of Good Women* (190).

[11]Ever since Manly ("Chaucer and the Rhetoricians"), scholars have debated Chaucer's knowledge of rhetorical theory and his deployment of rhetorical tropes. Reviews of scholarship, and personal positions, can be found in Howard (passim); Copeland (186-202); and Minnis (*Medieval Theory of Authorship* 160-210).

treatment of *inventio* as a problem in "finding," a problem defined, too, in Geoffrey's own Latin.[12] Translating the phrase, "Si quis habet fundare domum," as "For everi wight that hath an house to founde" (*Troilus* I.1065), Chaucer develops the original sense of invention as a form of architectonics: a form of structuring, linked to the processes of *ordinatio* and *compilatio* that would be put in practice by later medieval scribes and scholastics. As an example of *inventio* gone berserk, the *Tale of Sir Thopas* well exemplifies Geoffrey of Vinsauf's following advice: "non currit ad actum / Impetuosa manus," translated by Chaucer as, "Ne renneth naught the werk for to beginne / With rakel hond, but he wol bide a stounde" (*Troilus* I.1066-67). The only thing that dares to "bide a stounde" in *Thopas* is the hero's weary horse; the "rakel hond" that runs along here is the misguiding line of the Chaucerian narrator, who much like his hero, "renneth" on the byways of his romance.

In addition to his knowledge of Geoffrey of Vinsauf, Chaucer also would have been conversant in the Roman texts that stood behind the medieval definitions. The *De Inventione* and *Rhetorica ad Herennium*, both of which travelled under Ciceronian authorship in the Middle Ages, together with the *Ars Poetica* of Horace presented *inventio* as an act of rational discovery: a way of formulating cases and examples for forensic argument or literary exposition. For John of Garland, summarizing these traditions in his *Parisiana Poetria* in the thirteenth century, invention is the journey to such discoveries, a process of understanding the unknown: "Inuenire est in ignote rei noticiam ductu proprie rationis uenire" 'To invent is to come into knowledge of an unknown thing through the agency of one's own reason' (8-9).[13] Quoting the *Ad Herennium* to back this statement up, John avers that "Invention is thinking up things that are true or at least realistic (*uerarum et verisimilium*) to make your case plausible" (Lawler 8-9).

Inventio is the romance trope par excellence.[14] As the various texts I have quoted show, inherent in the idea of invention is the etymon *in + venire*, 'to come into,' 'to move towards.' The imagery of running or approaching in both John of Garland and Geoffrey of Vinsauf brings

[12]My discussion is pendant on Howard's exposition (134-37), in which he reviews the scholarship and the status of this passage as "a great favorite of Chaucer critics." I quote from Geoffrey of Vinsauf's Latin and the translation as printed in Howard (135).
[13]I cite Lawler's edition of John of Garland's *Parisiana Poetria* throughout.
[14]For stimulating remarks on the relationship between *inventio* and the origins of twelfth-century romance, see Vance.

out the physical sense of searching for topics and terms—a sense dramatized in the questing of romance narratives and, moreover, in the challenges to the romance hero to narrate his own story at its close. The Middle English romances that stand behind the *Thopas* draw out these embedded etymologies and narratives. *Sir Orfeo,* for example, begins as the narrator surveys the inheritance of Breton lay: "We redeþ oft and findeþ y-write" (1). Finding, here, is the search for proper material, much as the act of finding will control the hero's search for his abducted wife, his testing of his faithful steward, and the restoration of his kingdom (the verb "find" and its forms occurs more frequently than nearly any other verb in the poem).[15] The act of finding, too, permeates the exordia of many "literate" romances, as the narrator announces for himself or enjoins his reader to find something in the book that contains or provides the sources for his story.[16]

What I suggest is that the *Thopas* offers a romance of *inventio*. At one level, it literalizes the figurative language of the rhetorical tradition. As a search for something true or verisimilar, a journey after what John of Garland calls "ignote rei," Sir Thopas' own quest plays out on the topographies of fairyland the central motions of the rhetorical mind. But at another level, the performance of the *Thopas* reveals the narrator's own search for a topic that will acquit him in Harry Bailly's literary court. Unable to control his "rakel hond" or maintain the agency of his own reason, the narrator, much like Thopas' own horse, runs away with the story. The hero's ambling confrontations within the romance's fiction thus mirror the narrator's own lapses in invention, as both go in search of something they will never find.

This mirroring of fictive hero and Chaucerian teller extends itself to the broader relations between the two men and their adversaries. Thopas' encounter with the giant plays itself out, again, in the narrator's encounters with a hostile audience. The injunction that begins the Third Fit reifies the problem, as it goes beyond the convention of minstrel calls for silence to embrace the narrator's anxieties about the challenge to his work:

> Now holde youre mouth, *par charitee*,
> Bothe knyght and lady free,
> And herkeneth to my spelle;

[15]See the glossary entry in Bliss's edition.
[16]See the many examples quoted in Baugh.

Of bataille and of chivalry,
And of ladyes love-drury
Anon I wol yow telle.
(891-96)

By now, the narrator's relation to his audience is much like Thopas' relation to Olifaunt, where the physical aggression of the latter is transformed into the possible rhetorical aggressions of the former. With the exception of the one Knight on the Canterbury pilgrimage, this is no audience of knights and ladies "free"; and, for all Thopas' apparent confrontations with the monstrous, there are hardly any battles here, no clearly definable acts of chivalry. The encounter between the hero and the giant is a war of words, concluded as Sir Thopas ran away from Olifaunt's thrown stone. We never get to hear about the battle with the "geaunt with hevedes three" (842), nor do we learn of any "love-drury" other than Thopas' dreamt vision of his elf-queen.

The *Tale of Sir Thopas*, much like the *Squire's Tale*, is a story of deferred and dilated encounters. Nothing happens in either beyond the announcement that *something* will happen; and, indeed, for both, the only one who should hold his mouth is the narrator himself. Such an injunction, then, becomes the motive for the interruption of both stories: for the Squire, in the gentle paternalisms of the Franklin, but for the Chaucerian narrator, in the brusque confrontations of the Host. "Namoore of this, for Goddes dignitee" (919), he bursts in, blaring about his boredom and his aching ears and judging, "Thy drasty rymyng is nat worth a toord!" (930). In these aggressions, Harry Bailly comes off as little different from the giant Olifaunt, whose bloated threats not only challenge but infantilize Sir Thopas. "Child," the giant called him (810), a form of address turned to appellation by the narrator: "The child seyde . . ." (817). When the giant tries to drive him off by throwing stones, Sir Thopas escapes like a little boy retreating before a bully: "And faire escapeth child Thopas" (830). This childish Thopas stands as kin to the challenged Chaucerian narrator, earlier labelled "elvyssh" (703) and a "popet" (701) by the Host and now further demeaned by the Host's rude return.[17] The whole tone of the Host's response is charged with infantile abuse. His judgment of the *Thopas* as "drasty" (923, 930,

[17]The argument for both the childishness of Sir Thopas and of the Chaucerian narrator is made by Patterson ("'What Man Artow'?") though he does not treat the engagements with the Host in the infantilizing terms I offer here.

nicely glossed by the *Riverside Chaucer* as "crappy" [see the note to line 923 on p. 923]) resonates in its boyish scatology with the judgment that it is not worth a turd. His coinage "dogerel" (925), whatever the precise nature of its origin, also connotes the childish, with its onomatopoetics redolent of baby-talk.[18] The Host's anger is charged with oaths—God shows up three times in his dozen lines of abuse—and Chaucer, too, excuses himself "by Goddes sweete pyne" (936). These are, of course, the commonplaces of familiar idiom; yet, read against their romance model in the *Tale of Sir Thopas*, they reenact the oath-making of Olifaunt ("Child, by Termagaunt" 810) and the seemingly divine aegis controlling Thopas' retreat: "And al it was thurgh Goddes gras, / And thurgh his fair berynge" (831-32).

What matters most to Harry Bailly, though, is not so much the trite content of the *Tale of Sir Thopas*, but its sound. It is the "speech" he cannot stand, the "rym" (repeated four times) he cannot abide, and his "eres" that ache (923). The *Thopas* is a bunch of babble, and it recently has been suggested that the Host's "disgust" at Chaucer's "verbal form" contributes to the *Thopas–Melibee Link*'s understanding of the "narrowly conservative defense of writing . . . widespread throughout the Middle Ages" (Patterson, "'What Man Artow'?" 152-53). The challenge to the performance of the *Thopas* results in the orthodoxies of the *Melibee*; the retreat of the threatened teller of popular romance is to the comfortable allegories of translated prose. Now, to a certain extent, I agree with these claims and the tradition of reading the *Thopas–Melibee* section as a form of Chaucerian self-"quitting." And, I agree too with the argument that both tales, and the *Link*, share a concern with the dramatics of the abused child, a strategy of literary interest designed, as Patterson has crystalized it, to show how "Chaucer uses childhood to stage a problematic central to the act of writing" (164).

I think there are important features, however, that distinguish the loci of childhood and performance in *Thopas*. The oral nature of the *Tale* fits with its focus on the child-like qualities of the knight and the childishness of the teller. Together with the focus on the oral and the aural in the *Link*, and Harry Bailly's blend of baby-talk and glib scatology, the occasion of the *Thopas* and its reception draws us into the

[18]For the resonances of the Host's coinage, see Gaylord ("Chaucer's Dainty 'Dogerel'").

world of childish discourse itself.[19] It is a world that would have been familiar to late medieval readers who associated romance *avantures* with boyish tastes and children's entertainments. There is a sense in which the *Tale of Sir Thopas*, generically, fits into categories of boys' books: the kinds of stories that would be collected in the manuscripts of the fifteenth century and would have been condemned by educators of the sixteenth as puerile fancies, unfit for the learning child.[20]

The childishness of romance narrative, however, has a deeper history beyond the tastes of Chaucer and his later audiences. For Augustine, it is a form of literature intimately linked with the misapprehensions of the young boy. The first books of the *Confessions* detail the student Augustine's encounters with various temptations of adventure—with *errores* both poetic and personal. They detail, too, the realm of discourse in which such *errores* happen, a discourse of oral performance and aural reception. The story of the education of the young Augustine, though conforming to Late Antique Roman practice, is also charged with symbolic import. The quality of childhood in these early books is defined as the oral: crying babies, unlettered children, and reciting boys. Recitation, be it of the Roman drama or Virgilian epic, is central to early education, and Augustine makes much of his great embarrassments in school. He had to memorize the wanderings of Aeneas, a task inscribed into the romance structure of the *Confessions* itself and standing as the mediator between Dante and the Roman poet in the historical poetics of the *Commedia*.[21]

Perhaps this particular moment of Augustinian remembrance can explain the many resonances of orality and literacy, childhood and adult control, in Chaucer's poem:

[19]The medieval writer who explores the poetics of baby-talk most fully is, of course, Dante in various moments of the *Commedia* and the *De Vulgari Eloquentia*. For a review of Dante's explorations of childish babble in their literary, theoretical, and theological contexts, see Hollander, whose comments on the *Inferno* in particular may bear on my sense of Harry Bailly's "morally insufficient" response to both the *Thopas* and the *Melibee* (see 122-23, in particular).

[20]I have developed these associations in detail in *Chaucer and His Readers*.

[21]Though this is not the place to review the bibliography on the *Confessions* and its author's responses to romance, education, and Virgilian narrative, it would be worth acknowledging an overall debt to Mazotta's formulations of the various relationships among these issues and their impact on later medieval literary allegory.

> But if I ask how the name of Aeneas is spelt, *anyone who has learnt to read will give me the right answer,* based on the agreed convention which fixes the alphabet for all of us. If I next ask them whether a man would lose more by forgetting how to read and write or by forgetting the *fancies dreamed up by the poets*, surely everyone who is not out of his wits can see the answer they would give. So it was wrong of me *as a boy to prefer empty romances* to more valuable studies. In fact it would be truer to say that I loved the one and hated the other. But in those days 'one and one are two, two and two are four' was a loathsome jingle, while the wooden horse and its crew of soldiers, the burning of Troy and even the ghost of Creusa made a most *enchanting dream*, futile though it was.
>
> (34-35; bk. I, ch. 13; emphases mine)[22]

The childish Chaucerian narrator has found himself, much like the boy Augustine, to prefer the empty romances to schoolroom knowledge. His is the fantasy of romance performance—and it is within this fantasy's narrative that Thopas himself finds his motivations in an enchanting dream. The whole scene of the narrator's performance and the Host's interruption, I think, recapitulates many of these Augustinian concerns, and as in the *Confessions*, the proper response of Chaucer is, quite simply, to go back to school. His challenge is to move beyond the romance

[22]I cite Pine-Coffin's translation throughout. The translation is, admittedly, somewhat interpretive here, though I think the connotations he draws out of Augustine's vocabulary are intuitively right (especially in finding in Augustine's word "inania" the sense of empty romances and in considering "spectaculum uanitatis" as similarly empty dreams). For purposes of comparison, I offer the complete Latin quotation:

> at si quaram, quibus litteris scribatur Aeneae nomen, omnes mihi, qui haec didicerunt, uerum respondent et secundum id pactum et placitum, quo inter se homines ista signa firmarunt. item si quaeram, quid horum maiore uitae huius incommodo quisque obliuiscatur, legere et scribere an poetica illa figmenta, quis non uideat, quid responsurus sit, qui non est paenitus oblitus sui? peccabam ergo puer, cum illa inania istis utilioribus amore praeponebam uel potius ista oderam, illa amabam. iam uero unum et unum duo, duo et duo quattuor odiosa cantio mihi erat et dulcissimum spectaculum uanitatis equus ligneus plenus armatis et Troiae incendium atque ipsius umbra Creusae.
>
> (Knöll 20).

narratives of fantasy, *inventio*, and telling and to find himself in the texts of received knowledge.

II

To these ends, the announcement of the *Melibee* is framed in the self-consciousness of writing. From the sounds of *Thopas*, Chaucer moves to the *sentence* of *Melibee*. From the presence of the narrator, Chaucer moves towards the effacements of the transmitter. His comments in the *Link* attend primarily to the autonomy of texts: to the transmissions of material apart from authorial control or narrative presence. This is what I take to be the force of the allusion to the evangelists (943-52). Regardless of authorial agency, Chaucer seems to say, the gist or meaning of the story of the Passion remains the same: "Hir sentence is al oon" (952) 'the lesson is the same.' Indeed, this word "sentence," repeated five times by the narrator in nearly twenty lines (946, 947, 952, 961, 963), stands as the counterweight to the word "rym" and its forms of the Host's riposte. The iterations of the key term emphasize this shift from sounds to letters, from the verbal form to the inherent meaning of a performance. And, if the Host's reactions were keyed to establishing the genre of the narrator's performance—"rym dogerel," for example—so, too, Chaucer's announcement of his new tale hinges on denoting its participation in a class of narratives. This is a "tretys" (957, 963), a document, contract, prose text.[23] It exists for the apprehensions of the reader, not the listener, and there is a curious paradox raised by the appearance of this term and by the Chaucerian narrator's own excuses. At one level, he seems concerned with the aural appreciation of his tale: he is afraid of how he will be perceived to "varie . . . in my speche," that he will "tell" more proverbs than his audience has "herd" before, that he will not "the same wordes seye / As ye han herd." But at another level, Chaucer reinforces the impression that he plans not to *say* anything:

> . . . for, as in my sentence,
> Shul ye nowher fynden difference
> Fro the sentence of this tretys lyte

[23]On Chaucer's uses of the word "tretys," see Howard (59).

After the which this murye tale I write.
(961-63)

Chaucer invites his audience now to take on the mantle of the textual critic: to align themselves with something of the expectations of "correccioun" that, for example, governed the appeal to Gower and Strode at the close of the *Troilus* and informed the Parson's apology that, being "nat textuell," he would "stonde to correccioun" by members of the clerkly audience (see X 55-60). The business of "finding" difference between Chaucer's version and those currently in circulation differs, here, from the process of finding (*inventio*) controlling the selection of romance material. Rather, it requires the perusals of the text, the search through books that are the sole media of preservation for this kind of story. The *Tale of Melibee* is not *told* as much as it is *written*, and Chaucer's line may well seem, at first glance, as little more than one of the familiar nods we have come to expect from the *Knight's Tale*: "But of that storie list me nat to write" (A 1201). Such a lapse, taken either as forgetfulness on the part of Chaucer the reviser or as the evidence of "bookness" on the part of Chaucer the author, is one of the palpable fissures in the *Canterbury Tales*—one often read alongside the exhortation in the *Prologue* to the *Miller's Tale* to "Turne over the leef and chese another tale" (A 3177). There is a difference, though, between these earlier announcements of the poem's textuality and the announcement of the *Melibee* as something written. Unlike these other stories in the *Canterbury Tales*, the *Melibee* stands in a genealogy of translated, inherited texts. Its generic affiliations lie with the traditions of material directed at the literate, the learned, and the pedagogically minded. At stake, it seems to me, is not whether Chaucer intended the *Melibee* to be read as straight instruction, nor for that matter, for just whom it was directed. What is at stake is how the *Melibee* stands as instruction for the teller and his critic: how it may teach both Chaucer and the Host to respond to blunt threats with measured words and to turn from the tempting romances of the oral to the hard lessons of the written.

Melibee, for its medieval readers, was appreciated as a *compilatio*, a florilegium of moral texts, instructive quotes, and valuable citations.[24] The fifteenth-century scribes who transmitted it often filled in

[24]In his dissertation, Minnis suggests that, along with the *Tales* of the Monk and the Parson, "The *Tale of Melibee* can be regarded as a *compilatio*" (206), in

the margins with the names of the *auctores* cited, keying them by means of symbols or red highlights to the quotations within the text. Its status as a *compilatio* was also reinforced by the effect it had on later readers. Whether abstracted from the Canterbury frame or written in the complete manuscripts of the *Tales*, the *Melibee* appears unique in the many variations of its wording, its length, and its sheer weight of authorial citation.[25] Part of this phenomenon, certainly, is due to the prose nature of the *Tale* and to the greater possibilities of scribal error when unconstrained by the patterns of verse and rhyme. But part of this phenomenon, I believe, is due to the very staging and narration of the *Melibee* itself: a work presented as but one version of familiar, inherited material, a work self-consciously announced as longer than the others—and, hence, subject either to scribal truncation or to further augmentation by those who would seem to follow Chaucer's model.

---

whose manuscripts the margins "are filled with the names of the *auctores* cited. This practice may be understood to imply a literary judgment: these tales are being presented as repositories of *auctoritates*; Chaucer's text is being edited as a *compilatio*" (218). As far as I can tell, this material has not been included in *Medieval Theory of Authorship*. I have examined several of the manuscripts of the *Melibee* (some directly, some in facsimile). It is perhaps important that the Hengwrt Manuscript (perhaps the earliest complete manuscript of the *Tales*) offers very few marginal annotations, in keeping with its overall relative lack of interest in the mechanics of organization (in contrast, say, to the work of this same scribe in Ellesmere). The Helmingham Manuscript, which truncates the tale by about a third of its original length, annotates nearly all the citations of *auctores* with marginal names keyed in red to textual references. Manuscripts of Chaucer's ultimate source, Albertanus of Brescia's *Liber consolationis et consilii*, are similarly annotated; in "Rewriting Chaucer" I suggested that the fifteenth-century scribes of the *Tales* were continuing the practices of annotating this kind of work (319n30).

[25]This uniqueness proved nightmarish to Manly and Rickert in establishing a textual tradition for the *Tale*. See their discussion at II: 371-72. An interesting case of *Melibee*'s transformation is its appearance in the anthology, now Huntington Library MS HM 144, where it appears without its author's name or reference to the *Canterbury Tales* (save in a much later hand) and is headed "Prouerbis." In this manuscript, the *Melibee* ends with the following remarks: "They that this present and forseyde tale haue or shal Reede Remembyr the noble prouerbis that rebukyth Couetise and Vengeaunse takyng in truste of Fortune whiche hathe causyd many a noble Prince to falle as we may rede of them here folluyng" (fol. 99r). What, in fact, follows is the *Monk's Tale*, untitled and without Chaucerian reference, but with the running head "The Falle of Princis" (fols. 110-111v).

The *Melibee* begins with an appeal to texts, with a representation of the act of reading paralleling the Chaucerian narrator's own act of textual selection. After the initial attack on Melibee's house, wife, and daughter, and his discovery of the atrocity, Prudence tries to silence her husband's weeping: "This noble wyf Prudence remembred hire upon the sentence of Ovide, in his book that cleped is the Remedie of Love, here as he seith, / . . . (976). Each subsequent challenge, from Melibee's own doubts, to the contentions of his counsellors, to the appearance at the *Tale*'s close of the original "adversaries" (1730) is greeted by a demonstration of Prudence's wide reading. In fact, it would appear that Prudence can barely open her mouth without quoting a text or citing an authority, and this seems to me to be precisely the point. The lesson of the *Melibee*, beyond its specific instructions in patience and virtue, lies in the ability to read both appropriately and, as it were, appropriatively. Prudence demonstrates the ability to match the proverb with the problem and to displace physical confrontation with textual citation.

This is the situation of the *Thopas'* narrator when faced with the angry challenge of the Host, and to a certain extent, the *Tale of Melibee*'s own narrative enacts the Chaucerian strategy in the second half of the *Thopas–Melibee Link*. By turning from action to text, Chaucer defuses the threats of the Host, or for that matter, those of any audience potentially hostile to voiced performance. The "sentence" of the prose tale becomes the appeal to the "sententiae" of unassailable authorities. And the effect on Harry Bailly is, perhaps, to be best measured against Prudence's effect on Melibee's cruel adversaries: "And whan they herden the goodliche wordes of dame Prudence, / they were so supprised and ravysshed and hadden so greet joye of hire that wonder was to telle" (1733-34). Not only has Prudence "ravysshed" them into obedience, but she has transformed them from actors into readers, too. Their first response is to recall "the sawes of David the prophete" and draw on "the konnynge of Salomon" (1738). Melibee himself has also become something of a Prudential reader, quoting Seneca on forgiveness (1775). *His* transformation, by the *Tale*'s close, is to move from anger to citation, to become a man of "sentence" in both the judicial and the literary sense (see 1830), and to have "his herte . . . enclyne to the wil of his wif, considerynge hir trewe entente" (1871). As a new reader, Melibee follows his wife's will—a wife whose "entente" may be affiliated, by now, with the *ententes* of the Chaucerian narrator and the controlling appeal to *intentio auctoris* that constitutes the supreme excuse in medieval literary theory.

It would be no surprise to say that Harry Bailly mistakes the *Melibee*, much as he misreads nearly everything that comes his way. But his mistakings here fit him, again, into the narrative of authorial confrontation building from the invitation to the *Thopas*. Harry, first of all, learns nothing from the story; or to put the case more accurately, he learns exactly the opposite from what it seeks to teach. Instead of learning from the *Tale*, he finds in it a teaching for his own wife. Instead of seeking to incline himself to her will, he shows how his wife expects all others to do so:

> And if that any neighebor of myne
> Wol nat in chirche to my wyf enclyne,
> Or be so hardy to hire to trespace,
> Whan she comth hoom she rampeth in my face, ...
> (1901-4)

But the key problem for the Host, and the one that I think governs his whole response and ultimate retelling of the *Melibee*, is his mistake about the *Tale*'s mode of transmission:

> I hadde levere than a barel ale
> That Goodelief, my wyf, hadde *herd* this tale!
> (1893-94; emphasis mine)

If Goodelief (if that really is his wife's name)[26] were to get the story, then at the very least she should have read it rather than heard it: apprehended, as Harry Bailly surely cannot, that this has been, as Chaucer put it, a "murye tale I write"—not a telling but a treatise. In this signal mistake, Harry recasts the *Melibee* into his own oralist terms. The stately gestures of the prose allegory become, in his extended story of his wife, the broad strokes of the fabliau. The plethora of quotations becomes the fast-paced vernacularity of local dialogue. The Host's responses to the *Melibee*, together with his invitation to the Monk, constitute the longest single speech he offers in the *Canterbury Tales* (save for the single "quod he" of line 1924, the Host speaks without interrup-

[26]Early editions printed "gode lief" (thus, an epithet and not a name). For arguments and bibliography that this in fact is Harry's wife's name, see the *Riverside Chaucer* (928-29, note to line 1894).

tion from lines 1891 to 1964). Obsessively translating the events of *Melibee* into his own life, Harry sketches out a tale of domestic violence on the large scale, full of "grete clobbed staves" (1898) and knives, loud barking dogs, comparisons between Harry and a "coward ape" (to his wife) and a "wilde leoun" (to himself), and threats of murder, fighting, and mutilation. Even the oaths, commonplace though they may seem—Harry's "By Goddes bones" transformed in his quotation from his wife into her "By corpus bones"—signal in this environment the possibilities of violent dismemberment.

All the paradigms of *Melibee* are shifted here. Civic understanding becomes neighborly contention. The allegorically significant violence of the *Melibee*'s opening becomes the real, physical violence of the Host's family. Texts are lost in the welter of voiced anger. The Host recasts these paradigms to offer up not just a critique of the *Melibee* but a virtual rewriting of it. His narrative, with its intrusive first person pronouns, stands in marked contrast to the absence of an editorializing or reflective narrator in the *Melibee*. And, after the sustained textuality of the *Tale*, the Host's long speech takes us jarringly back to the oral world of personal performance and colloquial idiom. If there is a moment in the *Canterbury Tales* that may count as the "Host's Tale," this is it: a fabliau-style story of domestic challenge, a loud and boisterous tale of threats and counter-threats, a story full of the dehumanizings of beast similes and broken bodies.

This transformation of the *Tale of Melibee* reveals not just the Host's characteristic blindness to the forms of literary pedagogy but, read in the context of the broader theme of growth and orality controlling this portion of the *Tales*, shows him now far beneath the Chaucerian narrator in self-awareness. As I have suggested above, the narrator's turn from the oral performance of the *Thopas* to the textual transmission of the *Melibee* may represent, at one level, a kind of Augustinian turning from the recitations and romance obsessions of the boy to the responsive and responsible reading of the man. Augustine's remarks in the *Confessions* about "whether a man would lose more by forgetting how to read and write or by forgetting the fancies dreamed up by the poets" takes on a dramatic specificity for the characters in the *Thopas–Melibee* section of the *Canterbury Tales*. From the former to the latter tale, we move with Chaucer from the fancies of the poets to the knowledge of reading and writing. It is significant in this context that Prudence's first action, even before her recounting of Ovid's advice, is remembering. In recalling Ovid—"Prudence remembred hire upon the sentence of Ovide"— she shows us that central to the literary response to action is the need not to forget the knowledge of reading and writing. But this is exactly what Harry Bailly has forgotten. Unmindful of Chaucer's claims for writing or the lessons of his "sentence," unaware of the generic filiations of the *Melibee* or its traditional, instructional contexts, Harry blurts out a blunt retelling of the *Tale* as one of unrestrained violence and unbridled orality. The voice of Harry, like the voice of Goodelief, sticks in the ear now, and it may be fair to say that Harry Bailly is the one who has forgotten how to read and write and who has transformed *Melibee* into a fancy dreamed up by the fabulist he proves to be.

III

To this point, I have tried to outline a variety of ways of understanding the *Thopas–Melibee* section as dramatizing problems of orality and literacy in the *Canterbury Tales*: a shift from the presence of narrative voice to the absence of literate authorship; a shift from the childishness of the romance to the adult advice of texts; a shift from the identification with the child in *Thopas* to the identification of the adult in the figure of Prudence (see also Patterson, "'What Man Artow'?" 155). What I have tried to argue, too, is that the form of each tale is thematized within its narrative: for *Thopas*, a romance of orality, where the true subject of the story is the problematics of performance and its possible infantilizations of the narrator; for *Melibee*, a fiction of textuality, where we may be invited to suspend our understanding of the *Tales* as voiced performances, to read what is presented as another written version of an inherited text, and to find in that text a lesson in the art of reading—in particular, the art of reading the *Thopas–Melibee* section of the *Tales*. Finally, I suggested that the Host's response to the *Melibee* was to transform it into an oral performance of his own, a fast-paced, fabliau-style story of domestic violence.

In closing, I would like to contextualize this section somewhat further by suggesting a controlling pattern to Fragment VII of the *Canterbury Tales*. Long thought of as the "literature" fragment, this section of stories beginning with the *Shipman's Tale* and ending with the *Nun's*

Priest's raises the issues that many have seen as central to the Chaucerian project as a whole: narrative intention and reader response; generic diversity and the display of craftsmanship; the fascinations with the child and the problems of authorial identity; the autonomy of literature and the provocations of political action.[27] Fragment VII may also be appreciated as the "orality" fragment because of its tales' concern with the phenomena of speech, with teller–audience relationships, and with the many literary, cultural, and political contexts that constrain or challenge verbal self-presentation.

From the puns of the *Shipman's Tale* to the noise of the *Nun's Priest's*, the sound of human language controls the many diverse tales of Fragment VII. The well-known word play on "cosyn" and "cosynage" (kinship and trickery) and the fantastic triple pun on "taillynge" (with implications of commercial, sexual, and narrative control) present a verbal texture to the *Shipman's Tale* in which we can never be quite sure just what we hear.[28] The Prioress's story of the little boy who repeats *Alma redemptoris mater* without really understanding it shows us, now in a horrifying way, the price paid for words spoken without understanding. "I lerne song: I kan but smal grammere" (535), the older boy says to the clergeoun when asked to expound the meaning of the *Alma redemptoris*, affirming that the Prioress's is, in some controlling way, a fiction of illiteracy: a story about rote memorization, in particular, keyed to the young. So, too, after the *Melibee*, the Monk's seemingly oblivious recitation of one tragedy after another gets him in trouble—here, in the curt yet courtly interruption of the Knight. In the *Nun's Priest's Tale*, the childhood genre of Aesopic fable dovetails with a compilation of educative materials to produce a story whose moral, as Donald Howard aphorized it, tells us to open our eyes and shut our mouths.[29] From the loud rap on the door in the *Shipman's Tale* (213), through the ringings of the Prioress's *Alma*, the bobbings of Thopas' horse, the outbursts of the Host, the "clinking" of the Monk, and the unbridled barnyard noises at the end of the *Nun's Priest's Tale*,

[27]For arguments about the unity of Fragment VII, see Gaylord ("Sentence and Solaas"); Howard (271-88); and Patterson ("'What Man Artow'?" [esp. 162-64]).

[28]For a summary account of these puns, with citation of previous scholarship and commentary on their thematic import for the *Shipman's Tale*, see Patterson (*Chaucer and the Subject of History* 351, 360-62).

[29]"We would do better to keep our eyes open and our mouths shut" (Howard 286).

this Fragment rings in our ears more than any other section of the *Canterbury Tales*.

It rings, too, in the ears of Chaucer's audiences—not just the fictive aching Harry Bailly or impatient Knight but the historical community of English readers at the close of the fourteenth century. There has, of late, been a conspicuous revival of interest in the politics of Chaucer's making, and in particular, of the literary politics at work in the *Nun's Priest's Tale*.[30] In what is clearly Chaucer's single most explicit reference to contemporary events, the Rising of 1381 and the plague, critics have seen a poet struggling (or, perhaps, toying) with the provocations of social upheaval. Unlike his friend John Gower, who had addressed the Rising and the later challenges to dynastic control in the *Vox Clamantis* and the *Confessio Amantis*, respectively, Chaucer never seemed occupied with the fictional transformation of either popular dissent or royal tension. Some critics have, in fact, gone as far to suggest that the close of the *Nun's Priest's Tale* represents Chaucer's response to Gowerian political poetics: a transformation into humorous fable of the nightmarish cacophony of the *Vox Clamantis*.[31]

Whether or not Chaucer "quits" Gower at the close of Fragment VII, he has already "quit" himself. Having presented a small, child-like romancing persona in the telling of the *Thopas*, Chaucer has successively effaced the teller in the anonymities of *Melibee*, the dullness of the Monk, and the transparencies of the portrait-less Nun's Priest. Having presented a sequence of critical responses grounded in the oralisms of the Host, he moves beyond "quitting" to silence. The noises of the tales of Fragment VII, and the noise of Harry Bailly and his wife, give way to the loud clamor of the barnyard, perhaps that disturbing *vox populi* that the citizens of London heard in 1381. Oral performance has its dangers, Chaucer seems to say, not just in the embarrassments of an interrupted teller but in the threats of an angry mob. The plea that begins the last, fragmentary fit of *Thopas*—"Now holde youre mouth, *par charitee*"—may stand as the epigraph for Fragment VII as a whole. Within the drama of the *Tales*, the Host cannot hold *his*

[30]A phenomenon exemplified in the studies of Bishop; Travis; Ganim (113-17); and Justice.

[31]An intuition brilliantly articulated in Justice's reading of the *Tale* as a rewriting of Book I of the *Vox*, with Chauntecleer as Gower (chap. 5 of *Writing and Rebellion*).

mouth until the appearance of the Parson and the silencing of all before his sermon. But within Fragment VII, Chaucer holds his in the textualities of *Melibee*. We, too, must hold our mouths, I think, and follow the example of the *Nun's Priest's Tale*. For if its moral is in fact to keep our eyes open and our mouths shut, then what better state could we be in to read the very texts before us? Not in the clamor of the Rising, nor in the anger of the Host. Perhaps, with Augustine, we may put off the childishness of baby-talk and vacuous romances and turn to the letters on the page. When, at the moment of conversion in the garden, Augustine's eyes light on the page of the scriptures, they do so in silence: "Not in revelling and drunkenness, not in lust and wantonness, not in quarrels and rivalries" (178; bk. VIII, ch. 12). Such words may well stand as advice to Melibee, whose own name as we know means "drunk with honey"; to Harry Bailly and his own Goodelief; to the peasants allegorized at the close of the *Nun's Priest's Tale*; and perhaps, to us, for having lain aside the romance of orality and read the texts of understanding, we may find, with Augustine, that we have "no wish to read more and no need to do so" (idem).

Department of English
Stanford University

Works Cited

Baugh, Albert C. "The Middle English Romance: Some Questions of Creation, Presentation, and Preservation." *Speculum* 42 (1967): 1-31.

Bäuml, Franz. "Varieties and Consequences of Medieval Literacy and Illiteracy." *Speculum* 55 (1980): 237-65.

Benson, C. David. "Their Telling Difference: Chaucer the Pilgrim and His Two Contrasting Tales." *Chaucer Review* 18 (1983): 60-76.

Benson, Larry D., ed. *The Riverside Chaucer*. 3rd ed. Boston: Houghton, 1987.

Bishop, Ian. "*The Nun's Priest's Tale* and the Liberal Arts." *Review of English Studies* ns 30 (1979): 257-67.

Bliss, A.J., ed. *Sir Orfeo*. 2nd ed. Oxford: Clarendon, 1966.

Bowers, John M. "*The Tale of Beryn* and *The Siege of Thebes*: Alternate Ideas of *The Canterbury Tales*." *Studies in the Age of Chaucer* 7 (1985): 23-50.

Brockman, Bennett A. "Children and Literature in Late Medieval England." *Children's Literature* 4 (1975): 58-63.

—. "Robin Hood and the Invention of Children's Literature." *Children's Literature* 10 (1982): 1-17.

Burrow, John A. *Ricardian Poetry: Chaucer; Gower; Langland and the* Gawain *Poet*. London: Routledge, 1971.

—. "*Sir Thopas* in the Sixteenth Century." *Middle English Studies Presented to Norman Davis in Honour of his Seventieth Birthday*. Ed. Douglas Gray and E.G. Stanley. Oxford: Clarendon, 1983. 69-91.

—. "Four Notes on Chaucer's *Sir Thopas*." *Essays on Medieval Literature*. Oxford: Clarendon, 1984. 60-78.

Copeland, Rita. *Rhetoric, Hermeneutics, and Translation in the Middle Ages: Academic Traditions and Vernacular Texts*. Cambridge: Cambridge UP, 1991.

Crosby, Ruth. "Oral Delivery in the Middle Ages." *Speculum* 11 (1936): 88-110.

—. "Chaucer and the Custom of Oral Delivery." *Speculum* 13 (1938): 413-32.

Ganim, John M. *Chaucerian Theatricality*. Princeton: Princeton UP, 1990.

Gaylord, Alan T. "Sentence and Solaas in Fragment VII of the *Canterbury Tales*: Harry Bailly as Horseback Editor." *PMLA* 82 (1967): 226-35.

—. "Chaucer's Dainty 'Dogerel': The 'Elvyssh' Prosody of *Sir Thopas*." *Studies in the Age of Chaucer* 1 (1979): 84-104.

—. "The Moment of *Sir Thopas*: Towards a New Look at Chaucer's Language." *Chaucer Review* 16 (1982): 311-29.

—. "The 'Miracle' of *Sir Thopas*." *Studies in the Age of Chaucer* 6 (1984): 65-84.

Hollander, Robert. "Babytalk in Dante's *Commedia*." *Studies in Dante*. Ravenna: Longo Editore, 1980. 115-29.

Howard, Donald R. *The Idea of the* Canterbury Tales. Berkeley: U of California P, 1976.

Justice, Steven. *Writing and Rebellion: England in 1381*. Berkeley: U of California P, 1994.

Knöll, Pius, ed. *Sancti Aureli Augustini Confessionum Libri Tredecem*. CSEL Vol. 33. Vienna: F. Tempsky, 1896.

Lawler, Traugott, trans. and ed. *The* Parisiana Poetria *of John of Garland*. New Haven: Yale UP, 1974.

Leicester, H. Marshall, Jr. *The Disenchanted Self: Representing the Subject in the* Canterbury Tales. Berkeley: U of California P, 1990.

Lerer, Seth. *Chaucer and His Readers: Imagining the Author in Late-Medieval England*. Princeton: Princeton UP, 1993.

—. "Rewriting Chaucer: Two Fifteenth-Century Readings of the *Canterbury Tales*." *Viator* 19 (1988): 311-26.

—. "Classical Skepticism and English Poetry in the Twelfth Century." Diss. U of Chicago, 1981.

Manly, John M. "Chaucer and the Rhetoricians." *Proceedings of the British Academy* 12 (1926): 95-113.

—, and Edith Rickert. *The Text of the* Canterbury Tales. 8 Vols. Chicago: U of Chicago P, 1940.

Mazzotta, Giuseppe. *Dante, Poet of the Desert*. Princeton: Princeton UP, 1979.

Minnis, A. J. "Medieval Discussions of the Role of the Author." Diss. Queen's University, Belfast, 1976.

—. *Medieval Theory of Authorship*. London: Scolar, 1984.

Murphy, James J. *Rhetoric in the Middle Ages: A History of Rhetorical Theory from Saint Augustine to the Renaissance*. Berkeley: U of California P, 1974.

—. "Rhetoric and Dialectic in *The Owl and the Nightingale*." *Medieval Eloquence*. Ed. J. Murphy. Berkeley: U of California P, 1978. 198-230.

Olson, Glending. "A Reading of the *Thopas–Melibee* Link." *Chaucer Review* 10 (1975): 147-53.

Parker, Patricia A. *Inescapable Romance*. Princeton: Princeton UP, 1979.

Patterson, Lee. "'What Man Artow?': Authorial Self-Definition in *The Tale of Sir Thopas and The Tale of Melibee*." *Studies in the Age of Chaucer* 11 (1989): 117-75.

—. *Chaucer and the Subject of History*. Madison: U of Wisconsin P, 1991.

Pine-Coffin, R.S., trans. *Saint Augustine Confessions*. Harmondsworth: Penguin, 1961.

Silvia, Daniel S. "Some Fifteenth-Century Manuscripts of the *Canterbury Tales*." *Chaucer and Middle English Studies in Honour of Rossell Hope Robbins*. Ed. Beryl Rowland. London: Allen, 1974. 153-63.

Stanley, E.G., ed. *The Owl and the Nightingale*. 1960. Manchester: Manchester UP, 1972.

Travis, Peter W. "Chaucer's Trivial Fox Chase and the Peasants' Revolt of 1381." *Journal of Medieval and Renaissance Studies* 18 (1988): 195-220.

Turville-Petre, Thorlac. *The Alliterative Revival*. Cambridge: Brewer, 1977.

Vance, Eugene. *From Topic to Tale: Logic and Narrativity in the Middle Ages*. Minneapolis: U of Minnesota P, 1987.

Wyrchipe: The Clash of Oral-Heroic and Literate-Ricardian Ideals in the Alliterative *Morte Arthure*

Donna Lynne Rondolone

The alliterative *Morte Arthure*, composed about 1402 (Hamel, *Critical Edition* 62) by an anonymous poet of the Northeast Midlands, has received more attention and respect since William Matthews's 1960 book-length study of the poem, and it is now recognized as one of the great poems of the Alliterative Revival. Much of this attention has focused on Arthur, and the poem's modern audience has often responded to him in diametrically opposed ways; nor is there any consensus as to how a contemporary audience may have reacted to him. At one extreme is Matthews, who believes the poet was "a moralist" who portrayed Arthur from a very Christian perspective: like the Alexander of contemporary romances and treatises, Arthur is a military leader of great courage and decisiveness, but he is also a cruel tyrant infected with the deadly sin of pride. He dies despairing and unregenerate, without the self-knowledge which true contrition would have bestowed, and consequently, he personally—not impersonal Fortune—is wholly responsible for the destruction of his realm (68 ff., 135-41). At the other extreme is Larry D. Benson, who refutes Matthews's argument by citing contemporary historical references which approve of "cruel" behavior like Arthur's as necessary to a king's ability to maintain order in his realm (77-78). He interprets the poem as consisting of a tension

> between two goods, between the Christian detachment that is necessary for ultimate happiness even on this earth and the complete engagement with an earthly ideal that is necessary for heroism . . . . Arthur's fall is the result not of any flaw in himself but of a flawed ideal, the worldly ideal of heroic kingship that, like all worldly ideals, leads even its finest adherents to the inevitable turn of Fortune's wheel and a tragic fall.
>
> (80-81; 84)

Other interpretations of Arthur's character fall somewhere between these two extremes.[1] Despite their inconsistent and occasionally contradictory conclusions, however, all recognize within the poem a basic tension between one value system that encourages expansion, concrete action, and externalization and another that encourages contraction, passivity, and internal reflection. Arthur's heroic aggression is pitted against and ultimately succumbs to a larger impersonal, impeding force which seems to emanate from a Christianized platonic prime mover. Moreover, although we can see that the poet seems to be groping towards an Arthur who is more emotionally complex than the one-dimensional heroic Arthur of his chronicle sources, we never feel that the poet has achieved a coherent, integrated characterization because the forces of expansion and contraction which impinge upon Arthur seem to occur at awkward hard angles: one minute he is a humble vassal of God, and the next he is himself a godlike sovereign. His single combat with the St. Michael's Mount giant transports us into the otherworldly dimension of romance and psychomachia, but then his army's engagement with Lucius' forces volleys us into the very concrete community of the epic battle.

So how are we to account for our inconsistent responses to the poem in general and to Arthur in particular? I think the answer lies in the fact that the poet does indeed give us mixed signals, because he was unwittingly responding to contradictory pressures from his cultural environment: although he used written sources,[2] he was working in an oral (or at least oral-derived) medium in an age which was still essentially craft-literate. That is, although the centralized royal bureaucracy's in-

[1]See Finlayson; Lumiansky; Keiser; Patterson; and Hamel ("The Dream of a King").

[2]For a detailed discussion of the poet's use of sources, see Hamel (*Critical Edition* 34-52).

creasing use of written documents had been encouraging the spread of literacy for practical purposes, old oral habits of processing information persisted until printing could inexpensively supply every individual with his own copy (Clanchy 216, 230).[3] Since the conditions under which information is retained and processed in an oral or predominantly oral culture are fundamentally different from those in a literate culture, the structures of consciousness they generate reflect their distinct and often contradictory operations.[4] At the time and place of the *Morte Arthure*'s composition, the "noetic economy" (to borrow Walter Ong's elegant phrase) generated by chirographic technology was gradually encroaching upon that generated by oral conditions. I believe that the forces of expansion and contraction which scholars have intuitively recognized in the poem reflect the different structures of consciousness generated by oral and literate conditions, respectively. It will be helpful, then, to begin by briefly identifying the dynamics which distinguish the two "noetic economies."

In the absence of writing, the human memory has to be exploited in such a way that it can retain and transmit a large corpus of data without substantially changing it. This is accomplished largely through embedding information in a matrix of rhythm, alliteration, assonance, or other auditory pattern; the information then emerges as formulaic expressions within a familiar thematic setting (Ong, *Orality and Literacy* 34). Thus "thinking"—the manipulation of data—in an oral culture takes place in a narrative context: oral cultures are constrained to explore what we would call "concepts" (e.g., justice) within concrete, time-and-space-bound, agonistic frames of reference rather than dispassionately discussing them as abstract principles existing independently of practical human experience (Ong, *Orality and Literacy* 49-57; cf. Havelock, *Preface* 174, 180, 185; and *Greek Concept of Justice* passim).

These mnemonic limitations generate, among other things,[5]

[3]Ong points out that literate ways of thinking were not fully internalized until the Romantic movement (*Orality and Literacy* 41, 45) and discusses why the process took so long (*The Presence of the Word* 53-87).
[4]I use "structures of consciousness" to refer to modes of perceiving that determine how we think and feel, how we organize information, what kind of order we impose on the chaos of our experience, and how we conceive of ourselves.
[5]For example, an "oral style" characterized by repetition and parataxis. Although we literates tend to believe that these strategies normally produce only

the consumingly intense emotional nature of oral and oral-derived poetry.[6] The task of engineering fail-safe mnemonic support demands total kinesthetic and affective involvement. This demand probably stems not from cultural conditioning but from human physiology: most people, even highly educated literates, still find that words are easier to memorize if they are sung or spoken in rhythm. Such submersion in kinesthesia, along with the polarization of feelings inherent in agonistic narrative, means that a person in an oral culture cannot effectively distance himself from the information he hears. Because he has no breathing space to separate himself as knower or subject from knowledge or object, he cannot reflect on his own being as a unique self apart from the cultural matrix. Consequently, oral culture creates a personality structure which is relatively undifferentiated (Ong, *Orality and Literacy* 34-36; Havelock, *Greek Concept of Justice* 49-51; Russo and Simon passim). Eric Havelock describes the Homeric hero in terms which could also describe Gilgamesh, Beowulf, Roland, and Prince Igor: he is "a man to whom it has not occurred, and to whom it cannot occur, that he has a personality apart from the pattern of his acts" (*Preface* 199). In other words, the oral epic hero is fascinating in his breathtaking appearance, his hyperconfident boasts, and his incontrovertible physical strength, but he is not an intellectually or emotionally liberated individual, and so his options are severely limited—he has not chosen, nor could he choose, to be what he is or do what he does. Although his overwhelming presence mesmerizes us into believing that he is completely self-possessed, the hero's values are those of his community; his emotional and mental processes are initiated in a communal, usually agonistic context, and any inner doubt he might experience is automatically externalized as an outer conflict which is resolved through concrete action (Russo and Simon passim).

Mircea Eliade's studies of the mythologies of oral cultures reveal a similarly low level of differentiation: there is no hard-and-fast mutual exclusion of divine vs. human, eternal vs. temporal, or sacred vs. profane; instead, human beings have the power to experience the

---

tedium and imprecision, they enable oral epic poetry convincingly to express or elicit powerful feeling with extraordinary elegance. Ong describes how these strategies (which he calls "redundant or copious" and "additive rather than subordinative," respectively) operate in *Orality and Literacy* (37-41). For examples of such occurrences in *Beowulf*, see Irving (16 ff.).

[6]Ong describes this characteristic as "empathetic and participatory" (*Orality and Literacy* 45-46).

cosmic, the eternal, and the sacred in the here-and-now, which is re-endowed with the original order and forms established in the beginning. James Redfield notes that, in the *Iliad*, this need to repair and regenerate is expressed as the global transformation of chaos (disorder and formlessness) into cosmos (order and form). His description of this dynamic in the *Iliad* also accurately describes that in *Beowulf*:

> Purity is form; the impure is the formless, the deformed, and that which threatens the forms . . . . The epic does not make a contrast between the physical and the spiritual or between the personal and the social. Rather, it is expected that disorder on one level will be reflected in all and that when things are in order—*en kosmoi*—the order will be pervasive . . . . [The heroic ethic is] a pervasive drive for order, a need to rescue form from the formlessness of the world.
>
> (160-62)

In other words, the relatively undifferentiated state of the cosmos means that it cannot tolerate dissent anywhere, since anything foreign or out of place threatens the integrity of the whole. To protect that integrity, the cosmos needs a hero, someone whose correspondingly low level of differentiation is pristinely secure and inviolate, guarded perpetually by his stance of magnificent and absolute self-possession. The hero restores cosmic order in his own perfect image, whose smooth mirroring surface is never distorted by abrasive bits of unintegrated psyche. For example, Roland's uncompromising "prodece" is born of his innocence of inner moral conflict: his unscathed and rigid consciousness is entirely dedicated to defending the cosmos of the true God and Charlemagne, a cosmos which through his efforts remains like him, righteously pristine and unadulterated by paganism. This state of insistent and comprehensive lack of differentiation underlies what Thomas Greene calls the epic's "expansiveness":

> the epic universe is there to be invaded by the human will and imagination. Epic answers to man's need to clear away an area he can apprehend, if not dominate, and commonly this area expands to fill the epic universe, to cover the known world and reach heaven and hell.
>
> (9-10)

Arthur tries to do exactly this, to extend his influence "to fill the epic universe," until he is stopped by the news of Mordred's treason. This oral-heroic "expansiveness" comprises one pole of that basic tension identified at the beginning of this essay; the other pole is composed of the contraction into the isolated self, a restructuring of consciousness initiated by the gradual internalization of literacy.

With the advent of literacy the relatively undifferentiated nature of the cosmos and the hero begins to change, because writing restructures consciousness by removing the heavy burden placed on the memory (Ong, *Presence of the Word* 6-9; and *Orality and Literacy* 78-116). Since writing allows data to be placed onto an external, permanent, visual field, the mnemonic tactics of oral poetry can be relinquished: consciousness no longer has to be submerged in affect and kinesthesia, perpetually engaged in agonistic struggle, in order to gain access to information. With this new leisure, the human mind can slowly evolve from an embattled contestant into a dispassionate intellect free to reflect and develop the skills of abstraction and analysis.

This gradual internalization of literacy initiates a process of psychological differentiation in human beings which changes their perception of the self and the cosmos. The development of analysis and reflection permits the realization that there is an object, a "not-I," which exists in distinction to a subject, an "I" (Havelock, *Preface* passim). Mental and emotional processes, especially inner conflict, no longer have to be projected and embodied as personifications; they can be defined in abstract terms. Likewise, analysis and reflection allow the human subject to separate himself from the cosmos, which becomes an object that can be dispassionately examined. By the fourth century BCE in ancient Greece, this process had evolved to the point where Plato could divide the cosmos into mutually exclusive spheres of influence: the time-bound, concrete world of inconsistent human existence and the eternal, abstract world of ideas (Havelock, *Preface* 226-29). This model of a dichotomized cosmos found a permanent home in the writings of the church fathers and, through them, in western culture generally; it persists even now after the discoveries of quantum physics have demanded a new model of the universe.

The slowly evolving literate reconstruction of consciousness seems to have developed sufficiently by the fourteenth century to create a new kind of hero. First, he no longer must be memorable, so the chromatic intensity of his character can be toned down: he can become ordinary rather than extraordinary, tractable rather than incontrovertible. Concurrently, the developing ability to reflect and introspect further erodes the hero's rigid and pristine self-possession by encouraging the recognition of inner conflict and self-doubt.

John Burrow's description of the "Ricardian image of man," derived from the works of Chaucer, Langland, Gower, and the *Gawain*-poet (93-129), is consistent with how we would expect the oral epic hero to evolve under the growing pressures of literacy. In contrast to the oral epic hero, the literate-Ricardian protagonist, although he may be admirable and even a paragon of chivalry (like Gawain in *Sir Gawain and the Green Knight*), suffers inner conflict, self-doubt, and the humiliating realization that he has little significance and no power in relation to the cosmos, which is controlled by a transcendent, omnipotent, absolutely invulnerable deity which seems to have assumed the function and power of the oral epic hero (for example, Christ in the "vita de do-bet" section of *Piers Plowman*). Burrow notes the "unheroic" tone of Amans' words at the beginning of *Confessio Amantis* (96); I would add that Amans' outlook reflects the "literate" awareness of personal powerlessness and dysthymic lethargy:

> I may noght strecche up to the hevene
> Min hand, ne setten al in evene
> This world, which evere is in balance:
> It stant noght in my sufficance
> So grete thinges to compasse . . . .
> (i. 1-5; cited Burrow 96)[7]

The Ricardian protagonist—Troilus, Gawain, Amans, Will—must be more concerned with private inner experience, especially the intense yearning of romantic love or the hard introspective labor of identifying his sins, than with the gloriously single-minded, agonistic shaping of kingdoms and the cosmos by the force of his will. Even Troilus, whose deeds in battle might have had consequences of severe epic proportions for the Trojan conflict,[8] achieves nothing of political or cosmic significance. Instead, after several thousand lines of inner emotional storms generated by eros and betrayal, Chaucer flatly reports (without

[7]I cite Macaulay's edition of Gower's poetry throughout.
[8]Chaucer tells us that "For thousandes his [Troilus's] hondes maden deye, / As he that was withouten any peere, / Save Ector, in his tyme, as I kan heere" (V. 1802-04). I cite Benson's edition of Chaucer's works throughout.

mentioning a single sword-stroke) that Troilus is "despitously" slain by Achilles. He follows this bald statement with the image of Troilus' weightless soul being wafted into a static heaven; newly eviscerated and disengaged from the deeply felt experience of human companionship and conflict, the now thoroughly disembodied Troilus suddenly regards these feelings as alien and contemptibly ridiculous. Such a disinfecting, antiseptic passing contrasts with that of Beowulf, whose soul retains its visceral, uncompromising human dignity even in fiery transcendence, and whose palpable heroic presence continues to strengthen us earth-dwellers.

Burrow attributes the powerlessness of the Ricardian protagonist to the Lateran Council of 1215's mandate of annual confession (106-11), which created an enormous market for manuals instructing local priests in how to help a penitent apprehend the various species and subspecies of sins lurking furtively in the back of his mind. The literate tradition of scholastic moral philosophy rushed into this vacuum to provide a "comprehensive scheme of moral psychology which, like a reference grid on a map, would enable them [priest and penitent] to cover all the ground together systematically" (Burrow 107). The intensely literate nature of this exercise, with its lists and catalogues of abstractions essentially divorced from the concrete human lifeworld, profoundly changed the way individuals conceived of themselves.[9] The extent of this change is reflected in the inward focus and sense of powerlessness which dominate Ricardian protagonists, who are inevitably confronted with cosmically empowered antagonists. Burrow points out that these superhuman antagonists serve the same purpose as confessors: they thwart and dismantle all heroic pretensions with their devastatingly accurate prescience of the all-too-human protagonist's flaws (106-11). Moreover, they do not simply explain his faults to him; they persuade the protagonist to dramatize those faults to himself: Bertilak gets Gawain to accept the green girdle and Venus has Amans gaze at his own reflection in her mirror. When the awareness of his faults dawns on him, the protagonist feels overwhelmed with shame and humiliation and irremediably vulnerable to the antagonist's supernatural omniscience and (however gentle) trickery.

[9]Several studies have examined how confession influenced the process of self-reflection and contributed to the growth of self-awareness. See esp. Georgianna (79-119).

In his introduction, Burrow suggests that what he identifies as Ricardian "norms" "just do not apply" to the alliterative *Morte Arthure*, which must find its "place in a view of the period more comprehensive than mine" (10). I think Burrow is right that *Morte Arthure* needs a wider foundation than the one he builds, but many of the Ricardian traits he identifies are indeed in the poem, if in a less classical form. The wider foundation, I think, consists in regarding Ricardian "norms" as effects of the gradual internalization of literacy, which allows us to place them in a larger and slightly more flexible context. *Morte Arthure* is unique among poems of this period in that it demonstrates how the old oral-heroic values and the more recent literate-Ricardian values met and clashed. Although limitations of space prevent a thorough discussion of how this clash shapes the course of the entire poem,[10] we can examine three sections which are crucial for an understanding of Arthur's character: the beginning through Arthur's appointing Mordred as regent; Arthur's dream of Fortune; and Arthur's death.

The oral-heroic ideal collides with literate-Ricardian norms in the first twenty-five lines of the poem, a passage which reflects the platonic (that is, literate) division of the cosmos into two mutually exclusive realms: the eternal, divine, metaphysical world informed by a Christianized prime mover on the one hand, and the temporal, profane, physical world populated by human beings on the other. In the invocation (1-11), the poet emphasizes the transcendent nature of the "kyngdom of hevyne," where disembodied, and thus disinfected, souls hover perpetually in a nirvana-like orbit around the prime mover: the verbs the poet uses, "belde" and "byde," indicate that "blysse" is a kind of timeless, spaceless state in which one "is" but "does" nothing.[11] Lines 12-25, in contrast, emphasize the busy, concrete, agonistic nature of the sublunary realm. Here human beings are vibrantly, jubilantly corporeal: the poet uses concrete nouns, adjectives and verbs to state and restate the military deeds, firmly grounded in time and space, of the Round Table knights, who are "Doughty in theire doyngs" (20a), who "whanne wyth were," "Sloughe Lucyus" (23a), and "conqueryd . . . thorowe craftys of armes" (24). They are not only worthy to be remembered, but their extraordinary exploits have made them memorable, like the epic heroes Odysseus, Beowulf, and Roland. In fact, the significance of the enigmatic phrase "awke dedys" may be more accurately explained by

[10]For a fuller discussion of this issue, see my unpublished Ph.D. dissertation.
[11]I cite Hamel's edition of the Alliterative *Morte Arthure* throughout.

the poem's heavy oral "residue," which of necessity demanded heightened or bizarre—that is, memorable—characters and actions, than by any speculative reconstruction of the poet's artistic or didactic intentions. From this "oral" point of view, the discrepancy between the *OED* and *MED* definition of "awke" as "untoward, perverse" and their interpretation of its occurrence here as "odd, strange, marvelous," is essentially a non-issue: "awke" indicates primarily that these deeds are memorable in that they are extraordinary or bizarre. Thus Matthews's assertion that "awke" here indicates a deliberate, pejorative foreshadowing of the Round Table's sins (112-13; cf. Hamel, *Critical Edition* 254) is probably attributing too much intentionality to the poet; most likely he was reacting, pretty much automatically, to the residual demands of oral tradition. Nevertheless, the subtle mixing of layers or potentialities of meaning is peculiarly effective; like the dynamic image of a stone at the bottom of a shallow stream, it cannot tolerate analysis.

The only transition the poet has provided between these two realms is "heres" in line 11 and "here" in line 12. Otherwise they and the values they represent are butted one against the other in oral paratactic fashion. This tactic requires us to define for ourselves how the two worlds are related. Since the original reception of the poem was probably oral–aural—that is, it was most likely read aloud at social gatherings—its audience had to infer that relationship rapidly, without taking time to reflect. Very likely they assumed, as most of us do when we first read the poem (especially if we do so quickly) that the deeds of the Round Table knights, paragons of chivalry who "louede God Almyghty" (14b) were good works exemplifying the "vert[u]ous lywynge" (5b) which got one into heaven, and which were directed against the enemy's "schamesdede and synfull werkes" (3). We assume that Arthur and the Round Table knights act somehow in concert with God, and we affiliate ourselves with that holy alliance. What we have missed is the possibility that the literate-Ricardian ideal of "vert[u]ous lywynge" may not be the same as the oral-heroic ideal of "awke dedys"; the way in which an oral epic hero avoids "schame" and wins "wyrchippis" may, according to the literate-Ricardian ethos, constitute the commission of "schamesdede," especially if it does not acknowledge "wyrchip till Hym selvyn" (10).

The oral-heroic ideal emerges largely through the "werkes" and "doyngs" of Arthur himself, and his heroic nature is established right from the start: the catalogue of Arthur's subject realms downplays his right of inheritance and highlights his right to rule by virtue of conquest (26-51). Moreover, the security of his authority rests not so much on the external resource of a capable war machine (despite his later attribution of his kingship to his knights) as on his personal power. The *b*-verses of the catalogue emphasize that Uther's old empire could not have been reassembled without Arthur's incontrovertible will and impenetrable self-possession:

> Scathyll Scottlande by skyll he skyftys as hym lykys,
> And Wales of were he wane at hys will,
> Bathe Flaundrez and Fraunce fre til hym seluyn,
> . . . .
> By conqueste full cruell þey knewe hym fore lorde,
> . . . .
> Danmarke he dryssede all by drede of hym seluyn,
> Fra Swynn vnto Swetheryke with his swerde kene— . . . .
> (32-34, 43, 46-47)

In the next episode, in which Lucius' ambassadors demand tribute from Arthur, the poem narrows its focus from the entirety of Arthur's exploits to a particular incident in which we experience his forcefulness at close range. The terms of the quarrel between Arthur and Lucius have usually been seen as involving just war: does Lucius have the right to demand tribute and make war on Arthur? Does Arthur have the right to make war on Lucius? To date critics have reached no consensus on this question; for example, Matthews thinks Arthur's war is unjust from the start while Finlayson (*Morte Arthure*) believes Arthur's wars are justified until he begins his Italian campaign. It is practically impossible to decide confidently one way or the other, and in fact it is unnecessary to try, because the real terms of the quarrel are based on two different systems of determining legitimacy—one oral and the other literate. Lucius' claim to tribute is based entirely on the evidence of documents; his messenger attempts to intimidate Arthur with the literate authority of "credens," "targe," "notaries sygne," "rollez," and "regestre":

> 'Sir Lucius Iberius, the Emperour of Rome,
> Saluz the as sugett vndyre his sele ryche.
> It es credens, sir Kynge, with cruell wordez;
> Trow it for no trufles, his targe es to schewe.
> Now in this Newȝers Daye, with notaries sygne,
> I make the somouns in sale to sue for þi landys:

. . . .
Thy fadyr mad fewtee, we fynde in oure rollez,
In the regestre of Rome, who so ryghte lukez; . . . .'
(86-91, 112-13)

We can imagine that Arthur—having risked life and limb in order to consolidate his father's shattered kingdom and having earned his sovereignty with his own sweat and blood—must have been amazed at such an arrogant, effete assertion of imperial authority, and he must have regarded it with incredulous contempt. His enraged response to the senators reasserts the personal heroism on which his own sovereignty and the integrity of his kingdom rest:

The kynge blyschit on the beryn with his brode eghn,
Þat full brymly for breth brynte as the gledys;
Keste colours as kynge with crouell lates,
Luked as a lyon and on his lyppe bytes.
(116-19)

It is hard not to admire Arthur here; from the viewpoint of the oral-heroic ethos, Arthur's ferocity is an honest reaction to an outrageous counterfeit.[12] He defends his legitimacy by reasserting the tried truth of the heroic ethos, a defense that emerges brilliantly in the voiced plosive violence of the *b*-alliteration, which echoes that in lines 106-07. When the senators threatened that Lucius would "Bryne Bretayn þe brade and bryttyn thy knyghtys / And brynge the bouxsomly as a beste with brethe whare hym lykes," Arthur reacts with "breth," not fear, and assumes the identity not of a domesticated "beste" but that of an untamed "lyon," a reaction the senators apparently are not used to: they are literally knocked off their feet by Arthur's overwhelming heroic presence. Arthur's incontrovertibility and absolute self-possession are

[12]This episode calls to mind Clanchy's citation of the Earl Warenne's response to Edward I's *quo warranto* proceedings. Although the story may well be apocryphal, it aptly demonstrates the intensity of the clash of oral and literate standards: "The king disturbed some of the great men of the land through his judges wanting to know by what warrant [*quo warranto*] they held their lands, and if they did not have a good warrant, he immediately seized their lands. Among the rest, the Earl Warenne was called before the king's judges. Asked by what warrant he held, he produced in their midst an ancient and rusty sword and said: 'Look at this, my lords, this is my warrant! For my ancestors came with William the Bastard and conquered their lands with the sword, and by the sword I will defend them from anyone intending to seize them'" (21-22).

so concentrated in his face that his glare devastates the senators and disintegrates their cool pretension to ascendancy:

> 'Sir' sais þe senatour 'so Crist mott me helpe,
> Þe voute of thi vesage has woundyde vs all!
> Thow arte þe lordlyeste lede þat euer I one lukyde;
> By lukynge, withowttyn lesse, a lyon the semys.'
> (136-39)

Arthur's ability to dismantle imperial (that is, literate) authority and reassert his own (oral-heroic) authority is elegantly expressed in the senators' appropriately ironic cowering as dogs ("kenetez") "before þe kynge seluyn" (122) and assuming "bouxsomly as a beste" the humiliated posture which they had intended for him.

This image of the enraged Arthur glaring down upon the prostrate senators exemplifies the power differential in Arthur's relationships with others: it is agonistic and polarized, and it emerges not from an abstract investment of authority (such as that conferred by written documents) but from Arthur's own incontrovertible, impenetrable will. His apparently infinite self-possession gives him a god-like omnipotence; he becomes numinous—magnetically fascinating, repulsively terrifying, and certainly memorable. The senators, on the other hand, whose idea of authority is based on literate abstract legalism, cannot match Arthur's mesmerizing personal power. Although the poet never describes their appearance, we may well imagine them as bookish and physically ineffectual.

Later, in the Giant's Tower Council, Arthur's justification of a counterattack on Rome is based on the norms of the oral-heroic ethos (271-287). Except for the mention in line 274b of "cronicles," Arthur's argument is based on oral tradition, "as awlde men telles" (278b). Of course, we cannot make too much of either line, because the poet was no doubt most immediately concerned with satisfying each line's alliterative demands. The rest of Arthur's argument, however, is based on the oral-heroic standard that rights accrue to those victorious in battle: the winners earn an honest profit from honest fighting, much as whoever wins the trial by battle in the *Chanson de Roland* "at dreit" 'is in the right.' He asserts that his elders lost Rome only because there were no able-bodied warriors to defend it; his "ancestres" Belyn, Brenne, and later Constantyne won it fairly "be craftez of armes" (284).[13] In other words, the "euydens" Arthur adduces has practically nothing to do with written documentation: it is simply the right of victorious heroic warriors.

The feast Arthur gives for the Roman embassy reiterates, in slightly different terms, the point of the preceding episode: Arthur's physical presence, will, and absolute self-possession reassert the greater legitimacy of oral-heroic authority over literate authority. Arthur confronts the senator (presumably the spokesman for the Roman embassy) with a phalanx of food which he uses as an extension of his own heroic stature: such a plenitude of food is indigestible. As courtly and refined as the dishes are, their sheer number and concrete weight present an inexorable physicality which the senator could not begin to consume and assimilate to his own clerkly purposes.

Arthur, however, is in complete control of the visceral power which the feast represents: his very selfhood encloses it, possesses it, and shapes its energy according to his own heroic will. The poet emphasizes Arthur's control by framing his presentation of the feast with four formulas built on the word "self."[14] All four formulas— "Arthure hym seluyn" (172b), "þe kynge seluen" (176b), "þe kynge seluyn" (210b), and "þe Conquerour hym seluen" (216a)—focus our attention

[13]In his message to Lucius, Arthur again defines "ryghte" in agonistic terms; it is something to be demonstrated, not merely pronounced:

Comande hym kenely wyth crewell wordez,
Cayre owte of my kyngryke with his kydd knyghtez;
In caase that he will noghte, þat cursede wreche,
Com for his curtaisie and countere me ones!
Thane sall we rekken full rathe whatt ryghte þat he claymes,
Thus to ryot þis rewme and raunsone the pople:
Thare sall it derely be delte with dynttez of handez.
(1271-77)

[14]While Foley has brilliantly and convincingly demonstrated the need for caution in any attempt to reduce the complexity of traditional phraseology to simple formulaic templates, for our purposes Fry's elegant and practical definition of the Old English formula can be extended to the Middle English formula: the formula itself is "a group of words, one-half line in length, which shows evidence of being the direct product of a formulaic system" (204); the system is "a group of half-lines, usually loosely related metrically and semantically, which are related in form by the identical relative placement of two elements, one a variable word or element of a compound usually supplying the alliteration, and the other a constant word or element of a compound, with approximately the same distribution of nonstressed elements" (203).

on the unique personal power and self-possession which Arthur brings to the office of kingship. Arthur's authority is defined and constituted by his selfhood, by his personal embodiment of the oral-heroic ethos, not by any literate or abstract principle. Kingship belongs to "þe doughtyeste," "þe Conquerour," the man whose absolute self-possession can protect us much more effectively than we could protect ourselves. When Arthur sarcastically describes his display of power as "feble" (226a), the awe-stricken senator acknowledges that Arthur's "realtee" (228a) surpasses that of Rome. Hamel glosses "realtee" here as 'pomp, splendour' rather than 'sovereignty' (*Critical Edition* 491), but the context does not tolerate such a fine (that is, literate) distinction between concrete and abstract levels of meaning. Arthur has earned, and now guards, his kingship in physical, concrete, agonistic terms; his demonstration of sovereign power in those terms comprises the very essence of his sovereignty.

Thus far we have seen how Arthur is "ware in [his] werkes" (19a) and "doughty in [his] doyngs" (20a) on the battlefield and in court; among his other "awke dedys," however, is how he "dredde[s] ay schame" (20b), which his encounter with the Roman senators also illustrates. After the senator has "somonde" him, Arthur replies that no one has ever addressed him so impudently, but that he will "tak concell" before formally answering the charge:

> 'Thow has me somonde' quod þe kynge 'and said what þe lykes;
> Fore sake of thy soueraynge I suffre the þe more.
> Sen I [was] corounnde in kyth wyth crysum enoyntede,
> Was neuer creature to me þat carpede so large!
> Bot I sall tak concell at kynges enoyntede,
> . . . .
> Wyrke aftyre the wytte of my wyes knyghttes;
> To warpe wordez in waste no wyrchipe it were,
> Ne wilfully in þis wrethe to wreken my seluen.'
> (140-44, 149-51)

At first glance Arthur's response seems to be simply an admirable restraint of anger and a deliberate resistance to falling into the deadly sin of wrath. If, however, we read the passage with an awareness of the oral-heroic values which he has already demonstrated, we can see that Arthur's real concern here is his "wyrchipe." In fact, the last thing Arthur fears is anger—like that of Achilles or Beowulf, Arthur's anger is what has prospered him and his knights: through heroic wrath Arthur has created his kingdom and has successfully protected it from the Romans' first assault.[15] Moreover, Arthur's heroic anger is what he does as well as what he feels, because the oral-heroic ethos demands that he not simply experience it (and contemplate or "process" it, as we might), but become it, embody it, allow it to realize itself through him as the heroic conservator of social order.

But what does heroic anger have to do with *wyrchipe*? Within the oral-heroic ethos anger must be used appropriately, in such a way as to avoid "schame." Hamel glosses "wyrchipe" in line 150 as "honorable behavior" (*Critical Edition* 529). Although she makes fine distinctions in meaning among this and other occurrences of the word, the dominant ideas common to all its occurrences in *Morte Arthure* are those of 'honor' and 'esteem.' A perusal of the citations from Anglo-Saxon and Middle English works under the entry "worship" (sb.) in the *OED* shows that the meaning of ME "wyrchipe" does not seem to have changed from that of the OE "weorðscipe," "worth, respect, honour, dignity, glory" (Clark Hall 404), from which it derives.[16] But what exactly makes a man worthy or honorable? More to the point, how does Arthur avoid "schame" and become worthy and honorable?

First of all, Arthur implicitly defines "wyrchipe" in terms of concrete behavior, as any oral epic hero would: he refuses "To warpe wordez in waste" (150a); he also refuses "wilfully . . . to wreken my seluen" (151a). Hamel glosses "wilfully" as "in a self-willed way"

[15]Beowulf consistently transforms his rage into disciplined actions which protect the Danes and the Geats. Beowulf himself tells Hygelac how his anger enabled him to serve retributive justice to Grendel:

hyt ne mihte swā,
syððan ic on yrre uppriht āstōd.
Tō lang ys tō reccenne, hu i(c ð)ām lēodsceaðan
yfla gehwylces *o*ndlēan forgeald; . . . .
(2091b-94; I cite Klaeber's edition throughout)

'He [Grendel] could not do so [overcome Beowulf], after I stood
up in anger. It is too long to tell how I paid the people's enemy
a requital for every evil.' [translation mine]

While Achilles handles his anger less deliberately than Beowulf, the rage he feels at Patroclus' death is far more compelling than the slight Agamemnon has dealt him, and when it forces him to emerge from his sulk in order to avenge his friend, he turns the tide of war (incidentally, to be sure) to the Greeks' favor.

[16]See also the extensive citations in Bosworth-Toller under "weorþscipe" (1204).

(*Critical Edition* 528), which seems to contradict the poet's heroic portrait of Arthur, since his will, vivified by anger, is precisely what has prospered him and his people. An easy solution to this problem would be to decide that the poet used "wilfully" because it was alliteratively convenient, and that he did not consider how it affected his characterization of Arthur. However, the poet did have at least one alternative, "wekyrly" 'quickly' (2104), which would have satisfied the alliterative requirement in a neutral way. The answer to this problem lies in the passage's emphasis on control. Rather ironically, Arthur uses "wilfully" to indicate a loss of self-control, a loss of volition. Just as he declines to waste words, to lose control verbally, Arthur refuses to allow the contemptuous senator to provoke him into losing control physically. In retaining control over his temper—over his oral-heroic will and wrath—, Arthur retains control over the diplomatic contest; he maintains the integrity of the hospitality with which he has already bested the senators. The shame Arthur would incur in assaulting the senator would be commensurate with his own vulnerability to a simple diplomatic ruse.

Arthur's command to Kay to look out for "my wyrchipe" in preparing the feast for the Roman embassy emphasizes Arthur's ability to extend his self-control almost infinitely, so that his influence dominates other men's experience of power absolutely:

> He commande sir Cayous, 'Take kepe to thoos lordez,
> To styghtyll þa steryn men as theire statte askys:
> That they bee herberde in haste in thoos heghe chambres,
> Sythin sittandly in sale seruyde ther aftyr,
> That they fynd na fawte of fude to thiere horsez,
> Nowthire [of] weyn ne waxe ne welthe in þis erthe.
> Spare for no spyceryye bot spende what þe lykys,
> That there be largesce on lofte and no lake founden;
> If þou my wyrchipe wayte, wy, be my trouthe,
> Þou sall haue gersoms full grett þat gayne sall þe euere.'
> (156-165)

Arthur's "wyrchipe," his 'worth' and 'honor,' like his "realtee," his 'kingship,' is not simply an abstract ontological ideal; it is embodied in this concrete, subtly agonistic demonstration of his sovereignty—his ability to overwhelm, to stand above, from some inviolate place "on lofte"—that is personal as well as political. The senator can "fynd no fawte" in it, "no lake," no chink in the hospitality which Arthur is able to realize. When he reports to Lucius, the senator first extols Arthur's visceral, incontrovertible heroism, and then he explains that Arthur's concern for "wyrchipe allone" 'worthiness alone,' makes him incapable of being intimidated: "He wyll werraye, iwysse: beware ȝif þe lykes!" (546).

Wyrchipe, then, is both the integrity of the hero's will, the impenetrability of his self-possession, and others' recognition that the hero's personal power guarantees the integrity and safety of his social order. That is why Arthur does not want to "warpe wordez in waste" (150a): any *ineffectual* action would impugn his incontrovertibility, his personal power, upon which his own survival and that of his realm depend. That is also why winning "wyth were" comprises "wyrchippis many" (22). An anabolic, wholing action, it gathers together under the hero's cosmic protection that which would otherwise remain fragmented and chaotic. *Wyrchipe* neatly summarizes the oral-heroic value system, especially its imperative to create and maintain order by means of the hero's will, unadulterated by inner conflict and vivified by heroic anger.

The essence of the oral-heroic ethos is its reliance on human will and feeling and its assumption that these are powerful, effective agents for maintaining stability. While the poem betrays a preoccupation with this perception of the human condition, it also concerns itself with the literate-Ricardian ethos, whose fundamental assumption (as we shall see later) is diametrically opposed to the primitive humanism of the oral-heroic ethos. The struggle of these two ethical systems for ascendancy is implicit even in the invocation. Here the cosmos is split into two mutually exclusive halves: the divine, eternal, metaphysical "kyngdom of hevyne" (6b) of a perfect, Christianized, platonic prime mover and this "wrechyde werlde" (5a), the profane, temporal, concrete world of degenerate human experience. However, the prime mover, "grett glorious Godde" (1a), is not conceptualized (in a fully literate way) as some transcendent ontological essence or idea; it is personified as an earthly king. More specifically, this king is somehow comparable to Arthur. Although the poem does not deliberately do so, it cannot help but invite us to compare God, the king of heaven, and Arthur, the greatest king of the sublunary world in terms of what makes a king a king: "realtee" and "wyrchipe."

These terms are demonstrated largely through the narration of Arthur's actions and others' reactions to him, but they are also elegantly implied in the "self" formulas referring to Arthur which focus our perception of him through parataxis and redundancy. For example, the four "self" formulas which frame the feast for the Roman ambassadors juxtapose the heroic "self" (what Neumann has called the "Great Individual" [303]) with "Arthur" (172b), "kynge" (176b), "kyng" (210b), and "Conqueror" (216a). These reiterated identifications, embedded and repeated in a concrete, narrative context, form a composite portrait of Arthur as the greatest exemplar of the oral-heroic ethos.

However, the poet also refers to God by means of "self" formulas just as he uses them to refer to Arthur, and they define our perception of God through the same oral dynamics of parataxis and redundancy. They are concentrated in the invocation, which represents the metaphysical half of the dichotomized literate-Ricardian cosmos. In fact, the items which congregate around God's "self" and imply the terms of his sovereignty are all abstractions: "thurgh grace of Hym seluen" (1b); "in blysse wyth Hym seluen" (8b); and "bot wyrchip till Hym selvyn" (10b). Unlike Arthur, God is not defined through concrete action. While his grace has efficacy, we cannot watch it work; it seems to exist amorphously, apparently doing nothing. Moreover, our expected response to this inscrutable grace, "blysse," is neither agonistic nor concrete—it too is an inscrutable state of being, not doing. Finally, the context of "wyrchip"—"And wysse me to werpe owte som worde at this tym / That nothyre voyde be ne vayne, bot wyrchip till Hym selvyn" (9-10)—is the closest the invocation gets to anything like concrete action: the act of composing and reciting this poem is intended to acknowledge God's "honor" within "the kyngdom of hevyne" (6b) and the literate-Ricardian ethos. We have seen that in the oral-heroic ethos, *wyrchipe* refers to both the hero's incontrovertible will and others' recognition that the integrity of their society depends on that heroic will. Since in most other works of the Ricardian period the representations of the eternal, divine half of the cosmos are all incontrovertible—their power over human beings is absolute (e.g., Bertilak)—"wyrchip" here probably means just that: God's power is indisputable within the sub-lunary realm of human experience as well as within "the kyngdom of hevyne," a fact which we humans eventually have no choice but to acknowledge. In other words, the function and character of the human hero have been appropriated by God; somehow the struggle of the hero against his enemy, human or monstrous, has been replaced by God's assertion of divine superiority to human nature. After all, God is absolutely invulnerable in a way the mortal human hero can never be: God is non-physical and therefore eternal and utterly inviolate because he needs no defenses, nor can there ever be any effective offense against him. "[W]yrchip till Hym selvyn" (10), then, could very well mean the same thing as it does in reference to Arthur, but in a very different context: both the perfect incontrovertibility of God's will and our human recognition of his absolute power over us, along with the additional acknowledgement that human heroism is ephemeral and therefore specious. Any human claim to heroic power would then be arrogant and presumptuous. Clearly, then, *wyrchipe* and its appropriate investment are at the center of the conflict between the oral-heroic ethos and the literate-Ricardian ethos.

The poem first implies that the oral-heroic ideal of *wyrchipe* is arrogant and presumptuous when Arthur appoints Mordred as regent (625-92). This episode subtly undermines the oral-heroic ethos by demonstrating the blindness inherent in the relatively non-differentiated oral-heroic character in general and in Arthur in particular. Arthur's impenetrable oral-heroic will prevents him from recognizing Mordred's envy and human weakness, as only a more reflective, introspective—that is, literate—consciousness could do.

Like the scene depicting the feast for the Roman embassy, this episode emphasizes the oral-heroic nature of Arthur's kingship by portraying the interaction of Arthur and Mordred. Arthur's pronouncements take up most of the scene, and the uncompromising intensity and clarity of his statements reemphasize the extraordinary personal power which comprises the oral-heroic basis of his sovereignty. In the eight lines in which Arthur formally appoints Mordred as regent, ten first person singular forms stress not only Arthur's personal power but the extent to which that personal power shapes his public authority:

> 'I am in purpos to passe perilous wayes,
> To kaire with my kene men to conquere ȝone landes;
> To owttraye myn enmy, ȝif auenture it schewe,
> That ocupyes myn heritage, þe Empyre of Rome.
> I sette ȝow here a soueraynge, ascente ȝif ȝowe lykys,
> That es me sybb, my syster son sir Mordrede hym seluen,
> Sall be my leuetenaunte with lordchipez ynewe
> Of all my lele legemen þat my landez ȝemes.'
> (640-47)

Mordred's carefully deferential response to Arthur and his soft-spoken, submissive manner provide a striking contrast to Arthur's indomitable assertions:

> 'I beseke ȝow sir,   as my sybbe lorde,
> Þat ȝe will for charyté   cheese ȝow anoþer,
> For if ȝe putte me in þis plytte   ȝowre pople es dyssauyde;
> To present a prynce astate   my powere es symple.'
> (681-84)

Mordred's subservient posture before his uncle reminds us of the Roman senators' "Cowchide as kenetez" (122) before the leonine Arthur. Unlike Arthur, Mordred does not have the heroic will necessary to command authority; he appears to be as extraordinarily ineffectual as Arthur is incontrovertible. Actually, he is like the typical Ricardian protagonist: not merely aware of his limitations, he is absolutely convinced of his personal powerlessness, like Gower's Amans: "It stant noght in my sufficance / So grete thinges to compasse" (i. 4-5). Immediately after confessing his incompetence, Mordred adds that "When oþer of werre wysse   are wyrchipide hereaftyre, / Than may I for sothe   be sette bott at lyttill" (685-86). Rather than being "sette bott at lyttill," Mordred would like to be considered worthy, which requires, in accordance with the oral-heroic ethos, that he concretely prove his personal power and will in battle. The opportunity to do so is exactly what he requests in the next two lines; he has even prepared, at his own expense, a company of knights. Instead of receiving gratitude, however, like the barons at the Giant's Tower Council, Mordred gets a lecture on his duty not as a warlord but as Arthur's nephew, and then a threat: "That thow ne wyrk my will,   thow watte whatte it menes" (692).

We do not know the specifics of the punishment, but obviously Mordred does, as his humiliated Ricardian ego capitulates to Arthur's heroic will. Mordred has never had a chance to prove himself because he has always been dominated by his uncle's power—that is, Arthur's *wyrchipe*—and he has clearly learned his lessons of helplessness very well. While Arthur fights Lucius, however, Mordred compensates for his personal powerlessness by committing *lese majesté* and usurping Arthur's sovereignty as thoroughly as he can, both lands and queen, publicly and privately. In other words, Mordred desperately wants "wyrchipe allone" (541b), and so he steals it from the person most capable of mentoring him, but who will not because he is obsessed with it himself. In modern terms, Mordred suffers from pathologically low self-esteem, and his sense of powerlessness begets his violent one-upmanship; in late fourteenth-century terms, Mordred falls into the deadly sin of pride. Moreover, because of the limitations of his oral-heroic consciousness, Arthur cannot recognize Mordred's "worship envy" any more than he can recognize the potential for it in himself.

Nevertheless, during the following episodes which feature him, Arthur impeccably demonstrates the oral-heroic ideal condensed in *wyrchipe*: in his defeats of the St. Michael's Mount giant and Lucius, as well as his conquests of Metz, Como, and Milan, he uses his personal power to establish or restore social order, which ultimately benefits his subjects old and new (see esp. 3068-77 and 3128-33). During the Tuscan campaign, however, the poet shifts his focus from images of honest fighting intended to reestablish order to images of wanton, indiscriminate wasting:

> Into Tuskane he tournez,   when þus wele tymede,
> Takes townnes full tyte   with towrres full heghe;
> Walles he welte down,   wondyd knyghtez,
> Towrres he turnes   and turmentez þe pople;
> Wroghte wedewes full wlonke,   wrotherayle synges,
> Ofte wery and wepe   and wryngen theire handis,
> And all he wastys with werre   thare he awaye rydez—
> Thaire welthes and theire wonny[n]ges   wandrethe he wroghte!
> Thus they spryngen and sprede   and sparis bot lyttill,
> Spoylles dispetouslye   and spillis theire vynes,
> Spendis vnsparely   þat sparede was lange; . . . .
> (3150-61)

The destruction Arthur wreaks on Tuscany is unlike that inflicted on Metz and Como, because there is no mention of his "Reconsaill[ing] the comouns" (3130a) and rebuilding what has been destroyed. Rather, it is an end in itself, an all-consuming self-indulgence, and soon almost everyone in Europe knows it: "Fro Spayne into Spruyslande,   the worde of hym sprynges / And spekynngs of his spencis—   disspite es full hugge!" (3162-63). Even by oral-heroic standards, the *wyrchipe* that Arthur cares about so exclusively is now essentially identical to the brutal behavior of the giant of St. Michael's Mount: Arthur is using his heroic power to destroy, and others recognize that the integrity of their society is threatened, not protected, by that power.

The next episode, Arthur's dream of Fortune, continues this pejoration of oral-heroic values: it justifies Arthur's downfall by casting him as a usurper, a destroyer of social and cosmic order, motivated only by the deadly sin of pride. In the course of doing so, it also demonstrates how the literate-Ricardian ethos co-opts the human hero's role and confines it to the supernatural arena.

In their interpretation of the dream, the philosophers make no distinction between the treachery of Arthur's recent deeds and the integrity of his previous conquests:

> 'Freke' sais the philosophre 'thy fortune es passede,
> For thow sall fynd hir thi foo, frayste when the lykes.
> Thow arte at þe hegheste, I hette the forsothe—
> Chalange nowe when thow will, thow cheuys no more!
> Thow has schedde myche blode, and schalkes distroyede,
> Sakeles, in cirquytrie, in sere kynges landis.
> Schryfe the of thy schame and schape for thyn ende!'
> (3394-3400)

At the beginning of the poem Arthur's conquest of France provides clear evidence of his good character and his oral-heroic integrity:

> And he had couerede the coroun of the kyth ryche,
> Of all that Vter in erthe aughte in his tym—
> . . . .
> Bathe Flaundrez and Fraunce fre til hym seluyn . . . .
> (28-29, 34)

But 3400 lines later it is evidence of his evil character and literate-Ricardian "cirquytrie" (3399a). The philosophers' strategy of alluding to Arthur's defeat of Frollo, which pre-dates the events recounted in the poem, retroactively condemns Arthur's earlier conquests, which the poem unquestionably presented as admirable and honorable; those glorious achievements are lumped indiscriminately with his most recent aggressions and assimilated to their heinousness. We are thus forced to see Arthur's entire heroic career from a profoundly shifted perspective, from which it appears as nothing but a series of "vnresonable dedis" (3452b).

The poem does not account for this egregious inconsistency or for the sudden shift in Arthur's behavior. The reason for this deficit (a deficit only according to fully literate consciousness and conventional literary taste) is that the poet's method of composition was dominated by residual oral habit: even with pen in hand, he could not conceive of logically and systematically representing the complex, turbulent course which the contending currents of Arthur's thoughts and feelings might be taking. Rather, he could only represent what he could visualize: Arthur's interactions with people and things in an external, concrete, agonistic landscape. Having the philosophers baldly identify Arthur's sin is the closest he could get to representing an intrapsychic process. However, from our perspective of fully internalized literacy, we can see that what has changed is not so much Arthur's behavior (even taking the Tuscan "chevauché" into account) or his thoughts and feelings; what has changed drastically is the ethical context in which he is being judged. The literate-Ricardian ideal of "vert[u]ous lywynge" is not the same as the oral-heroic ideal of "awke dedys": the way in which Arthur avoids "schame" and wins "wyrchippis" constitutes, according to the literate-Ricardian ethos, the commission of "schamesdede."

Moreover, Arthur's potential to commit "schamesdede" is not restricted to the sublunary plane; in the literate-Ricardian construction of the universe Arthur poses a future threat, one with potentially cosmic consequences. After he has conquered Rome, Arthur declares that he intends to "graythe ouer þe Grette See with gud men of armes / To reuenge the Renke that on the Rode dyede" (3216-17). However, the prescient philosophers inform Arthur that such is not his destiny; rather, the task of avenging Christ will fall to Charlemagne and Godfrey (3422-23; 3426-31). In short, Arthur intends to usurp the destinies of both Charlemagne and Godfrey, an action which would also rob Fortune of her role in orchestrating Christian eschatological history. While Arthur's usurpation of Frollo's kingdom is of merely earthly significance, his proposed usurpation of the two other Worthies' destinies, and thus of Fortune's agency, could affect the entire cosmos: Arthur would be challenging the theological construction of the dichotomized literate-Ricardian cosmos. In violating sublunary boundaries of time and space, he would be misappropriating the transcendent, providential nature of God, abducting it from its supernatural sphere of influence, rendering it earthbound, and perhaps even reducing it to his personal aggrandizement.

While this drive to extend order throughout the cosmos is the cornerstone of the oral-heroic ethos, Arthur's literate-Ricardian philosophers identify it as "cirquytrie" (3399a), the species of pride defined by Chaucer's Parson as "Presumpcioun."[17] However, beyond their explicit condemnation, the poem covertly degrades the oral-heroic ethos. Fortune and the philosophers work in tandem as literate-Ricardian "confessors" to undermine oral-heroic values.

Fortune is essentially an agent of God: she herself swears "be Criste þat me made" (3385b), and her angelic descent from heaven (3250 ff.) certainly suggests a providential role. She seems to personify the eschatological force that not only administers death but directs the destinies of those chosen to execute providential history. It is evidently Fortune's responsibility to guarantee that history will evolve through the Pagan and Jewish ages to its Christian fulfillment; accordingly, Fortune must see that Arthur inaugurates the Christian age, but she must also make sure that he does not interfere with the destinies of Charlemagne or Godfrey.

In this literate-Ricardian worldview, God is the real hero whose indisputable will comprises the ability to *be* autonomously and invulnerably, and who *ex officio* controls everything that is not similarly autonomous. Arthur's dream of Fortune contrasts this absolutely static, eternal power to *be* with the temporal and therefore relatively inconsequential power to *act*. Moreover, any human action can be counteracted by one of God's agents (literate-Ricardian "confessors") who demonstrate the superiority of God's being by neutralizing the effects of human endeavor. Thus Fortune erodes the careers of all human rulers, even those of the Nine Worthies.

Accordingly, Fortune's declaration that Arthur does not control his own destiny implies that his oral-heroic will is at best merely incidental to the success he experiences:

> 'The aughte to wirchipe my will,   and thow wele cowthe,
> Of all the valyant men   that euer was in erthe;
> Fore all thy wirchipe in werre   by me has thow wonnen.
> I hafe bene frendely, freke,   and fremmede till oþer—
> That has þow fownden, in faithe,   and fele of þi biernez.
> Fore I fellid down sir Frolle,   with frowrede knyghtes;
> Forethi the fruytes of Fraunce   are freely thynne awen.
> Thow sall þe chayere escheue: I chese þe my selfen
> Before all þe cheftaynes   chosen in this erthe!'
>
> (3340-48)

[17]Cf. the *Parson's Tale*: "Presumpcioun is whan a man undertaketh an emprise that hym oghte nat do, or elles that he may nat do; and this is called surquidrie" (402).

Fortune's greater will, her ability to control the outcome of Arthur's endeavors, is consistent with her larger role as agent of God and orchestrator of providential history. The philosophers, however, without explaining how they infer this conclusion from Fortune's declaration, tell Arthur that he himself is responsible for that same outcome (see 3398-99, 3403-04, and 3452-53). This contradiction subverts the oral-heroic ethos: first, Fortune deflates the ethos by trivializing Arthur's ability to act and the significance of his intention; she renders his heroic will into inconsequential wishful thinking, so that his heroic actions are no longer meaningful and authentically powerful. Thus both Arthur's heroic "will" and his heroic "wyrchipe" are presumptuous illusions. Their apparent consequences are not his at all, nor do they even have a human provenance; they are in reality supernaturally determined phenomena which originate in a supernatural source.

The philosophers further undermine the oral-heroic ethos not merely by urging Arthur to confess his sinful actions, but particularly by emphasizing his sinful state of being: Arthur is in a state of "cirquytrie" (3399a), which is "thy schame" (3400a); he ought to "kaste in thyne herte" (3406b) and "amende thy mode" (3454a). Quite clearly, his feelings—especially that heroic wrath that is the *sine qua non* of oral-heroic consciousness—are not merely blameworthy but the source of all Arthur's trouble.

Moreover, the portraits of the Nine Worthies in Arthur's dream seem designed to devalue the Worthies' oral-heroic posture, especially the typically oral-heroic conflation of personal power and political authority. All six Pagan and Jewish Worthies' *ubi sunt* speeches focus on their lost personal and public sovereignty; Joshua's is typical:

> 'I was in Surrye a syr   and sett by myn one
> As souerayne and seyngnour   of sere kynges londis.
> Now of my solace, I am   full sodanly fallen,
> And for sake of my syn   ȝone sete es me rewede!'
> (3312-15)

Before these individual complaints, and immediately after Arthur's vision of Fortune, they explain as a chorus that they have been damned for carousing at the expense of the commons (3270-77). That is, before the "confessor" Fortune forced them into the more introspective literate-Ricardian consciousness, the Worthies had single-mindedly used their heroic will and power not to create and preserve social order, but to destroy it, all in the pursuit of a degenerate form of *wyrchipe*. Moreover, the Worthies' chorus accurately reflects Arthur's "chevauché" through Tuscany, and the similarity implies that Arthur will suffer the same fate as the Pagan and Jewish Worthies unless he "amende . . . [his] mode" (3454a) before it is too late—that is, unless he recognizes and confesses his "cirquytrie" before he dies. Whether he does or not, though, the Worthies' laments, Arthur's scorched-earth Tuscan campaign, and the philosophers' pejorative reassessment of his earlier honorable conquests all have the same purpose: to dissolve the normally absolute distinction between the hero and the violator. Both use oral-heroic will, wrath, and power to destroy, not to create, order.

The philosophers devalue Arthur's oral-heroic posture in yet another way. Although they admit that he will be celebrated by future generations for his heroism (3439-45), their attitude is like that of Old Age in *The Parlement of the Thre Ages*:

> Now hafe I neuened ȝow the names of nyne of þe beste
> Þat euer were in this werlde wiste appon erthe,
> And the doghtyeste of dedis in thaire dayes tyme;
> Bot doghteynes when dede comes ne dare noghte habyde.
> (580-83)

Old Age is a kind of *memento mori* figure who disabuses Youth and Middle Age of their illusions of worldly power. Both he and Arthur's philosophers clearly represent the literate-Ricardian world view, in which any human effort to assert power for any purpose is certainly futile—primarily because human beings are vulnerable to death—and insubordinate, because to make such an effort in the first place is to subvert the authority and omnipotence of the supernatural. That is, since the literate-Ricardian ethos regards all assertions of human power as surely ineffectual and probably blasphemous, and since the oral-heroic ethos grows out of the need to assert human power in order to ward off the forces of entropy, any oral-heroic behavior must be sinful, specifically the deadly sin of *cirquytrie*. In contrast, within the oral-heroic ethos, escaping death by means of heroic courage is as appropriate as accepting death with heroic courage. Someone who is not "fæge" 'fated to die' might perish for lack of such courage, and, as Beowulf advises Unferth, the supernatural might even assist someone who demonstrates it: "Wyrd oft nereð / unfǣgne eorl, þonne his ellen dēah!" (572b-73).

In other words, it is always worth fighting because you do not know if you are destined to die until you die fighting. This is the fundamental difference between the oral-heroic ethos and literate-Ricardian ethos; as Thomas Greene notes, the oral-heroic construction of the supernatural approves of the human exercise of power:

> [t]he subject of all epic poetry might thus be said to be politics, but a politics not limited to society, a politics embracing the natural and the fabulous worlds, embracing even the moral or spiritual worlds they sometimes shadow forth, and involving ultimately the divine. The implications expand to suggest, if not frankly to assert, a cosmic power struggle. The heroic act assumes its highest prestige by its divine authorization . . . .
>
> (17-18)

In contrast, the literate-Ricardian conception of the supernatural disapproves of such resistance and is constantly enforcing the injunction that human beings must feel and be essentially helpless. In the oral-heroic ethos, the process of coming to terms with mortality celebrates and honors human nature because that nature is endowed with the power and will to *act*; in the literate-Ricardian ethos, that same process humiliates and shames human nature because it is not endowed with the ability to *be* autonomously and invulnerably. Accordingly, the philosophers' final advice to "þe doughtyeste þat euer was duelland in erthe" (3443) is simply "And mekely aske mercy for mede of thy saule!" (3455).

However, Arthur never does so. Although he finally admits that all his good earthly fortune was a gift of God, Arthur never confesses the sin of *cirquytrie* that provoked Fortune's vengeful abandonment of him:

> 'I thanke þe, Gode, of Thy grace with a gud wyll,
> That gafe vs vertue and witt to vencows þis beryns
> And vs had grauntede þe gree of theis gret lordes!
> He sent vs neuer no schame ne schenchipe in erthe,
> Bot euer ȝit þe ouerhande of all oþer kynges.'
>
> (4296-4300)

What the poet dramatizes instead is Arthur's very self-possessed provision for a peaceful succession:

> 'Constantyn, my cosyn, he sall the corown bere

Alls becommys hym of kynde, ȝife Criste will hym thole.
Beryn, fore my benyson, thowe berye ȝone lordys
That in baytaille with brondez are broghte owte of lyfe;
And sythen merke manly to Mordrede children,
That they bee sleyghely slayne and slongen in watyrs—
Latt no wykkyde wede waxe ne wrythe one this erthe!
I warne fore thy wirchipe, wirke alls I bydde.'
(4316-23)

Clearly, Arthur's oral-heroic commitment to "wyrchipe allone" (541b) has not completely disintegrated: his oral-heroic will and wrath still enable him to delegate action which will protect the social order of which he has been the guarantor.

In any case, the mere fact of his death seems to be more consonant with oral epic than with Ricardian verbal art; Ricardian protagonists, like Amans or Gawain, survive their ordeals only to live with the constant awareness of the shamefulness and powerlessness of their human nature. While Arthur does learn from his encounter with his Ricardian "confessor" Fortune that his human power and *wyrchipe* are limited, he continues to exercise them until the moment of his death. This lesson is entirely consistent with Greene's observation that the epic struggles to find some equilibrium between heroic expansion and "tragic contraction of capacity and control" (16): "The hero learns—and the reader [or listener] with him—wherein lies his power and to what degree, and wherein lie his limitations and to what degree. The conclusion formalizes these discoveries" (17).

What does the conclusion of *Morte Arthure* "formalize"? Despite the undoubted finality of Arthur's death, there is no formally stated resolution of the ethical and existential questions raised by the conflict of the oral-heroic and literate-Ricardian ethoi. However, Arthur does ensure a peaceful succession, and in that sense his *wyrchipe* has survived his personal mortal span. Although Arthur the man must die, the *wyrchipe* he bequeaths as a hero survives—or at least it will survive if Constantine has the impenetrable will and extraordinary personal power to carry it.

I suggested earlier that the expansive and contractive forces in the alliterative *Morte Arthure* reflect oral and literate structures of consciousness, respectively. Now I must qualify that statement: the literate-Ricardian viewpoint in *Morte Arthure* seems to be the result of reconstructing the older epic perception of the tragic, constrictive dimension of human existence according to Christian tradition, whose platonic nature was at least partially determined by rudimentary literate skills of analysis and reflection. The result is an extreme dichotomization of the universe into mutually exclusive realms: the eternal, divine, metaphysical realm in which only God exercises influence; and the temporal, profane, physical realm influenced by God perpetually and by men only so long as they live. True *wyrchipe*, which we have already identified as the power to create, maintain, and restore order—in short, the power to influence—can therefore be found only in God, the sole being capable of exercising influence eternally.

Yet the poet, like the Arthur he portrayed, does not seem to have been fully converted to this view of the universe or of human nature. His dramatization of Arthur's last moments betrays a felt conviction in the indomitability of the human spirit, an intimation of something that is not intimidated by the inevitability or even the imminence of death. Perhaps in this way the poet created Arthur in his own image: despite the platonic Christian tradition's abstract, intellectually constructed devaluation of human feeling, something in both poet and Arthur recognized that heroism is not a commodity subject to decay but a choice coeval with individual human consciousness, and that the choosing is itself a heroic act.

Department of English
University of Pennsylvania

Works Cited

Benson, Larry D. "The Alliterative *Morte Arthure* and Medieval Tragedy." *Tennessee Studies in Literature* 11 (1966): 75-87.

—, ed. *The Riverside Chaucer*. 3rd ed. Boston: Houghton, 1987.

Bosworth, Joseph. *An Anglo-Saxon Dictionary*. Ed. T. Northcote Toller. London: Oxford UP, 1954.

Burrow, John A. *Ricardian Poetry: Chaucer; Gower; Langland and the* Gawain *Poet*. London: Routledge, 1971.

Clanchy, M.T. *From Memory to Written Record: England 1066-1307*. Cambridge, MA: Harvard UP, 1979.

Clark Hall, J.R. *A Concise Anglo-Saxon Dictionary*. 4th ed. Cambridge: Cambridge UP, 1960.

Eliade, Mircea. *Myth and Reality*. Trans. Willard R. Trask. New York: Harper, 1963.

—. *The Myth of the Eternal Return: or, Cosmos and History*. Trans. Willard R. Trask. Bollingen Series XLVI. Princeton: Princeton UP, 1971.

Finlayson, John, ed. *Morte Arthure*. Evanston: Northwestern UP, 1967.

—. "The Concept of the Hero in *Morte Arthure*." *Chaucer und seine Zeit: Symposion für Walter F. Schirmer*. Ed. Arno Esch. Tübingen: Niemeyer, 1968. 249-74.

Foley, John Miles. *Traditional Oral Epic: The* Odyssey, Beowulf, *and the Serbo-Croatian Return Song*. Berkeley: U of California P, 1990.

Fry, Donald K. "Old English Formulas and Systems." *English Studies* 68 (1967): 193-204.

Georgianna, Linda. *The Solitary Self: Individuality in the* Ancrene Wisse. Cambridge, MA: Harvard UP, 1981.

Greene, Thomas. *The Descent from Heaven: A Study in Epic Continuity*. New Haven: Yale UP, 1963.

Hamel, Mary. "The Dream of a King: The Alliterative *Morte Arthure* and Dante." *Chaucer Review* 14 (1980): 298-312.
—, ed. Morte Arthure: *A Critical Edition*. New York: Garland, 1984.
Havelock, Eric A. *Preface to Plato*. Cambridge, MA: Harvard UP, 1963.
—. *The Greek Concept of Justice: From Its Shadow in Homer to Its Substance in Plato*. Cambridge, MA: Harvard UP, 1978.
—. *The Literate Revolution in Greece and Its Cultural Consequences*. Princeton: Princeton UP, 1982.
Irving, Edward B., Jr. *Rereading* Beowulf. Philadelphia: U of Pennsylvania P, 1989.
Jenkins, T. Atkinson, ed. *La Chanson de Roland*. Boston: Heath, 1924.
Keiser, George R. "The Theme of Justice in the Alliterative *Morte Arthure*." *Annuale Mediaevale* 16 (1975): 94-109.
Klaeber, Friederich, ed. Beowulf *and the* Fight at Finnsburg. 3rd ed. Lexington: Heath, 1950.
Lumiansky, Robert M. "The Alliterative *Morte Arthure*, the Concept of Medieval Tragedy, and the Cardinal Virtue Fortitude." *Medieval and Renaissance Studies: Proceedings of the Southern Institute of Medieval and Renaissance Studies, Summer 1967*. Ed. J.M. Headley. Chapel Hill: U of North Carolina P, 1968. 95-118.
Macaulay, G.C., ed. *The English Works of John Gower*. Vol. I. EETS os 81. London: Oxford UP, 1900.
Matthews, William. *The Tragedy of Arthur*. Berkeley: U of California P, 1960.
Neumann, Erich. *The Origins and History of Consciousness*. Trans. R. F.C. Hull. Bollingen Series XLII. New York: Pantheon, 1954.
Offord, M.Y., ed. *The Parlement of the Thre Ages*. EETS os 246. London: Oxford UP, 1959.
Ong, Walter J. *The Presence of the Word*. 1967. Minneapolis: U of Minnesota P, 1981.
—. *Orality and Literacy: The Technologizing of the Word*. London: Methuen, 1982.
Patterson, Lee W. "The Historiography of Romance and the Alliterative *Morte Arthure*." *Journal of Medieval and Renaissance Studies* 13 (1983): 1-32.
Redfield, James M. *Nature and Culture in the* Iliad: *The Tragedy of Hector*. Chicago: U of Chicago P, 1975.

Rondolone, Donna Lynne. "The Clash of Oral-Heroic and Literate-Ricardian Ideals in the Alliterative *Morte Arthure*." Diss. U of Pennsylvania, 1992.

Russo, Joseph, and Bennett Simon. "Homeric Psychology and the Oral Epic Tradition." *Journal of the History of Ideas* 29 (1968): 483-98.

The Alliterative *Morte Arthure* As a Witness to Epic

Britton J. Harwood

If it is true by definition that dominant and subordinate groups within every society use texts both to secure their own cohesion and to mold consciousness within the wider society, then our knowledge of the identity and functioning of these texts even within late medieval England seems far from complete. I wish to propose here that the alliterative *Morte Arthure*, composed perhaps between 1399 and 1402 (Benson, "Date" 29), stands in a special relationship to one class of such texts, offering a privileged access to the means of socialization within preliterate English society. In fact, the *Morte Arthure* presents a paradox that can likely be dissolved only in tandem with the question of socialization. On the one hand, the poem was likely composed in writing, for the reader can follow the poet's use of one written text after another. On the other hand, a stronger case for oral composition can be made for the *Morte Arthure* than for any other long poem in English. This paradox may disappear if we entertain the idea that the poem provides in its entirety a facsimile or simulacrum of an epic. Although early critics sometimes classed the poem with epic, only recently has research disclosed the bearing of epic on acculturation. Consequently, they lacked a powerful means for dealing with the peculiar textuality of this poem.

Morte Arthure offers only a simulacrum of epic, for a great deal of the poem can be traced to written sources. The epic text it models, to the contrary, must have been transmitted orally. For my present purpose, it will not matter whether the earlier, exemplary text was an actual Arthurian epic, Continental or Welsh in provenance, lying in an eleventh- or twelfth-century form behind the written chronicles used by the *Morte Arthure*-poet, or whether it was a nonArthurian epic, English in origin, the ordonnance of which the poet shaped chronicle material to imitate.[1] In either case, the poem modeled by the *Morte Arthure* would have been the "tribal encyclopedia" (to adopt Eric Havelock's phrase [*Preface* 66]) of a society that, in many respects, was still preliterate. I shall try to make good on this proposal chiefly through considering the specific nature of the poet's reshaping of his written sources.

Geoffrey Shepherd has called the alliterative poets of late medieval England "no spokesmen for an oral culture," even while "the mnemonic use of verse is less submerged" in their poems than it was "in contemporary verse of a more bookish kind" (5). The *Morte Arthure*-poet, however, stands out from this group precisely because he makes alliteration as a "mnemotechnique" (Shepherd 5) speak out for "oral culture" itself. Alliterative poets recall "the great *gestes* of antiquity," their alliterative meter fixing in the memory "moral, political, religious, sanitary, and behavioral commonplaces" (idem).[2] But the *Morte Arthure*-poet alone among them writes a work whose form becomes its theme; for its form is a representation of epic and therefore of that form through which "oral culture" preserved itself as a whole.

[1]On oral narratives of various complexity as sources for Geoffrey of Monmouth, see, for example, Bloch (95-108). "Already in eleventh-century Wales Arthur was in process of becoming the vortex to which were drawn the heroes of originally independent saga-cycles" (Bromwich 47). When Alcuin advised Hygebald at the end of the eighth century to ignore heathen poetry, or Alfred in the next century made a habit of memorizing vernacular poetry, or William of Malmesbury or John of Wallingford in the twelfth and thirteenth centuries took down stories from oral narratives, these poems transmitted by voice may have been epic in structure and were at least sometimes lengthy (see C. Wright 21, 30-31; Kelly 60; and Wilson 24, 31-32, 48-52).

[2]On the *Morte Arthure* as written within a "poetics of memory" (Shepherd 8), cf. esp. Vance: "[t]he closer Roland approaches to the moment of his death, the more the action of the poem tends toward pure commemoration. Almost surreptitiously, an unmistakable substitution of priorities takes place as a heroics of memory displaces a heroics of the sword" (64). The same may be said of Arthur, beginning with his eulogy for Gawain (3956-92). (I cite the poem throughout from Hamel's splendid and indispensable edition.) The villain, too, imitates, as Vance puts it, "the actions of the poet" (65): Arthur is anticipated in commemorating Gawain, of course, by Modred (3875-85).

I

At the time writing assumed at least some of the communicative and storage functions performed by oral poetry, a demand for jongleur entertainment apparently continued, possibly perpetuating "the traditional . . . methods of the improvising art" (Lawrence 176). Among these may have been alliteration. We cannot rule out the possibility that the *Morte Arthure*-poet was such a minstrel, because nothing is known of his life but the district, perhaps, where he grew up (McIntosh 238). Nevertheless, while he might have had alliteration as a minstrel habit, he has demonstrably immersed himself within books, only to write a poem in which the alliterative mnemotechnique itself is constructed as an inevitable and functional element.[3]

The *Morte Arthure* was not orally composed.[4] Oral composition implies the use of formulas, but the formulas of the *Morte Arthure* (see Waldron 796) do not imply oral composition. Neither does the possibility that Robert of Thornton or an earlier scribe reconstructed the poem from memory. J.L.N. O'Loughlin maintains that comparing the

[3]Johnson, in discussing formulaic thrift in the *Morte Arthure* and hence the way "function-word" adjectives occur with specific nouns, finds that "*Real* occurs six times in [the poet's] formulaic system, *riotous* five; but the two words do not compete with each other, for *riotous* is last found at line 1527 and *real* first occurs at line 1762" (260). If the poet had actually composed out of a formulaic system that had become preconscious for him, this phenomenon would seem to be inexplicable. Thus he is to be distinguished from poets whose work has a "similarity of content or structure . . . due to the mode of composition, not to direct dependence of one poem upon another" (Curschmann 41). The *Morte Arthure*, I suggest, is directly imitative of another poem. It is in this antecedent, rather, that similarity derives from a "mode of composition."

[4]I take "oral composition" to mean that a poet's selection of formulas coincides with the moment of delivery, not simply that the poem "reaches its audience through the medium of recitation," in which case "a manuscript in the background would not alter its oral character" (Finlayson, "Formulaic" 391; citing M. Parry 144). Baugh rejected the notion that the six "Matter of England" romances that he examined were orally composed: where the French originals could be identified, the English poets followed them with such fidelity as to suggest that the sources were lying open in a manuscript before them ("Improvisation" 431). Although the sources of the poet of the *Morte Arthure* are numerous, he too occasionally translates.

Thornton manuscript with the Winchester, which shares an ancestor with the Thornton (one that is not, however, the poet's prototype),[5] shows that "whole passages . . . have been transposed, half-lines have been substituted from other contexts, names altered or introduced from other romances, words and phrases changed to the detriment of meter and sense, passages omitted or clumsily patched over" (522-23). Such evidence suggests mnemonic reconstruction by the Thornton scribe. That would not imply, however, that the poet himself had composed *Morte Arthure* orally or that, composing it in writing, he had depended chiefly on his memory.

For example, in the Mt. St. Michael episode, the poet departs from all four of his chronicle sources (Geoffrey of Monmouth's *Historia*, Wace's *Roman de Brut*, and Laȝamon's and Robert Manning of Bourne's adaptations of Wace) to have Arthur himself, not Bedevere, listen to the old nurse's account of the giant's fatal rape of her young charge. The poet departs as well in making this victim the wife, not the niece or daughter, of Arthur's cousin, the duke of Brittany. Either change might have come from forgetting the earlier texts. Nevertheless, the poet is very likely reading, not remembering, when he makes "a Templere" Arthur's first source of news about the giant (841), because the change moves from vagueness to specification. The news had been brought simply by "an hende cniht" in Laȝamon (12,802).[6] (In the three other chronicles, there is no source at all.)[7] Although it is possible that the poet consistently relies just on his memory of the chronicles, his very process of making choices among versions, like the process of collating passages within a single text, is a literate habit. It makes little difference in principle, then, whether he is choosing among four remembered versions or among four that are in front of him. Unlike the oral poet who has in his head "a basic plot which he will deliver to his audience directly," the "moment of composition" for the *Morte Arthure*-poet, which is a deliberative moment, is not "the moment of delivery" (Finlayson, *Morte Arthure* 24-25).

The written word is no alien medium for him, for he surely found much of his material through reading. In addition to Wace's *Brut*

[5]On textual relations between the Winchester and the Thornton manuscripts, see Hamel ("Introduction" 4-14).
[6]I cite Brook and Leslie's edition of the Caligula version of Laȝamon's *Brut* throughout.
[7]See Geoffrey (471, l. 1); Wace (11,416); and Manning (12,277).

and the other early chronicles, he seems to draw on some later ones, like the Chandos Herald's *Vie du Prince Noir* and Walsingham's *Chronicon Angliae* (Finlayson, "Date" 631-33, 637). Alexander narratives like *Li Fuerres de Gadres*, *The Wars of Alexander*, and "The Vows of the Heron" apparently provided details like some in the foraging expedition, Alexander's portrait among the Nine Worthies, and the vows taken in the Giant's Tower (Matthews 35, 45, 40; Finlayson, "Two Minor Sources" 133). An English version of a French Charlemagne romance has supplied incidents for Gawain's meeting with Priamus (Finlayson, "*Sir Ferumbras*" 380-86). Corinne Saunders has proposed that the landscape in the dream of Fortune comes from two separate scenes in the *Roman de Thebes* (452). Mary Hamel takes the use of "Malebranche" as an epithet to mean that the poet has read the *Inferno* ("Dream" 304). The Vulgate *Mort Artu* may have inspired the climactic duel with Modred (Matthews 180). Writing is obviously no alien part of the *Morte Arthure*-poet's culture.

Nevertheless, he is at pains to compose as if it were and as if composition for him were oral. Using Milman Parry's criteria of paratactic fluidity, formulaic density, and formulaic thrift, James Johnson and Valerie Krishna have shown that at least the *Morte Arthure* among Middle English poems "comes closer than *Beowulf* does to possessing the qualities singled out by Parry as the marks of 'traditional' poetry" (Krishna 83). By contrast with *Beowulf*, where Krishna finds necessary enjambment in forty-one percent of the lines, Parry reported that only a little over one-fourth of Homer's lines were syntactically incomplete; and, according to Albert Lord, only 14.9% of 2,400 lines of Yugoslav oral poetry show necessary enjambment (Krishna 66, 68; citing Lord "Homer"). Surprisingly, even fewer lines in the *Morte Arthure*—only twelve percent, according to Krishna—are enjambed: "[n]ot only does the *Morte Arthure* fall within Parry and Lord's range for oral poetry, but it is at the extreme of this range, paralleling most closely the 'normal,' less sophisticated Southslavic poets" (69).

The *Morte Arthure* is not only strongly end-stopped and paratactic. It is formulaically dense. Parry defined the formula as "a group of words, usually one half-line in length, which is regularly employed to express a given essential idea" (80). The group is not a formula unless it occurs at least twice in the same poem (72). Citing Johnson's unpublished dissertation on the *Morte Arthure*, Krishna reports that 1,863 of the poem's second half-lines and 717 of its first half-lines are repeated exactly, or nearly so, within the poem, yielding "a density of 29.7 percent straight formulas" (75; citing Johnson, "Formulaic Diction" 43-45). Adopting Joseph Duggan's threshold of twenty percent as strong evidence of oral composition, she finds the figure for the *Morte Arthure* "very striking," "almost identical to the average density of straight formulas in the ten epic poems in Duggan's study" (75).[8]

"Thrift" was Parry's word for a system of noun-epithet formulas. Because the epithet varied for each formula while the noun remained constant, the system provided a formula for each kind of metrical slot. Johnson finds thrift in the *Morte Arthure* because

> the number of adjectives fitted into the adjustable slot . . . for any specific alliterative requirement [that is, a requirement that the line alliterate on *f*, for example] is quite limited . . . . When more than one adjective for a particular alliterative requirement has been used, the frequency of occurrence of these adjectives is usually unequal—one word will be used several times, others as little as once.
> ("Formulaic Thrift" 256)

For some initial sounds, only one choice of adjective is available (idem 259). Krishna reports that there are 221 alliterating expressions for Arthur in the poem. In the *f* alliterating slot, Arthur is designated five times, four times by the same expression and once by a variant. In the *s* slot, he is designated ten times, nine of them by the same expression, once by a variant. In *w*, Arthur is designated six times by the same expression, once by a variant (78-79).[9]

By the criteria of pervasive parataxis, formulaic density, and formulaic thrift, then, *Beowulf* would appear to be the lettered poem,

[8]"Johnson has indexed full-line repetitions in the *Morte Arthure*, and a count of the first 3,182 lines shows 129 full-line repetitions in the *Morte Arthure*, 14 more than in the same number of lines in the *Iliad*" (Krishna 76). She points out that there are only 33 whole-line repetitions in *Beowulf* (75).

[9]Krishna contrasts the *Morte Arthure* with *Beowulf*. She cites William Whallon as reporting that alliterating kennings appear there 78 times for the eponymic character, far fewer than the 221 occurrences in the *Morte Arthure* and therefore providing far less opportunity for violations of thrift. But Krishna shows that thrift is actually violated far more often in *Beowulf*. For example, "In the F alliterating slot, Beowulf is designated 5 times by 5 different expressions" (79).

Morte Arthure the oral one.[10] Nevertheless, the highly literate person who composed *Morte Arthure* wrote it out. He may have dictated it, but not because he could not write. Even in his specific use of formulas, he betrays the habits of literacy; for the poem is written not simply in alliterative long lines but with "four-line consecutive alliteration" (Vaughan 7, 3). These quatrains are "actual compositional structures," occurring with "remarkable consistency," into which some forty-five percent of the verse paragraphs in the poem (as marked by rubrics or initial letters) can be subdivided (Vaughan 7, 3, 8).[11] Such structures reveal an interest in planning and consistency that seems to work against meeting the need for memorizability. "The real and essential 'formula' in orally preserved speech," Havelock has written, "consists of a total 'situation' in the poet's mind," a series of standardised images following each other in his memory in a fixed order (*Preface* 82).

Composed from written sources and within the habits of literacy, the *Morte Arthure* is paradoxically preeminent in meeting the tests for oral composition. It seems to be oral because the poet wishes it to appear that way.[12] Rather, that is the way he wishes it to sound. Part of his purpose, I suggest, was *trompe-l'oreille*—giving his work the sound of the orally composed, orally transmitted poem that he was reshaping his written sources to imitate. He does not use some third technique transitional between oral and written;[13] rather, he simulates orality in writing.

[10]Krishna suggests, rather, that *Beowulf* represents an early, the *Morte Arthure* a late phase "in the evolution of an oral composition" (82-83). This seems puzzling. For oral composition to be possible at all, most lines would have to be paratactic, the reliance on formulas would have to be heavy, and each metrical slot would have to offer few choices within the poet's system of formulas. The only "evolution" that would seem to be possible would occur by contact with literacy. Krishna herself calls it surprising that some Middle English poems, and the *Morte Arthure* in particular, come "closer in all respects than does *Beowulf* to Parry's original description of a traditional poem" (64).

[11]See also Ritzke-Rutherford on a new formulaic element, the "cluster," a "recurrence of loose collocational word groups not subject to the confines of one or two consecutive lines of poetry" (73). In the introduction to his edition of the *Morte Arthure*, Finlayson had observed that "many formulas cover a line or even a group of lines" (26). Cf. Finlayson ("Formulaic" 384, 387).

[12]Cf. Waldron, who calls the poem "decidedly unliterary in appearance" (800).

[13]Cf. Lord: "[o]nce the oral technique is lost, it is never regained. The written technique, on the other hand, is not compatible with the oral technique, and the two could not possibly combine, to form another, a third, a 'transitional' technique" (*Singer* 129). The movement to literacy seems to be inscribed in the

The poem imitated by the *Morte Arthure* was orally composed because it was an epic. Before considering the *Morte Arthure* in relation to the function and therefore the structure of epic, we should briefly consider some previous generic placements of the work.

II

If modern criticism emphasizes specific structures, considerable from either a spatial or a temporal viewpoint, in thinking about genres (Frye 77), then like many other medieval narratives the *Morte Arthure* does not announce its genre in that sense. The poem calls itself a "storye" (25), a "romance" (3440), and a "cronycle" (3445). It is "storye" (*historia*) in the rhetoricians' sense of claiming to be based on actual events (Strohm 321), "romance" because it is written in the vernacular, and "cronycle" because it takes up its "actual events" in the order they happened. In the same vein, it calls one of its own sources, Wace's *Brut*, "romawns" (3200) and another of its sources, Laȝamon's version of Wace, a "cronycle" (3218).[14] Similarly, the poet of *The Wars of Alexander* calls his source (one of three redactions of the *Historia de preliis Alexandri Magni*) both "þe romance" (488, 1201, etc.), although it is Latin, and "þe cronaclis" (1064).[15] Recent critics uniformly deny that the *Morte Arthure* is a romance in any strong sense (Everett 64, 67; Matthews 95-96; Finlayson, *Morte Arthure* 9), even though, "unlike . . . the earlier epic or the later ballad, [the poem] is primarily clerkly, learned, and . . . exists in and depends on books" (as Larry Benson observes of romances in general [*Art and Tradition* 6]). When recent

poem itself, where, within the space of a few lines, the poet names alternative means of storage: "as chronicles telles" (274), "as awlde men telles" (279).

[14]I am assuming that the *Morte Arthure*-poet takes the placement of the Wheel of Fortune dream from Arthur's dream in Laȝamon that Modred is destroying his hall (13,982-14,018). I do not see the basis for Patterson's claim that the poet uses "romance" and "chronicle" to distinguish "two streams of Arthurian writing" ("Romance" 213). It is the present "storye" itself, not necessarily transformations of it, that will be esteemed among kings and knights as "romance" and rehearsed by kings and clerks in futurity as "chronicle" (*Morte Arthure* 3440-45).

[15]I cite H. Duggan and Turville-Petre's edition of *The Wars of Alexander* throughout.

critics assign the poem to a form, some, following William Matthews, have settled upon tragedy; others—John Finlayson most notably—have chosen the *chanson de geste*.

A broad definition of "tragedy" can no doubt capture the poem. If falling "out of heigh degree / Into myserie" (*Monk's Tale* 7.1976-77)[16] includes defeat and death, no matter how nobly borne, then Arthur, who is fatally wounded by Modred and discovers that the rebels have killed all his "trewe lordys" (4281), is no less tragic than Julius Caesar, who, in Chaucer's Monk's telling, was manly enough in his dying to remember his modesty (2711-18). This is no more than to say that mortality itself is our tragic lot.[17] Having been ordered by his father to adhere to Arthur, no matter what, Idrus refuses to leave the hard-pressed king and rescue his father: "He es eldare than I, and ende sall we bothen: / He sall ferkke before and I sall come aftyre" (4151-52). If mortality, then grief; and extended laments, "for a long time . . . regarded as an essential part of tragedy," occur several times in the poem (Haas, "Laments" 52).

But Matthews and others have argued that the poem is tragic in a stronger sense. In the Trecento, humanists like Mussato and Petrarch linked a fall from happiness with the intervention of Fortune, who was confusingly viewed sometimes as capricious, sometimes as subordinate to the justice of God (Haas, "*Monk's Tale*" 54-57, 60). Perhaps because Matthews mistakenly thought "the dream of fortune . . . was almost certainly the poet's own invention" (it actually appears in the Vulgate *Mort Artu*, just before the final battle with Modred [176.56-79]), he construed it as "the key to the structure" imposed by the poet. "The genre is the tragedy of fortune" (105), and Arthur's losses punished him for "mounting cruelty, covetousness, and imperialistic ambition" like Alexander's (128). When Arthur turned into Tuscany (3150), R.M. Lumiansky maintained, he lost his magnanimity and became obsessed with conquest for its own sake (110-12): "We sall be ouerlynge of all þat on the erthe lengez!" (3211).[18] It is difficult,

[16]I cite Benson's edition of Chaucer's works throughout.

[17]Cf. Benson, who denies that the poem is tragic in any Aristotelian sense: "[t]he hero, like all men, will inevitably fall to death or wretchedness even though he be flawless, for the lesson of medieval tragedy is simply that man is not the master of his own destiny" ("Medieval Tragedy" 79).

[18]Peck, who contrasts Arthur's motives in the two halves of the poem, sees the turning point of the poem in the "rhetorical finality" of lines 2371-74 (168). These lines are spoken by the narrator in his own person, and it is not easy to

however, to see Arthur's proud ambition as a key to the *Morte Arthure*'s originality, since it has been part of the chronicle story from the beginning, like Modred's treachery and Arthur's death: "And when this [namely, that all the kings of the world were afraid of him] was notified unto Arthur, his heart was uplifted for that he was a terror unto them, and he set his desire upon subduing the whole of Europe unto himself" ('Cumque id arturo notificatum esset extolens se quia cunctis timori erat totam europam sibi subdere aflectat' [9.11]).[19]

Moreover, there is perhaps no tragedy unless the protagonist discovers his own criminality and unless his suffering takes the form of guilt. It is true that, in bewailing Gawain's death, Arthur says that his knight has died "for syn of myn one" (3986). Further, as the king helplessly watches the killing of Ewayne, he deeply wishes he could lay down his own life for his knights (4157-60). Bereft of his peers, he figures himself as "a wafull wedowe þat wanttes hir beryn" (4285). It is essential to the kind of poem that the *Morte Arthure* is, however, that the dying Arthur at the next moment can survey his career with satisfaction:

> 'I thanke þe, Gode, of Thy grace with a gud wyll,
> That gafe vs vertue and witt to vencows þis beryns
> And vs has grauntede þe gree of theis gret lordes!
> He sent vs neuer no schame ne schenchipe in erthe,
> Bot euer ʒit þe ouerhande of all oþer kynges.'
> (4296-300)

---

find in them something less than his usual endorsement of British actions. As Boren will (314-15), Lumiansky appears to believe that the poet disapproves of Arthur's accepting child hostages (111). But already in the chronicles (e.g., Wace 2915), the Romans had sent child hostages to Belinus and Brennius. The hospitality extended to the hostages by Arthur (3208-209) exemplifies the very magnanimity Lumiansky thinks Arthur has already lost. O'Loughlin located Arthur's "*hamartia*," 'crime' in "his begetting of Mordred" (254). But neither in the chronicles nor in the *Morte Arthure* has Arthur fathered Modred. Other recent critics who see the poet faulting Arthur include Hamel ("Dream"); Howard; Janssen; and Twomey. Even Finlayson, who correctly places the poem with *chansons de geste*, sees the poet linking Arthur's fall to "a series of conquests which have no definite connection with his professed reason for going to war" ("Concept" 265). But contrast Keiser, who points out that these were avowed in the early council at the Giant's Tower ("Justice" 97). For other arguments that Arthur has not behaved unjustly, see esp. Vale; Eadie; and Obst.

[19]I cite Griscom's edition of Geoffrey's *Historia Regum Brittanniae* throughout.

At the end, as George Kane has remarked, "there is no trace or suggestion of melancholy or defeat" (*Middle English* 69). This satisfaction could not be further from the guilty nastiness with which Pandarus, at the end of a poem actually identifying itself as "tragedye," projects his own bad conscience on to Criseyde, whom he says he hates, or the guilty nastiness with which the narrator there goes off to Christ in a snit, for Christ "nyl falsen no wight" (*Troilus* 5.1786, 1722-23, 1845). The *Morte Arthure* shows Arthur's character "subdu'd / To what it works in, like the dyer's hand" (6-7).[20] Political leaders soon learn the principle of the double effect, the difference in their case being that each of the offsetting effects is a matter of life and death.[21] Arthur has no penchant to discover and contemplate eternal things; and if this lack makes him tragic in the Christian perspective, it is not at all clear that the poet believes it dims his kingly success (cf. Benson, "Medieval Tragedy" 78-84). Divine judgment no doubt falls evenly on royal "cirquytrie" and private, and that judgment is inscribed in the poem. But the pride of a king can galvanize a nation, or at least its ruling class; and the poem shows that as well.

A "philosophre" makes Arthur's "cirquytrie" and the resulting loss of innocent life the implicit reasons why Fortune has come to hate him (3394-400). Even if the judgment were explicit, however, taking it as an overarching moral framework for the poem would be not only to forget that the same scholar goes on to make Arthur the ninth "of þe nobileste namede in erthe" (3439), but to ignore how tangential such a framework would be to much of the *Morte Arthure*.[22] No doubt when Priamus blames his own "cyrqwitrye" for his loss to Gawain (2616-17), this can be seen to anticipate Arthur's fatal pride and thus to lodge the whole foraging expedition within the moral frame. But the contents of the foraging episode are various. For instance, Priamus' followers use nine lines to resign from the service of the Duke of Lorraine, complaining he has not paid them (2925-33). Such variety, or digressiveness, makes no easy fit within an overarching tragic action. In its own way,

[20]I cite Shakespeare's Sonnet 111 from Booth's edition.
[21]Patterson observes that "[t]he pathos of monarchy solicits our political consent" (*Negotiating* 230).
[22]Cf. Eadie's remark: "[t]he point to recognise, in literary terms, is that Arthur is not operating on a level where religious judgements pertain at all" (5). Cf. Dean (115n).

in fact, it seems to have more to do with the rest of the poem than the "cyrqwitrye" does.

The digressiveness has been (unfavorably) noticed more than once. Matthews thought it diverted "attention from the main narrative and from the principal theme" (178; cf. Everett 65). There may be more than one way to think about digressiveness, however. Havelock, writing about epic, acknowledges that "[d]idactic or encyclopedic elements that may be there . . . are incidental to the epic purpose and likely to weigh as a drag on the narrative. However," he goes on to say, "we are going to explore the argument that the precise opposite may be the case; that the warp and woof of Homer is didactic, and that the tale is made subservient to the task of accommodating the weight of educational materials which lie within it" (*Preface* 61). Earlier observations that the *Morte Arthure* is epic (Kane, *Middle English* 70; O'Loughlin 524) were right, I think, but most so because it, too, makes the tale of Arthur subservient to didactic, encyclopedic digressions. Pointing to a concern "with nationalism, the glories of war, with warrior-heroes and a warrior king," to a preoccupation with a group rather than an individual, and to a structure similar to the *Roland*'s, Finlayson has likened the *Morte Arthure* to a *chanson de geste* (*Morte Arthure* 11, 7, 13). If the *Roland* is the *Iliad* of the French (Gautier 2: 794), then Finlayson, too, is calling the English poem an epic. Yet the force of the suggestion cannot be fully understood if it does not reach to episodic structure and therefore to the function and, in one sense, the nature of epic.[23]

[23]Matthews tries to refute the claim that the poem is an epic. Although the society described by the poet "existed theoretically eight centuries earlier," the poet nevertheless "invests it with the values and habits of his own time: his representation of kingship, loyalty, war, arms, shipping, empire, agrees with the ideas of the fourteenth century as they appear in the contemporary textbooks and in the conduct of affairs" (97). Cf. Benson ("Medieval Tragedy" 77). Matthews believes this argues against epic. But contrast Bakhtin:

> The world of the epic is the national heroic past: it is a world of 'beginnings' and 'peak times' in the national history, a world of fathers and of founders of families, a world of 'firsts' and 'bests.' The important point here is not that the past constitutes the content of the epic. The formally constitutive feature of the epic as a genre is rather the *transferal* of a represented world into the past, and the degree to which this world participates in the past.
>
> (13; my emphasis)

III

Epic poetry carried a burden that was lifted only by printing and by a system of instruction in reading and writing the vernacular language. To know whether there is a place in any part of the fourteenth century that epic poetry must fill means to consider whether there is any sense in which fourteenth-century England is preliterate. M.T. Clanchy shows that, in the second half of the thirteenth century, peasants, both free and unfree, were using charters to convey land. This implies that they understood these Latin documents, just as their use of seals for authentication does (50-51). At the turn of the century, there is reason to believe that most aristocrats are at least minimally literate. Clanchy uses a case in the court of King's Bench to show that, "from a random sample of thirteen gentlemen of Norfolk at the end of the thirteenth century, ten could read an entry in a chronicle, two could not, and one's ability is unrecorded" (225). The literacy of English kings from Henry I onward "inevitably gave the baronage and gentry a motivation to learn some Latin," in Clanchy's view, "both to avoid looking foolish at court . . . and to have sufficient understanding of the written demands, expressed in Latin, which began to pour from the royal Chancery and Exchequer" (235).

Yet possession of a modicum of Latin by perhaps a majority of the population did not mean that most people in 1300 could read or write English or French, because elementary instruction "started from Latin." Not until well after 1300 was either Middle English or French "sufficiently standardized, or well enough established as a literary language, to become the basis of elementary instruction in reading and writing" (Clanchy 233). Neither did the proliferation of documents in England mean that any appreciable portion of the population could become acculturated through reading.[24] Where in the tenth century documents were never extensive enough to threaten "to supplant purely

---

Cf. Havelock (*Preface* 121-23).

[24]"Maybe half the population could read, in medieval England and throughout Latin Christendom, if by reading is meant the ability to recognize the written words of the best-known prayers" (Clanchy 13).

oral forms of conducting the affairs of the realm" (Keynes 244), by the fourteenth century surviving records of the central administration include ordinances, law books, Exchequer and Chancery enrollments, wardrobe accounts, and thousands of documents given under the privy seal (Tout 1: 36-62). Nonetheless, "the strong element of professionalism" in the literate skills that produced these documents also meant, as in earlier ages, that most members of the ruling class did not need to practise these skills on their own behalf (McKitterick, "Introduction" 4). Some of the professionals were clerics who made careers within the bureaucracy; others were the "court squires" who, increasingly from the reign of Edward I, as Janet Coleman has described them, were "administrative, unwarlike men." Many of the country gentry were also "experienced administrators, rising lawyers, prosperous businessmen" (58-59), at least from the reign of Edward III. These, like the free tenant farmers or franklins, were a literate group (idem). All such literacy, however, whether deeply clerical or mainly practical, could not, before printing and schools, have been the principal means of socialization.

In fact, the literacy of burgesses or rural landowners, when not required in administration or business, seems to have been directed chiefly to private devotional reading, as attested by the edifying books they left in their wills (Coleman 23). Devotion was the aim, too, of the Latin and music taught by the grammar schools (Albert Parry 72, 216), whether these were attached to cathedrals, monasteries, colleges, hospitals, guilds, foundations, towns, parishes, or chantries (Hepple 13-19). One Dominican held that instruction for boys should be centered on faith, habits, and "scientia," which he defined (following Bernard of Clairvaux) as the desire for eternal life (Corbett 28). Vincent of Beauvais insisted that girls of noble parents be instructed "in letters and good morals" (Gabriel 38). With the exception of a guild at Stratford, no institution but the Church seems to have established a school in England before the fifteenth century.[25] In considering whether, early in the fourteenth century, there were social functions that only epic poetry could have performed, "the really significant point," to adapt Clanchy's ob-

[25]See Albert Parry (125). In the middle of the fifteenth century, the Inns of Court and Chancery included subjects other than the law, such as history, music, and even dancing (Emden 535). Within the context of guild schools, which appear in the same century, "a new middle class" was demanding a curriculum better suited to the needs of children who did not intend to "enter the ministry" (McMahon 99).

servation, "is not the proportion of the population which could read (in whatever sense), but the fact that the dynamic of literacy was religious" (13). Since it was religious, it led in general to Latin. And for knights, burgesses, and peasants of the fourteenth century, Latin could no more have served the purposes of acculturation than it did in the eleventh; for it "was a foreign language," and "books were not generally available" (Clanchy 247).[26]

Thus, fourteenth-century English society is neither exclusively literate nor oral. Albert Parry distinguished three stages that should be attached to the term "writing." They hold for reading as well. The second of the three bears on the centuries that led to the *Morte Arthure*. It is an evolutionary stage where writing has a practical value "as a means of communication and for business purposes" (75). Thus, when Havelock describes for early Greece, not three stages, but three social areas dependent on oral communication, only the first of these has been taken over by literacy even in late-medieval England. This is "the area of current legal and political transactions; the issuance of directions which would accumulate as precedents" (*Preface* 120). The second and third must have continued to depend on the oral transmission of epic poetry.[27] These are "the continual re-telling of the tribal history, the tale of the ancestors and how they behaved as models for the present. This historical task would be the special province of the minstrels. And finally there would be the continual indoctrination of the young in both tale and precedent through recital" (idem 120-21). Such continual indoctrination, partly into the knowledge of a nation (Gautier 1:11), is not the instruction "in fide, moribus, et scientia" that the Church called for. But the transnational Church never supplied all cultural needs. No doubt, as Ward Parks allows, by the later fourteenth century "undiluted, primary orality was largely a thing of the past, even among illiterates." Yet, as he cautions, "one must not forget how slowly monumental his-

[26]Obviously they were not nonexistent. Humphrey de Bohun, earl of Hereford and Essex from 1336-61, commissioned the translation of *Guillaume de Palerne* into alliterative English, perhaps so that the romance might instruct nonFrench-speaking dependents of his in Gloucestershire in "the virtues of 'gentilesse' and 'cortaysie'" (Turville-Petre 41). In the next century there were "feudal manuals," evidently peculiar to England, that not only incorporated a family's genealogy but served as a reference work for the gentry, partly by summarizing English history (T. Wright ix-xi).

[27]On the oral dissemination of *chansons de geste*, see esp. Gautier (1:6); Riquer (304-306); and Rychner (10).

torical changes occur" (675). The movement from orality to literacy could not be achieved "with any degree of thoroughness among a cultural majority" except with universal education (idem).

The immemorial existence within epic poetry of a system of socialization inspired suspicion and even hostility in the Church, of course, as evidenced by surviving clerical satire at the expense of jongleurs.[28] As Joseph Duggan remarks, "[t]he fact that jongleurs . . . perpetuated the conceptions of history of the illiterate majority, whose collective memory was preserved in orally transmitted tales, made them a threat to that segment of society that privileged the written word" (757). The *Morte Arthure* comes close to demystifying ideas of God and the Church as part of a national ideology. "Churchmen of the high Middle Ages," Duggan goes on to say, "saw the jongleurs as rivals to their own—literate—view of history informed by the relationship between God and man" (idem). The Church barely tolerated the best jongleurs and never went further than giving them the benefit of a doubt (Gautier 2: 25; cf. Chambers 1: 38-41, 55-59). Langland, for example, who has to allow that he himself is a minstrel of sorts, generally tars all kinds of jongleurs with the same brush that he uses on the most vulgar:

> þoo þ*a*t feynen hem foolis, and wiþ faityng libbeþ
> Ayein þe lawe of oure lord, and lyen on hemselue,
> Spitten and spuen and speke foule wordes,
> Drynken and dreuelen and do men for to gape,
> Likne men and lye on hem þat leneþ hem no ȝiftes,
> Thei konne na moore mynstralcie ne Musik men to glade
> Than Munde þe Miller of *Multa fecit deus*.
> . . . .
> Ac [mynstralcie and murþe] amonges men is nouþe
> Lecherie, losengerye and losels tales . . . .
> (B.10.39-50)[29]

While Langland may have watched these "foolis" more often in taverns than in manor houses, they form something of a mass even with the many minstrels who traveled with Edward III, whose registers show that "Roland le Fartere" was well rewarded by the king's progenitors for the service of making a leap, a whistle, and a fart. In the previous

[28]On distribution of the terms "jongleur" and "minstrel," see Crosby (91n3).
[29]See also B.13.224-34. I cite Kane and Donaldson's edition of the B version of *Piers* throughout. The standard analysis of Langland's treatment of minstrels is Donaldson (136-55).

reign, John de Colon, a Lombard minstrel, received three shillings "for making his minstrelsy, with snakes, in the presence of the king" (Bullock-Davies 134, 32). Similar gifts went to acrobats, fools, taborers, psaltery-players, trumpeters, vielle-players, pipers, jugglers, and messengers.

At points, however, Langland is at least neutral on a kind of jongleur who seems to have been distinguishable within this entertaining mass. "Clerkes and knyhtes welcometh kynges munstrals" (C.7.97);[30] and the content of their acceptable songs may be revealed in one of the very lines where Langland turns minstrelsy into a figure for poverty, illiteracy, and physical handicaps. An unlettered man should tell you rich, Langland writes, of the sufferings of Christ, "And fithele the withoute flaterynge of god Friday þe geste" (C.7.107). "Gestes"—deeds and accounts of them—cause Thomas de Cabham, bishop of Salisbury (d. 1313), to make his single exception as he goes about reprobating entertainers. Classifying entertainers into three kinds ("histrionum genera"), he damns the first two in their entirety. Among the third (musicians and singers), those are condemned who contribute to lechery. Those are not, however, who confine themselves to singing "gesta principum et vitam sanctorum," the deeds of heroes and the lives of saints (Chambers 2:262). If late-medieval English society is in some important ways preliterate, then a lineage must go back from these acceptable jongleurs to the bards whom Hesiod called the servants of the muses, who chant "the mighty deeds of former men / And the blessed gods" (*Theogony* 100-101; cited and trans. Havelock, *Preface* 64).

The jongleur who specialized in *chansons* of such *gestes* seems to live at least in memory during the second half of the fourteenth century. In Langland's, perhaps, as we have seen. The *Wynnere and Wastoure*-poet erects a certain standard:

> Whylome were lordes in londe þat loued in thaire hertis
> To here makers of myrthes þat matirs couthe fynde
> And now es no frenchipe in fere bot fayntnesse of hert,
> Wyse wordes withinn þat wroghte were neu*er*
> Ne redde in no romance þat eu*er* renke herde.
> Bot now a childe appon chere withowtten chyn-wedys
> Þat neu*er* wroghte thurgh witt thies wordes togedire
> Fro he can jangle als a jaye and japes telle
> He schall be lenede and louede and lett of a while

[30]I cite Pearsall's edition of the C version of *Piers* throughout.

> Wele more þan þe man that made it hymseluen.
> (19-28)[31]

These exemplary "makers of myrthes" are the "chanteurs sévères," those who devoted themselves exclusively to a national epic, that Gautier saw as surviving even in a weakened and discolored form into the fourteenth and fifteenth centuries, at least in France (2: 27). The Dominican John Bromyard, writing in the second quarter of the fourteenth century, presumably had first-hand knowledge of this sort of "mimus," whose task he likened to that of the "herraldus" and "menestrallus," namely, "the glorification of the deeds of noble knights" (Owst 11). As Cabham starkly contrasted the jongleur of the "gesta principum" with the singers of lecherous "cantilenas," so the *Wynnere and Wastoure*-poet opposes him to those who tell "japes"—stories whose disconnection from tradition may be figured by the youthfulness of the downy-skinned teller. King Dindimus in *Alexander B* makes a similar distinction. He says that he and the other Brahmans deplore "any tale þat turneþ to bourde":

> But whanne we meven our mynde mirþe to here,
> We raiken to oure romauncus and reden þe storius,
> Þat our eldrene on erþe or þis time wroute.
> (466-68)[32]

And where in France the Round Table was dismissed as a frivolous subject in favor of Roland or William of Orange, so in England, conversely, if there was a national epic, Arthur was its hero, and stories like "the book of Launcelot de Lake" were contrasted with it as fictitious and therefore useless.[33]

The solace provided by *chansons de geste* was allowable in Cabham's view since it was "utilis" (Chambers 2: 263). Because certain

[31]I cite Trigg's edition of *Wynnere and Wastoure* throughout. Salter has recently questioned the traditional dating of *Wynnere and Wastoure* to 1352 (40-52). In a forthcoming essay, however, Professor Carter Revard will advance new reasons for believing that the poem alludes specifically to the Statute of Treasons of 1352 and for linking the composition of the poem to a visit by the Black Prince to Chester in 1353 (personal communication).

[32]I cite Magoun's edition of the *Gests of Alexander*.

[33]The presence of a "book" does not, of course, imply private reading. Baugh remarks that "a minstrel reading a romance [aloud to an audience] would have had plenty of precedent" ("Middle English Romance" 22).

jongleurs sang perhaps for the sake of information ("forte ad informationem"), not just recreation, they were excepted, in a thirteenth-century treatise, *De septem sacramentis*, from a general condemnation (cited J. Duggan 733). The narrator of the English version of *Parténopeus de Blois* recommends "gestes" to the unlettered person exactly because something might be learned:

> To the lewed also, pa*r*de,
> Is goode su*m*-tyme for to here.
> For by herynge he may lere
> Thynge þ*at* fryste he ne knewe;
> And to soche folke olde þynge ys new,
> Whanne hyt ys i*n* gestes songe,
> Or els in p*ro*se told wyth tonge.
> (21-27)[34]

Epic gives this information in a certain form, which we should next consider, before turning at last to the alliterative *Morte* as an imitation of epic form and function.

IV

If civilization relies on the maintenance of a collective memory, how is this accomplished before printing and without schooling, except for what the Church provided? Late-medieval England is not early Greece, if for no other reason than that some of the storage functions of language—retention of a knowledge of the laws, for example, or of the actions of jurors, or of the grants of estates—have been taken over by documents. But how, in late-medieval England, is the national history accessibly stored for all members of the community? How does the community call each of its members to take her or his place within a network of custom and usage? In short, before the printing press, not to speak of the electronic media, and before a reconception of elementary and secondary schooling, how does a community constitute itself? The question that Havelock asked for the Hellenes seems to me equally pressing for the English: in "a situation where documentation remained

[34]I cite Bödtker's edition of *Partonope of Blois*.

minimal, how is the apparatus of this civilization preserved? We speak here of the public and private law of the group, its proprieties and its traditions, its historical sense and its technical skills" (*Preface* 41).

In his survey of medieval education, Nicholas Orme offers the usual answer to this question, namely, that customs and beliefs were absorbed at home (1)—"left," in Havelock's words, "to the unconscious mind of the community and to the give and take between the generations without further assistance" (*Preface* 41). If Havelock is right, however, the tradition always requires embodiment in some verbal archetype, "a performative utterance on an ambitious scale which both describes and enforces [the] overall habit pattern, political and private, of the group . . . . It will include repeated examples of correct procedure and also rough definitions of standard technical practices which are followed by the group in question" (*Preface* 42).[35] What, then, was this "performative utterance on an ambitious scale" for late-medieval England?

In seeking such an "utterance," we shall be looking both for a story capable of giving the group its identity and also for a certain kind of digressiveness.

[35]In a recent discussion of oral epic, John Miles Foley has taken up Havelock's notion of the "oral encyclopedia" (95). Cf. Coleman (164). The existence of such large performative utterances may help to account for the importance of musical performance within aristocratic education in the Middle Ages, carried out when youths were sent "to the households of great nobles or great ecclesiastics" (Albert Parry 121, 117). The *Morte Arthure* refers to such an education when Arthur reminds Modred, "Thowe arte my neuewe full nere, my nurree of olde / That I haue chastyede and chosen, a childe of my chambyre" (689-90). The physical pleasures of singing and dancing were mobilized to assist in memorization, for "the recital of the tribal encyclopedia . . . was also a tribal recreation" (Havelock, *Preface* 152). Nourishment and nurture may well have been still associated in the late Middle Ages, when old and young may still have sat down "at common mess tables and perhaps spent considerable time there. . . . A purely poetic *paideia*, to be effectively transmitted, requires only regular occasions for performance" (Havelock, *Preface* 124). Instruction in harping and other forms of music did not make a jongleur of the youth, whose lot in life was different. But music would have enabled a participation in the performance of poetry that seems still, in the late Middle Ages, to have been "fundamental in adult recreation." Pleasure was exploited "as the instrument of cultural continuity" (Havelock, *Preface* 37, 157). That jongleurs performed in aristocratic halls does not imply, of course, that they did not sing as well to mixed audiences at crossroads and in squares.

The stronger "the sense of common ethos shared by communities who speak a common tongue," Havelock writes, "the more urgent is the need for the creation of a great story which shall compendiously gather up all the little stories into a coherent succession, grouped around several prominent agents . . . . Only the over-all plot of a great story can serve, a plot memorized in thousands of lines but reducible to specific episodes which shall yield specific examples" (*Preface* 175-76). In England, the "great story" would necessarily tell of Arthur, whom Geoffrey had made the conqueror of the Romans as well as of the Saxons: "[i]n consequence . . . the 'Saxons' came to think of their country as England, and to make Arthur their national hero, in the same way as Charlemagne was the national hero in France" (Ker 117; cf. Havelock, *Muse* 11). Because epics work "to conserve the group mores," the persons who act in them "must be the kind of men whose actions would involve the public law and the family law of the group," "political" in a general sense, because their actions "will send out vibrations into the farthest confines of this society" (Havelock, *Preface* 167-68). Epics give paradigms of "accepted practice or proper feeling," by contrast with "what may be unusual or improper and excessive or rash. So far as the bard's own invention is concerned, this is more likely to show itself when his characters depart from the accepted *nomos* and *ethos* than when they conform" (idem 87).[36] By Hesiod's word "nomoi," Havelock means not just what will develop as statute law in Greece but "the force of usage and custom before it was written down" (idem 63). An analogous conception for English society would include, but not be limited to, the common law. "*Ethea* are not less binding than *nomoi* but are more personal; the word may originally have denoted the way a human being lived in his 'haunts.' If so, it could be easily extended to cover the mores of the human haunt which is the household and family" (idem 63).[37]

[36]The "psychodynamics of the memorizing process" require *agents* (e.g., gods who behave vividly) to explain events, because historical causes and effects cannot be abstractly analyzed: see Havelock (*Preface* 169; cf. 94-95). A good example of this, I think, is the appearance in the *Morte Arthure* of Fortune ("a duches dereworthily dyghte in dyaperde wedis" [3251]) to explain historical change. Such an explanation would contrast with the analysis that writing makes possible—e.g., the analysis of political science and the social order in books 7 to 10 of Vincent of Beauvais' written encyclopedia. See Gabriel (16).
[37]Perhaps the outstanding instance of *ethea* within the first thousand lines of the *Morte Arthure* is the extended expression of grief that the poet gives Arthur and

The digressiveness of primary epic follows the character of knowledge orally stored. Such knowledge is "time-conditioned," "not simply true for all situations and so timeless." Events and data are retained within "disjunct episodes," each worded so as to "retain a high content of visual suggestion" and joined to each other paratactically (Havelock, *Preface* 180-81).[38] The parataxis follows from the memorable content, which is at odds with rising levels of generalization or arrangement according to logical relationship. Moreover, the epic poet "continually restates and rehandles the *nomos* and *ethos* of his society as though from a modern standpoint he were not quite sure of the correct version" (idem 92). Thus the episodes also admit of a degree of contradictoriness among themselves, for the tradition, being repetitive, is "subject to variant versions" (idem 186).[39] Because in an oral culture "the hoarded usages of society tend also to assume the guise of hoarded techniques," the poet digresses into procedures. These occur only as part of a general education (idem 83); they are only "typical and general, not detailed enough to cover an actual operation" (idem 124). Havelock compares the "bard"—in our case, the jongleur—with

---

Guinevere upon parting (697-708, 715-16). This inscribes the *mos* that love is to be found only within marriage. It moves forward and changes, as well as expands, three lines in Wace about friends saying farewell (11,202-204). Laȝamon, in two lines, places all the grief among those related by blood (12,743-44). Finlayson, believing that such scenes have no place in a *chanson de geste,* suggests an influence from the Chandos Herald's life of the Black Prince ("Date" 636).

[38]Such visual suggestion, esp. effects of violence, helped orators to remember, Vance observes (53-54; citing Yates 1-27). Thus, in a highly functional sense, "without a war, there can be no *chanson de geste*" (Vance 61).

[39]If the *Morte Arthure* imitates epic and thus aspires to a disjunctive, paratactic character, the critic cannot, with any confidence, use the customary techniques of New Criticism to recover authorial intention. For example, the poet may not intend Arthur to think of himself as guilty simply because, having been responsible for the weeping of the widows of Tuscany, he goes on, in his last lament, to compare himself "to a woeful widow" (contrast Haas, "Laments" 125). The same may be said of Jutta Wurster's attempt to draw parallels between the narrator and the philosopher who interprets Arthur's second dream (55); or of Benson's argument for a "tension . . . between two goods" as a pattern informing many details of the poem ("Medieval Tragedy" 75, 80, 83-84). Moreover, proposals like Lumiansky's for an evolving character in Arthur might not make a good fit with epic. As Bakhtin observes about the individual in such "high distanced genres," "he is a fully finished and completed being. . . . He has already become everything that he could become, and he could become only that which he has already become" (34).

> a man living in a large house crowded with furniture, both necessary and elaborate. His task is to thread his way through the house, touching and feeling the furniture as he goes and reporting its shape and texture. He chooses a winding and leisurely route which shall in the course of a day's recital allow him to touch and handle most of what is in the house. The route that he picks will have its own design. This becomes his story, and represents the nearest that he can approach to sheer invention.
>
> (*Preface* 88-89)

If there is an "oral encyclopedia" in late-medieval England, then, its narrative line will be supplied by the career of Arthur. It will be episodic and paratactic, and its narrative line will continually motivate digressions, which, among themselves, will canvass English culture from a certain viewpoint. It will be serenely unaware of its own internal contradictions. It will chant in a single dialect, unriven by any multiplicity in point of view. The *Morte Arthure* seems to point to such a poem, as a necessarily rapid and selective survey of its first thousand lines will suggest.

V

Morte Arthure begins at the place in Wace where Arthur has spent nine years in subduing and ruling Norway, Denmark, and Gaul and other French territories. The English poet eliminates all detail: "Qwen that the Kynge Arthur by conqueste hade wonnyn / Castells and kyngdoms and contreez many" (26-27). Soon thereafter, however, where Wace names several French territories taken by Hoel, who commands half the English force under Arthur (10,109-12),[40] the English poet expands the list (30-47), including all the lands that were once (he says) controlled by Uther (29). In expanding it, he reaches back to Ireland, Flanders, Gotland, Norway, and Denmark, some of Arthur's earlier conquests in Wace. Some territories that he adds, however (for example, Hainault, Brabant, Flanders, and Holland), are new altogether.

[40]I cite Arnold's edition of Wace's *Roman de Brut* throughout.

In effect the English poet has created an eighteen-line catalog. As Havelock says of a passage in the *Iliad*, "[w]e cannot call it a digression for it is wholly relevant to its context, but it constitutes nevertheless a leisured pause in the tale" (*Preface* 83). The *Morte Arthure*-poet's catalog would not do for a gazetteer of western Europe, or for a complete list of English possessions at any time, or for a map.[41] Yet it serves general education by being a paradigm of all those things. The catalog moves concentrically from Argyll (in southwestern Scotland), the Orkneys and other outlying islands, Ireland, Scotland, and Wales, to lowland counties and French provinces and towns, interspersed in two waves with the names of more distant regions—first Gotland and Greece (37), then Norway, Germany, Austria, Denmark, and Sweden (44-47). Thus it gives a sense of closer and farther.[42] The places in France it particularly adds to Wace (Guienne, Bayonne, Bordeaux, Toulouse, Provence, Valence, Vienne, and Normandy), as well as Navarre, also added, invoke English possessions and successes: Normandy and Toulouse from the days of Angevin domination from the Channel to the Pyrenees; Guienne and the towns of Bayonne and Bordeaux, ceded to England in 1360 as part of the Treaty of Bretigny; Navarre, associated with the Black Prince's great victory in 1367 at Nájera; and Provence and the towns on the Rhone, repeatedly harassed by English forces. Thus the catalog makes implicit and unavoidable the fact, from time out of mind, that England has straddled the sea.

The English poet then condenses the chronicles with a few deft lines (48-63): Arthur parcels out conquered territories to his supporters, relaxes back in Wales, and founds Caerleon, described at length by both Geoffrey and Wace but dispatched in the *Morte Arthure* in four lines (60-63). The English poet then shifts the scene to Carlisle. In the chronicles, the feast that is to follow marks Pentecost and Arthur's coronation. The *Morte Arthure* omits the coronation and vastly abbreviates Wace in other ways, omitting the long list of people attending the feast, for example, and the games played as part of the celebration (Wace 10,249-322, 10,521-88). Wace's amplification of the table service at the feast and other details are reduced to a few general lines (74-77).

[41]Cf. Havelock (*Preface* 80-83, 124). As Banks remarked long ago, the poem "is often uncompromisingly technical" (125). Cf. Finlayson (*Morte Arthure* 22); and Patterson ("Romance" 212-13).

[42]In two later additions to the chronicles, the poem will sketch the geography of northern Italy (558-69) and of central Europe (618-23).

The *Morte Arthure* does retain, however, the ranks of those attending, and adjusts the order as it is found in Wace ("cuntes, . . . ducs" [10,243-44]) to reproduce—with gaps and within the constraints of alliteration—the English peerage. It adds the distinction between knight bachelor and knight banneret (Keen 168):

> dukez and dusperes of diuers rewmes,
> Erles and ercheuesqes and oþer ynowe,
> Byschopes and bachelers and banerettes nobill
> Þat bowes to his banere, buske when hym lykys.
> (66-69)

Through the pleasure of hearing this poem, people of all ranks would thus imperceptibly absorb one of "the usages of the political apparatus" (Havelock, *Preface* 75).

Then, as in the *Iliad* itself, the narrative action begins with a major feud, demands by the Roman emperor. The English poet uses no more space than Wace for the New Year's Day intrusion of the Roman messengers, but he works his paideutic, encyclopedic changes. Because public usage, the *nomoi*, include "courte thewes" (21), he takes what Wace says once—that the twelve elders "saluerent" 'salute' Arthur (10,632)—and repeats it with variation over several lines (82-84); for the greeting upon entering a room was rigorously prescribed by courtesy manuals (Nicholls 119). Similarly, he will add a line, once the envoys have an answer from Arthur, in which they will again bow to the king and this time ask for "coungé" 'dismissal' (479).

The *nuncius* to Arthur, a senator, proceeds to state Lucius' grievances: Arthur has plundered and murdered the emperor's loyal vassals and is contumacious himself. Hence the passage (86-115) is strictly relevant to the narrative. Nonetheless, it introduces certain essential cultural practices. First, the (oral) epic reports, paradoxically, that the culture depends on writing. The poet finds in Wace that one of the elders simply hands Arthur a "chartre" (10,638), which Wace then summarizes in direct discourse. (In Laȝamon no writing mediates the challenge at all.) In the *Morte Arthure*, the senator *speaks* a summons to Arthur; oral forms "were preserved and ossified when documents were introduced" (Clanchy 272). Nevertheless, he produces a document that the poet has him refer to repeatedly. Citing the formal opening of it, the senator says to Arthur that the emperor

Saluz the as sugett vndyre his sele ryche.
It es credens, sir Kynge, with cruell wordez;
Trow it for no trufles, his targe es to schewe.
Now in this Newȝers Daye, with notaries sygne,
I make the somouns in sale to sue for þi landys.
(87-91)

On the principle dating from Henry II "that no one need answer for his freehold without a royal writ" (Clanchy 91), receipt of this piece of writing would ordinarily make Arthur liable. That it is a writ, a command, the senator reinforces with the word "somouns" (91, 104). ("'Thow has me somonde' quod þe kynge," a few lines later [140].) The senator calls attention to the introductory clause certifying the messengers (the "credens") and twice to the imperial seal with which the notary has authenticated the writ (Vale 33-34). The details of this document, then, *as* document introduce one of the important techniques of royal government. It stands metonymically for written communication at the outset of a poem that commemorates hearing.

Second, the English poet modifies the rule that Arthur supposedly has broken; and repetition of the emperor's accusation continually recalls this rule, which happens to be the rule constitutive of feudalism. In Geoffrey, the emperor complains that Arthur withholds "tributum" he was ordered to pay; he also occupies lands, thereby interrupting the flow of tribute that their kings had been paying to Rome (9.15). Wace (and Manning translating Wace) also gives the emperor's essential grievance as loss of tribute. The *Morte Arthure* appears to develop Laȝamon, however, for the latter recasts the grievance in feudal terms (cf. Vale 35): "Þu haldest al þi kine-lond a þire aȝere hond" (12,371). The Roman thane wants to know whether Arthur is prepared to make an act of homage—to say whether he will acknowledge that Lucius is king over him, and whether he will "his mon bicumen" and "hine for lauerd icnawen" (12,380). In the *Morte Arthure*, Lucius claims that Uther received his lands from Lucius' predecessor: he held them because he had "mad fewtee" (112). Thus, there is nothing automatic about Arthur's holding them in his turn. If he wants them, he must "sue" for them (91), on the principle that the fief had reverted to the grantor, since the grantee (Uther) had died, and his heir, Arthur, had not sought confirmation from the grantor within a year and a day (see Critchley 17). No feudal principle seems to have been more central than that no grant of land was absolute.

In the chronicles, Arthur's barons rage out against the insulting demand, and the king himself must remind them of their obligation to recognize the envoys' immunity. While this ethic is fully retained in the *Morte Arthure*, it is a frightened Roman who must beg, "Misdoo no messangere" (126); for the king himself is furious. The poet expands a single line in Laȝamon (where Arthur leaps to rescue the Romans "swulc hit a liun weore" [12,400]) into a description of the king's terrifying countenance, his eyes wide and burning, his face pale with anger (116-24). The Romans, cowering like small hounds, call him a lion themselves (136-39). The perilousness of kings is something the dominant class uses epic to teach all of society; and if Arthur puts his anger away for a while (144), yet, as we see when he finally sends the slain Lucius to Rome as the demanded tribute (2342-64), it is only to cherish "resentment in his heart till he bring all to pass"—as Calchas said of Agamemnon (*Iliad* 1.81-83; cf. Havelock, *Preface* 69).[43]

Moreover, by letting the Romans state one ethic, the *Morte Arthure* permits the king to focus on a second, the obligation to splendid, self-destructive consumption, or "largesce" (163). In the "leisured pause" that follows, the narrative action becomes a convenience for representing at least one phase of the custom that, above all, defined nobility (Harwood 483-85). Just as the English will vanquish the Romans in conventional battle, so the *Morte Arthure* first sees that they defeat them at the banquet table within that sublimated form of aggression, the obligatory gift (cf. 3162-63 and Harder 51). Thus, the poem turns the messengers into recipients—having spoken for the emperor, they now get to eat for him—and therefore witnesses: for seven nights you will linger here "in solace," Arthur tells them, "To see whatte lyfe þat wee leede in thees lawe lanndes, / Forby þe realtee of Rome, þat recheste was euere" (153-55).

[43]Hence, modern judgments against Arthur's arbitrariness or vindictiveness—Peck (158), for example, or Twomey (138-42)—assume the relevance of an analytic tradition, stretching back to Plato, that would arrive at the idea of justice (and so of a just war). But my claim is that the *Morte Arthure* imitates communication under preliterate circumstances, where such analysis remains marginal. When the envoys report to the emperor, much briefer praise of Arthur in the chronicles is expanded into lines 530-45, which state the ideal qualities in a king—strength (expressed in part by "crewelle lates" [536]), wisdom, and generosity. Two other *nomoi* are dramatized by Modred, when, in the *Morte Arthure* alone, he attempts to decline the regency: he is modest (684) and reluctant to avoid combat (685-86).

This ironic modesty is the first of his aggressive gifts. By moving the feast from Arthur's coronation, where it occurs in the chronicles and where no enemy is present, the poem in its *paideia* brings the competitive character of "largesce" to the surface. Thus, after the profusion of dishes (176-205),[44] Arthur secures an admission of defeat: force yourselves, he asks the envoys, to have a little more to eat, even though the food doesn't amount to much. "Sir," the senator replies, "There ryngnede neuer syche realtee within Rome walles!" (228-29). Epic motifs, Havelock points out, are "social-political: they continually recall and itemize the rules of order to be followed in such things as . . . conducting a banquet" (*Muse* 58).[45] Consequently, until literacy (rereading, that is) makes analysis possible, law and practice—*nomos* and *techne*—run into each other. Public traditions like the obligatory gift are inseparable from such technical matters as the order of courses at a meal or modes of cookery, over which the poem has taken the occasion to linger.

Once the company has dined, Arthur and his men withdraw to ponder a response to the emperor. Although the *Morte Arthure* shortens the speeches that follow (Cador's and Hoel's are twice as long in Laȝamon, for example), it repeats and amplifies the fact of a royal *consilium*. Even before the banquet, when Arthur tells the envoys not to expect a quick answer, the *Morte Arthure* adds a passage describing "the king in council":

> Bot I sall tak concell at kynges enoyntede,
> Off dukes and duspers and doctours noble,

[44]On splendid feasts as Arthurian tradition and contemporary practice, see respectively Keiser ("Structure" 136); and Harder (53). The custom of the gift is communicated also in the *Morte Arthure*'s modification of the debate in the Giant's Tower. Beginning with Aungers', the shorter but more numerous speeches there are changed under the influence of "The Vows of the Heron," as Finlayson has shown ("Minor Sources"). The pattern established from Aungers' on comprises the statement of a harm done by the Romans and a vow of vengeance. By contrast with the simultaneity of warfare, where opposing individuals or troops fall upon each other at once, vows, like boasts and insults, are exchanged and therefore timed and thus fall within the economy of the gift (Harwood 487).

[45]Havelock also mentions here "arming for battle." The *Morte Arthure* expands to twenty lines a passage in Laȝamon where Bedevere arms before ascending St. Michael's Mount (12,879-85). In the later poem, of course, it is Arthur who does so.

Offe peres of þe parlement, prelates and oþer,
Off þe richeste renkys of þe Round Table;
Þus schall I take avisemente of valiante beryns,
Wyrke aftyre the wytte of my wyes knyghttes.
(144-49)[46]

When in fact Arthur goes "to concell" (243) in the Giant's Tower, we hear "he wendes / Wyth justicez and juggez and gentill knyghtes" (245-46). When the council is over, the twelve days of Christmas have elapsed, and the envoys finally get their answer, it is prefaced by a reminder "Of peris of þe parlement, prelates and oþer" (416). Surrounded by his *curia* Arthur is still "the kyng in his concell" as he delivers his answer, although the parliament was over (417). When Arthur actually calls for military service from his lords a few days afterwards, he is once more "in his kydde councell" (626); and when he later makes Modred "leuetenaunte," the *Morte Arthure* expands the chronicles by placing the announcement in parliament:

In the palez of ȝorke a parlement he haldez
With all þe peres of þe rewme, prelates and oþer;
And aftyre þe prechynge in presence of lordes,
The kyng in his concell carpys þes wordes . . . .
(636-39)

Collectively, these passages touch on most of the groups summoned to parliament in the later fourteenth century. "Prelates" (146, 416, 637) are the lords spiritual, particularly the two archbishops and the nineteen bishops, but perhaps also abbots and priors. The lords temporal, in addition to the dukes and earls, included a varying number of barons, "men of substance" (McKisack 186)—"þe rycheste renkys." Edward III summoned thirty-eight barons in 1376, for example. "A third and smaller group always found in parliament comprised officials and administrators" (McKisack 187). These are the "doctours noble" (145) and the "justicez and juggez" (246) who go into the tower with Arthur. And if the poem, which communicates (in the episode of St. Michael's Mount, for instance) the significant difference between well-born and ill-born, has no place for burgesses, the "wyes knyghttes" (149)—the "gentill kynghtes" (246)—may represent the knights of the shire.

[46]Contrast the shorter passages in Wace (10,727) and Laȝamon (12,415-17).

Beyond giving a paradigm of parliament, however, the poem repeats with variations that the king by public custom is always "the kyng in his concell"(639), to whom his vassals owe, in return for their fiefs, attendance at court and advice. They are accustomed, not only to being obliged to give counsel, but to expect that they will be asked.[47] The right to be consulted and even to withhold consent (when scutage or aid is being levied, except in a few cases) is granted to the magnates in that species of *nomos*, England's first statute, the Great Charter. (Thus, when putting the question of Modred's regency, Arthur tells the parliament at York, "Ascente ȝif ȝowe lykys" [644].) A complicated division of the feudal *curia regis*, one evolution of which is parliament, partly accounts for "how much more highly organized was the English government than any other of the time" (Baldwin 6-7). The poem serves the purposes of general education by giving a sense of that complexity.

The complexity includes the administrative bureaucracy and the courts; and war poem though it is, the *Morte Arthure* will find a moment to consider them. The digression is motivated by the appointment of Modred as regent. "Chauncelere and chambyrleyn chaunge as þe lykes," Arthur instructs him,

> Audytours and offycers ordayne thy seluen,
> Bathe jureez and juggez and justicez of landes;
> Luke thow justyfye them wele that injurye wyrkes.
> (660-63)

Three of the great officers of state are the chancellor, the treasurer, and the keeper of the privy seal. The last, who gains importance under Edward III because he is given portfolios for diplomacy and war (Tout 5: 55-56), is not in the poet's list, since the privy seal will travel abroad with Arthur. The remaining two great officers are, from the household, the steward and the chamberlain. The stewardship, traditionally filled in Arthur's house by Kay, has already been allotted its moment (156-65). Given the primacy of the chancellor and thus the poet's need to alliterate on "c," the chamberlain may stand in here for the treasurer, for the lands that supported the chamber were merged under Edward III into

[47]"Concell" as a sort of motif occurs at 259, 291, 305, 344, where it is used by or of each of the first several speakers, including Arthur himself.

the Exchequer.[48] The courts, too, are taken up—not just those limited by their commissions or to hearing cases in the first instance (for example, the itinerant justices, "justicez of landes"), but also, perhaps, the Great Council itself, where anyone could seek the king's justice without a writ (663).[49] Finally, the digression commemorates the custom that all these officers serve at the pleasure of the king (660). When parliament sent word to the young Richard in 1386 that it wished him to dismiss his chancellor and treasurer, he replied that "he would not at their request remove a scullion from his kitchen" (McKisack 443). (Soon afterward, he fired his chancellor nonetheless.)

On hearing that Arthur plans to attack,[50] Lucius continues the great feud by assembling an army. In fashioning his imitation epic, the *Morte Arthure*-poet finds a catalog already in his chronicle sources, as the emperor summons the component troops. The poet makes two changes, however, the first of these for at least two reasons. First, he more than doubles the territorial names found in Wace. This brings into better balance the Roman and the English forces, so far as the numerousness of place names gives an impression of absolute strength.[51] The

[48]On the other hand, "chambyrleyn" and "audytour" are specific Exchequer offices (see Tout 4: 163). The poem sketches the royal administration with a few strokes, scarcely a complete picture, of course. For example, the wardrobe of the household is not mentioned. It had functioned periodically as a war treasury earlier in the century, but in later years "was mainly a court office concerned with the expenditure of the royal household" (McKisack 217). A digression later in the poem does, however, touch on the privy wardrobe (distinct from both the great wardrobe, which was another storehouse, and the wardrobe of the household); located in the Tower, it housed stocks of weapons (2622-27). Arthur's "wardrop of Walyngfordhe" (4203) seems to resemble one of the numerous "small wardrobes in various places where the king or queen were likely to visit" (Tout 4: 181).

[49]One of the public customs introduced digressively relates to justice—specifically, to permitting a criminal who has fled to sanctuary to leave the kingdom under stringent conditions. See Neilson (384-85) on the restrictions Arthur imposes on the envoys (445-66).

[50]Arthur's attack will follow the route taken by the returning envoys themselves (494-502). As G.B. Parks has pointed out, "[t]he authentic road to Rome is obviously the core of the journeys mentioned in the poem" (167), and thus part of the geography of the "oral" encyclopedia.

[51]To this end, the poet omits anything comparable to Wace 11,133-62, where Arthur in his turn summons people loyal to him. The poet has already transferred the troop numbers appearing in Wace's passage to the episode in the Giant's Tower where a sequence of Arthur's followers pledge specific forces. On

fuller list also gives a sense, within an encyclopedic purpose, of northern and eastern Europe (Lithuania and Albania, for example), northern Africa, and the Near East, just as earlier catalogs had sampled geography closer to home. In a comparable way, beyond providing, in the catalog of the ships, "a rough description of the Mycenaean confederacy," Homer goes on to give "a Trojan list of allies" (2.821-77), "for it enlarges the geographic perspective" (Havelock, *Preface* 122-23).

The second change is subtler and perhaps less certain. Wace and Laȝamon are not very clear about the grounds on which Lucius summons foreign lords to Rome. Presumably, he is their overlord; hence, he can issue an order: "Reis e cuntes e dux manda" (*Roman de Brut* 11,086). He also offers an inducement, however: they should come if they wish to cover themselves with honor (11,088-89). Laȝamon includes the prospect of conquests and booty, and the orders go perhaps only to those who love the emperor (12,648-50). In the *Morte Arthure*, by contrast, we hear that the emperor's letters intimidate these vassals—"For drede of his daungere they dresside þem sone" (579)—, for the letters cite a specific sanction: "All thate faillez on þe felde be forfette fore euere" (585). This is a feudal levy; and the passage, for all its exoticism, inculcates the essential theory of feudalism: "every medieval fief, by definition, owed service, usually military service" (Critchley 23). The fief was only a conditional grant, as we have seen, and could be taken back if the service was not performed: "[t]here was no reason for confiscation more just than the refusal of the grantee to perform the service due, said the *Libri Feudorum*" (idem).

Not just the theory but also the contemporary practice of feudalism must be learned; and the passage may include a contradiction parallel to the one that actually obtained in medieval Europe, where from the 1220s at least kings contracted with aristocrats for troops, and the aristocrats recruited individual warriors by contract, too: "[t]he men who went to war with or on behalf of a great baron can hardly ever be shown to have been his feudal tenants" (Critchley 38). For Richard's Scottish expedition of 1385, he issued writs of summons to raise the feudal levy for the last time in England in the fourteenth century. But "the force which accompanied Richard across the Border was a contract army of the normal type" (McKisack 235); and Richard quickly renounced any attempt to collect fines because feudal services had not

---

the poet's sources for his additions to Lucius' allies, see esp. Hamel ("'Christening'" 299); and Matthews (183-84).

been performed. Similarly, although Lucius issues writs of summons, the "sowdanes that were sekyre *sowdeours* to Rome" are there for pay (593; my emphasis); for "solde" means 'wages' or 'hire.'

Before we conclude this rapid canvass of the first thousand lines by briefly considering some purposes to which the poet has turned both Arthur's shipboard dream and the giant of St. Michael's Mount, we might touch on a last instance of the poet's taste for *techne*, the movement of the army to Barfleur.[52] For all that the English were (and are) a sea-faring people, as no national poem could refrain from saying, the cost of building and maintaining a navy deterred English kings from possessing more than a small squadron of ships. Hence, when the need arose, "large numbers of merchant vessels were impressed ad hoc." The procedures were simple enough. Royal officers "were dispatched to the ports" (Allmand 87-88). Accordingly, the *Morte Arthure* adds this to the chronicles: Arthur "sendez furthe sodaynly sergeantes of armes / To all hys mariners on rawe to areste hym schippys" (632-33).

When the king arrives at Sandwich, the poet expands a single couplet in Wace ("La furent les nefs amenees / E les maisnees assemblees" [11,191-92]) into this scene:

> Thare the grete were gederyde wyth galyarde knyghtes,
> Garneschit on þe grene felde and graythelyche arayede:
> Dukkes and duzseperez daynttehely rydes,
> Erlez of Ynglande with archers ynewe.
> Schirreues scharply schiftys the comouns,
> Rewlys before þe ryche of the Rounde Table,
> Assingnez ilke a contree to certayne lordes
> In the southe on þe see banke, saile when þem lykes.
> (721-28)

The poem pauses here over the organization of the army. In England, having contracted with the king to provide large numbers of men, the highest nobility ("dukkes and duzseperez") filled command positions. The armigerous gentry, often county office-holders ("schirreues"), subcontracted with the magnates to provide recruits and held lesser com-

[52]Cf. Barnie: "[t]he parallel between Arthur and Edward is achieved not by means of an exact identification of particular campaigns, but by the consistent description of Arthur and his conquests in terms of fourteenth-century English military practice. Through the steady accumulation of realistic detail the poem achieves an aura of contemporaneity quite unique in fourteenth-century English romance" (148).

mand posts (Allmand 70-71). Moreover, by juxtaposing the archers with the magnates, who are certainly mounted, the poet touches on a balance between archers and men-at-arms. The combination of archers and (dismounted) men-at-arms had given the English two great victories, at Crécy in 1346 and at Poitiers ten years later. A traveling army requires commodities of all sorts, and the *Morte Arthure*-poet expands the "stuffe" going on board to comprise, not just the horses and weapons that he finds in Wace, but tents and other cloths, cloth sacks, chests, and cloaks. Wace's simple "chevals" (12,000) becomes "trappyde stedes" (731), "haknays and horsez of armez" (734). (Manning did nothing to amplify Wace, and Laȝamon had omitted the passage altogether.)

The *Morte Arthure*'s intense engagement with the navigational passage in Wace, as the English army crosses to France (11,205-33), is far from inconsistent with the poem as "tribal encyclopedia," for it would be difficult to imagine how anyone could set out to give his hearers a sense of what it means to be English without soon turning to the sea. "The navigational directives in the first book of the *Iliad* are only typical and general, not detailed enough to cover an actual operation," Havelock has written. "But they provide a paradigm for any Greek boy who will have to deal with the sea as a way of life" (*Preface* 124). In fact, the *Morte Arthure*-poet found at this point in Wace, who was born on the Channel island of Jersey, after all, and lived for a long while at Caen, near the sea in Normandy, a wealth of navigational detail not comparable to anything in the first book of the *Iliad*—a series of terms closer in their technicality, perhaps, to those when Priam's sons take "the mule-yoke, a box-wood yoke with a knob thereon, well-fitted with guiding-rings," so that Priam may carry ransom in a wagon for Hector's body and then bring the body home with him again (24.267-69).

Manning dealt with the passage rapidly and perfunctorily. Laȝamon had virtually passed over it altogether. But the *Morte Arthure*-poet writes an episode as long as Wace's and refines it, it seems, in the direction of even greater technicality. In lieu of Wace's single term, "la nef," he offers "coggez and crayers" (738), "floynes and fercostez and Flemesche schyppes" (743). He adds the detail that the mariners must "prouen theire depnesse" (746) in order, as Hamel points out in a note in her edition, to deal with the silted-up harbor at Sandwich (281n746, 750); and he adds the details of dinghies being hauled aboard and of porthole covers slammed shut. Where the mariners in Wace steer by the stars, evidently without much conviction, the English poet adds as a complication that the night clouds over, and the mariners must look to their needle and stone. Even then there is the same anxiety as in Wace, and all the ships suddenly strike their sails for the night. In the hands of the English poet, this passage hangs from the storyline like the union jack.

VI

To conclude, I should like to take up together the king's dream of the dragon and the bear and the fight that then follows between Arthur and the giant of St. Michael's Mount. One of the alternate interpretations of the dream, offered by the clerks whom Arthur consults, links it to a battle "with somme gyaunt," of course (825). I shall be concerned with the changes the poet makes to the episodes as he finds them in Geoffrey and Wace, for Laȝamon seems to be used just at one point.

Although, as Paul Branscheid pointed out (191), the *Morte Arthure* clarifies and unifies the St. Michael's Mount episode in several ways (assigning another giant's belt of beards to this giant, for example, and dropping Arthur's reminiscence of the other contest altogether), the English poet sometimes enlarges and otherwise modifies both episodes. These changes all take the direction of communicating that most fundamental of the *nomoi* of late-medieval English society, adherence to the idea of the natural inferiority of the peasantry, the rural direct producers, or in a narrower and clearer form, maintenance of the time-honored idea of a decisive gap between gentle people and servile. The intention of the epic poet is to communicate "a single and unified world view, obligatory and indubitably true for heroes as well as for authors and audiences" (Bakhtin 35). Epics are not dialogical. It does not follow, however, that medieval English society itself is unified and single or that epic is somehow under a dispensation from intervening within the social contest. (Neither does it follow, of course, that the poet succeeds, without internal contradiction, in communicating "a single and unified world view.") As every Englishman knew, if only from the poll tax of 1380, wars cost very large amounts of money. It is hard to see how a general education could be complete that did not acknowledge, however gingerly, the sphere in which wealth comes to be created in the first place. This means acknowledging the vast agrarian majority. When the poem deals with it explicitly, all is quiet in the country:

> Pouerall and pastorelles   passede on aftyre
> With porkes to pasture   at the price ʒates;
> Boyes in þe subarbis   bourden ful heghe
> At a bare synglere   that to þe bente rynnys.
> (3104-107)

In the two present episodes of intense struggle, however, the poem by indirection calls upon its audience to take up a class position.

In Geoffrey, the predations of the giant have been limited to the rape of Helena, Duke Hoel's niece, and the death and destruction he has inflicted on those who have pursued him. Wace adds to the rape the sufferings of the peasant population. The giant has destroyed their homes, stolen their property, and carried off their wives and children. The peasants hide from him in the woods. Because the laborers are in such disarray, the fields lie unworked:

> Mult veïssiez les païsanz
> Maisuns vuider, porter enfanz,
> Femes mener, bestes chacier,
> Es munz munter, es bois mucier.
> Par bois e par deserz fuient
> E encor la murir cremeient.
> Tute esteit la terre guerpie,
> Tute s'en ert la gent fuïe.
> (11,309-16)

The *Morte Arthure* changes this. Called three times a "carle" (1063, 1107,1165) and sharing none of the interests of the ruling class ("For bothe landez and lythes   full lyttill by he settes; / Of rentez ne of rede golde   rekkez he neuer" [994-95]), the giant kills and eats his social betters: "He has fretyn of folke   mo that fyfe hondrethe / And als fele fawntekyns   of freebornne childyre" (844-45).

The English poet modifies Wace, not only by identifying the giant as a peasant, but using a composite of beasts to describe him (cf. Patterson, *Chaucer* 262-64).[53] The closest antecedent to him in English

[53]On the *descriptio* of the giant, see esp. Finlayson ("Giant"; "Hero" 260-62). As Arthur, Kay, and Bedevere are riding from the British encampment towards

is the giant herdsman in *Ywain and Gawain*, the translation evidently made about 1325-50 of Chrétien's *Yvain*, where the herdsman is a "cherle" (268)—a "vilain" (294, 314).[54] While no animal in the later text matches one in the earlier—the *Morte Arthure* giant is hook-nosed like a hawk, for instance, the herdsman is snub-nosed like a cat—each *descriptio* is a bestial montage. Since washing is carefully prescribed for the well-born (Nicholls 33, 91), the carl is extravagantly filthy (1061-63, 1091-93), not least with his matted hair (1078). The knotted hair may identify him with Chrétien's vilain, whose mustache is "tortiz" (305), but surely separates him from the well-born, who use combs. (The royal beards collected by the giant are all "crispid and kombide" [1003].) It is this tangled hair that identifies the bear with the carl. The bear comes with "lothely lokkes," "All with lutterde legges, lokerde vnfaire, / Filtyrde vnfrely" (778-80).[55] By contrast, the victorious dragon wears chain mail like Arthur's (766-67, 769) and is "clene" in scales and claws (766, 772).[56] "Enamelde full faire" (765), it rears up like all the arts of civilization against brute hatred and rage. The fight between dragon and bear is class warfare, interpreted from one side.

The carl rejects all the inhibitions that society exacts ("he will lenge owt of lawe" [996]). He has not checked his oral sadism (the *Morte Arthure* takes a single line from Laȝamon [12,816] and makes the giant lavishly cannibal), and the giant's sense of smell is undiminished, as if he has always gone on all fours. (The widow urges Arthur to stay downwind of the giant in hunting him down [1039-40].) Because

---

St. Michael's Mount, the *Morte Arthure*-poet adds to the chronicles a scene of nature (920-32). This finds a place in the "encyclopedia" for English birds particularly: worm-fowl, seed-fowl, and birds of ravine are all there. However, the catalog at the same time is an introduction of creatures for whom the question of justice does not arise; by contrast, when animals become metaphoric in the case of the carl, they represent the fallenness of human beings, for whom the question of justice *does* arise.

[54] I cite Foerster's edition of Chrétien's *Yvain* throughout.

[55] Possibly, the bear also represents Arthur himself, for the dream is ambiguous. (If it were not, Arthur would not have to consult "two phylozophirs.") For some of the complexities, see Göller ("Dream").

[56] It is just possible that the dragon's "tatterede taile with tonges so huge" (821), which signifies the people traveling with Arthur in his fleet, would have been recognized as the swallow-tailed pennants carried by knights. (At the point of the knight's promotion to banneret, the tails are cut away—that is, the pennant is squared off.)

the carl has not covered his genitals—goes "breklesse" (1048)—Arthur may cut them off for that reason (1123). (It may not be too much to suggest that, in the imaginary of the text, the unconscious aristocratic wish to consume the peasantry figuratively is inverted and literalized in the carl as cannibal.)

If one nation's great legendary feud with another is exploited as a convenience for acculturating the young (and reminding the old of what it means to be English), the king's "syngulere batell" with the giant would seem to bear on that feud only slightly. The episode, nonetheless, is, in an important sense, the foyer of the poem. In it, the poet lingers over no single custom. Rather, it is the leisured pause in which all the *nomoi* are there in their negative. It triumphs ideologically over the peasantry, sublimely ignoring the contradiction that it tries to place a historical group outside culture. And reciprocally, the very disgust for the peasantry that it activates, and that its hearers experience historically, is levied to make fearful the prospect of living outside the social altogether.

Department of English
Miami University

Works Cited

Allmand, Christopher. *The Hundred Years War*. Cambridge: Cambridge UP, 1988.

Arnold, Ivor, ed. Le Roman de Brut *de Wace*. 2 vols. Paris: Société des Anciens Textes Français, 1938-40.

Bakhtin, M.M. *The Dialogic Imagination: Four Essays*. Ed. Michael Holquist. Trans. Caryl Emerson and Michael Holquist. Austin: U of Texas P, 1981.

Baldwin, James Fosdick. *The King's Council in England During the Middle Ages*. 1913. Gloucester, MA: Peter Smith, 1965.

Banks, Mary M., ed. *Morte Arthure*. London: Longmans, 1901.

Barnie, John. *War in Medieval Society: Social Values in the Hundred Years War, 1337-99*. London: Weidenfeld, 1974.

Baugh, Albert C. "Improvisation in the Middle English Romances." *Proceedings of the American Philosophical Society* 103 (1959): 418-54.

—. "The Middle English Romances: Some Questions of Creation, Presentation, and Preservation." *Speculum* 42 (1967): 1-31.

Benson, Larry D. *Art and Tradition in* Sir Gawain and the Green Knight. New Brunswick: Rutgers UP, 1965.

—. "The Alliterative *Morte Arthure* and Medieval Tragedy." *Tennessee Studies in Literature* 11 (1966): 75-87.

—. "The Date of the Alliterative *Morte Arthure*." *Medieval Studies in Honor of Lillian Herlands Hornstein*. Ed. Jess B. Bessinger, Jr., and Robert R. Raymo. New York: New York UP, 1976. 19-40.

—, ed. *The Riverside Chaucer*. 3rd ed. Boston: Houghton, 1987.

Bloch, Marc. "Tradition ou littérature: les origines du cycle Arthurien." *Revue de Synthèse* 1 (1931): 95-111.

Bödtker, A. Trampe. *The Middle-English versions of* Partonope of Blois. EETS os 109. London: Oxford UP, 1912.

Booth, Stephen. *Shakespeare's Sonnets*. New Haven: Yale UP, 1980.
Boren, James L. "Narrative Design in the Alliterative *Morte Arthure*." *Philological Quarterly* 56 (1977): 310-19.
Branscheid, Paul. "Über die Quellen des stabreimenden *Morte Arthure*." *Anglia* 8 (1885): 179-236.
Bromwich, Rachel. "The Welsh Triads." *Arthurian Literature in the Middle Ages: A Collaborative History*. Ed. Roger S. Loomis. Oxford: Oxford UP, 1959. 44-51.
Brook, G.L. and R.F. Leslie, eds. *Laȝamon*: Brut. EETS os 263, 277. Oxford: Oxford UP, 1963, 1978.
Bullock-Davies, Constance, comp. *Register of Royal and Baronial Domestic Minstrels, 1272-1327*. Woodbridge: Boydell, 1986.
Chambers, E.K. *The Medieval Stage*. 2 vols. Oxford: Oxford UP, 1903.
Clanchy, M.T. *From Memory to Written Record: England 1066-1307*. 1979. 2nd ed. Oxford: Blackwell, 1993.
Coleman, Janet. *Medieval Readers and Writers, 1350-1400*. New York: Columbia UP, 1981.
Corbett, James A. *The "De instructione puerorum" of William of Tournai, O.P.* Notre Dame: Medieval Institute, 1955.
Critchley, John S. *Feudalism*. Boston: Allen, 1978.
Crosby, Ruth. "Oral Delivery in the Middle Ages." *Speculum* 11 (1936): 88-110.
Curschmann, Michael. "Oral Poetry in Medieval English, French, and German Literature: Some Notes on Recent Research." *Speculum* 42 (1967): 36-52.
Dean, Christopher. "Sir Gawain in the Alliterative *Morte Arthure*." *Papers on Language and Literature* 22 (1986): 115-25.
Donaldson, E. Talbot. Piers Plowman: *The C-Text and Its Poet*. New Haven: Yale UP, 1949.
Duggan, Hoyt N. and Thorlac Turville-Petre, eds. *The Wars of Alexander*. EETS ss 10. Oxford: Oxford UP, 1989.
Duggan, Joseph J. "Social Functions of the Medieval Epic in the Romance Literatures." *Oral Tradition* 1 (1986): 728-66.
Eadie, J. "The Alliterative *Morte Arthure*: Structure and Meaning." *English Studies* 63 (1982): 1-12.
Emden, A.B. "Learning and Education." *Medieval England*. Ed. A.L. Poole. 2 vols. Oxford: Clarendon, 1958. 515-40.
Everett, Dorothy. "The Alliterative Revival: (i). The Alliterative *Morte Arthure* and Other Poems." *Essays on Middle English Liter-*

ature. Ed. Patricia Kean. 1955. Oxford: Clarendon, 1964. 46-67.

Finlayson, John. "Two Minor Sources of the Alliterative *Morte Arthure*." *Notes and Queries* ns 9 (1962): 132-33.

—. "Formulaic Technique in *Morte Arthure*." *Anglia* 81 (1963): 372-93.

—. "Arthur and the Giant of St. Michael's Mount." *Medium Ævum* 33 (1964): 112-20.

—, ed. *Morte Arthure*. Evanston: Northwestern UP, 1967.

—. "*Morte Arthure*: The Date and a Source for the Contemporary References." *Speculum* 42 (1967): 624-38.

—. "The Concept of the Hero in *Morte Arthure*." *Chaucer und seine Zeit: Symposion für Walter F. Schirmer*. Ed. Arno Esch. Tübingen: Niemayer, 1968. 249-74.

—. "The Alliterative *Morte Arthure* and Sir Ferumbras." *Anglia* 92 (1974): 38-86.

Foerster, Wendelin, ed. *Yvain (le chevalier au lion)*. 1942. Manchester: Manchester UP, 1984.

Foley, John Miles. "Man, Muse, and Story: Psychohistorical Patterns in Oral Epic Poetry." *Oral Tradition* 2 (1987): 91-107.

Frappier, Jean, ed. *La mort le roi Artu*. Geneva: Droz; Paris: Minard, 1964.

Friedman, Albert B. and Norman T. Harrington, eds. *Ywain and Gawain*. EETS os 254. London: Oxford UP, 1964.

Frye, Northrop. *Anatomy of Criticism: Four Essays*. Princeton: Princeton UP, 1957.

Furnivall, F.J., ed. *Robert Manning of Bourne*. The Chronicle. 2 vols. London, 1887.

Gabriel, Astrik L. *The Educational Ideas of Vincent of Beauvais*. Notre Dame: Medieval Institute, 1956.

Gautier, Léon. *Les épopées françaises*. 2nd ed. 4 vols. Paris, 1878-82.

Griscom, Acton, ed. *Geoffrey of Monmouth*. Historia Regum Britanniae. 1929. Trans. Sebastian Evans. Rev. Charles W. Dunn. New York: Dutton, 1958.

Göller, Karl Heinz. "The Dream of the Dragon and Bear." *The Alliterative* Morte Arthure: *A Reassessment of the Poem*. Ed. Karl Göller. Cambridge: Brewer, 1981. 130-39; nn177-79.

—, ed. *The Alliterative* Morte Arthure: *A Reassessment of the Poem*. Cambridge: Brewer, 1981.

Haas, Renate. "The Laments for the Dead." *The Alliterative* Morte Arthure: *A Reassessment of the Poem*. Ed. Karl Göller. Cambridge: Brewer, 1981. 117-29; nn176-77.

—. "Chaucer's *Monk's Tale*: An Ingenious Criticism of Early Humanist Conceptions of Tragedy." *Humanistica Lovaniensis* 36 (1987): 44-70.

Hamel, Mary. "The Dream of a King: The Alliterative *Morte Arthure* and Dante." *Chaucer Review* 14 (1980): 298-312.

—. "The 'Christening' of Sir Priamus in the Alliterative *Morte Arthure*." *Viator* 13 (1982): 295-307.

—, ed. Morte Arthure: *A Critical Edition*. New York: Garland, 1984.

Harder, Henry L. "Feasting in the Alliterative *Morte Arthure*." *Studies in Medieval Culture* 14 (1980): 49-62; nn156-57.

Harwood, Britton J. "*Gawain* and the Gift." *PMLA* 106 (1991): 483-99.

Havelock, Eric A. *Preface to Plato*. Cambridge, MA: Harvard UP, 1963.

—. *The Muse Learns to Write: Reflections on Orality and Literacy from Antiquity to the Present*. New Haven: Yale UP, 1986.

Hepple, Richard B. *Medieval Education in England*. London: Bell, 1932.

Howard, Douglas. "Kingship and Conquest: Tragic Conflict in *Morte Arthure*." *Indiana Social Studies Quarterly* 31 (1978): 29-38.

Janssen, Anke. "The Dream of the Wheel of Fortune." *The Alliterative* Morte Arthure: *A Reassessment of the Poem*. Ed. Karl Göller. Cambridge: Brewer, 1981. 140-52; nn179-81.

Johnson, James D. "Formulaic Diction and Thematic Composition in the Alliterative *Morte Arthure*." Diss. U of Illinois, 1969.

—. "Formulaic Thrift in the Alliterative *Morte Arthure*." *Medium Ævum* 47 (1978): 255-61.

Kane, George. *Middle English Literature*. London: Methuen, 1951.

—, and E. Talbot Donaldson, eds. Piers Plowman: *The B Version*. London: Athlone, 1975.

Keen, Maurice. *Chivalry*. New Haven: Yale UP, 1984.

Keiser, George R. "Narrative Structure in the Alliterative *Morte Arthure*, 26-720." *Chaucer Review* 9 (1974): 130-44.

—. "The Theme of Justice in the Alliterative *Morte Arthure*." *Annuale Mediaevale* 16 (1975): 94-109.

Kelly, Susan. "Anglo-Saxon Lay Society and the Written Word." *The Uses of Literacy in Early Medieval Europe*. Ed. Rosamond McKitterick. Cambridge: Cambridge UP, 1990. 36-62.

Ker, W.P. *Epic and Romance: Essays on Medieval Literature*. 2nd ed. London: Macmillan, 1931.

Keynes, Simon. "Royal Government and the Written Word in Late Anglo-Saxon England." *The Uses of Literacy in Early Medieval Europe*. Ed. Rosamond McKitterick. Cambridge: Cambridge UP, 1990. 226-57.

Krishna, Valerie. "Parataxis, Formulaic Density, and Thrift in the Alliterative *Morte Arthure*." *Speculum* 57 (1982): 63-83.

Lawrence, R.R. "The Formulaic Theory and Its Application to English Alliterative Poetry." *Essays on Style and Language: Linguistic and Critical Approaches to Literary Style*. Ed. Roger Fowler. London: Routledge, 1966. 166-83.

Loomis, Roger Sherman, ed. *Arthurian Literature in the Middle Ages: A Collaborative History*. Oxford: Clarendon, 1959.

Lord, Albert B. "Homer and Huso III: Enjambment in Greek and Southslavic Heroic Song." *Transactions of the American Philological Association* 79 (1948): 113-24.

—. *The Singer of Tales*. Cambridge, MA: Harvard UP, 1960.

Lumiansky, Robert M. "The Alliterative *Morte Arthure*, the Concept of Medieval Tragedy, and the Cardinal Virtue Fortitude." *Medieval and Renaissance Studies: Proceedings of the Southeastern Institute of Medieval and Renaissance Studies, Summer 1967*. Ed. J.M. Headley. Chapel Hill: U of North Carolina P, 1968. 95-118.

McIntosh, Angus. "The Textual Transmission of the Alliterative *Morte Arthure*." *English and Medieval Studies Presented to J.R.R. Tolkien on the Occasion of His Seventieth Birthday*. Ed. Norman Davis and C.L. Wrenn. London: Allen, 1962. 231-40.

McKisack, May. *The Fourteenth Century, 1307-1399*. Oxford: Clarendon, 1959.

McKitterick, Rosamond. "Introduction." *The Uses of Literacy in Early Medieval Europe*. Ed. Rosamond McKitterick. Cambridge: Cambridge UP, 1990. 1-10.

—, ed. *The Uses of Literacy in Early Medieval Europe*. Cambridge: Cambridge UP, 1990.

McMahon, Clara P. *Education in Fifteenth-Century England*. Baltimore: Johns Hopkins UP, 1947.

Magoun, Francis P., Jr., ed. *The Gests of King Alexander of Macedon*. Cambridge, MA: Harvard UP, 1929.

Matthews, William. *The Tragedy of Arthur*. Berkeley: U of California P, 1960.

Murray, A.T., trans. *The* Iliad. 2 vols. Cambridge, MA: Harvard UP, 1924-25.

Neilson, George. "Three Footnotes." *An English Miscellany Presented to Dr. Furnivall in Honor of His Seventy-Fifth Birthday*. Oxford: Clarendon, 1901. 382-85.

Nicholls, Jonathan. *The Matter of Courtesy*. Woodbridge: Boydell, 1985.

Obst, Wolfgang. "The Gawain–Priamus Episode in the Alliterative *Morte Arthure*." *Studia Neophilologica* 57 (1985): 9-18.

O'Loughlin, J.L.N. "The English Alliterative Romances." *Arthurian Literature in the Middle Ages: A Collaborative History*. Ed. Roger S. Loomis. Oxford: Clarendon, 1959. 520-27.

Orme, Nicholas. *Education and Society in Medieval and Renaissance England*. London: Hambledon, 1989.

Owst, G.R. *Literature and Pulpit in Medieval England*. 2nd ed. Oxford: Blackwell, 1961.

Parks, George B. "King Arthur and the Roads to Rome." *Journal of English and Germanic Philology* 45 (1946): 164-70.

Parks, Ward. "The Oral-Formulaic Theory in Middle English Studies." *Oral Tradition* 1 (1986): 636-94.

Parry, Albert W. *Education in England in the Middle Ages*. London: U Tutorial P, 1920.

Parry, Milman. "Studies in the Epic Technique of Oral Verse-Making. I. Homer and Homeric Style." *Harvard Studies in Classical Philology* 41 (1930): 73-147.

Patterson, Lee. "The Romance of History and the Alliterative *Morte Arthure*." *Negotiating the Past: The Historical Understanding of Medieval Literature*. Madison: U of Wisconsin P, 1987. 197-230.

—. *Chaucer and the Subject of History*. Madison: U of Wisconsin P, 1991.

Pearsall, Derek, ed. Piers Plowman *by William Langland. An Edition of the C-Text*. Berkeley: U of California P, 1979.

Peck, Russell. "Willfulness and Wonders: Boethian Tragedy in the Alliterative *Morte Arthure*." *The Alliterative Tradition in the Fourteenth Century*. Ed. Bernard S. Levy and Paul E. Szarmach. Kent, OH: Kent State UP, 1981. 153-82.

Riquer, Martin de. *Les chansons de geste françaises*. 2nd ed. Trans. Irénée Cluzel. Paris: Nizet, 1957.

Ritzke-Rutherford, Jean. "Formulaic Microstructure: The Cluster." *The Alliterative* Morte Arthure: *A Reassessment of the Poem*. Ed. Karl Göller. Cambridge: Brewer, 1981. 70-82; nn167-69.

Rychner, Jean. *La chanson de geste: essai sur l'art épique des jongleurs*. Geneva: Droz; Lille: Giard, 1955.

Salter, Elizabeth. "The Timeliness of *Wynnere and Wastoure*." *Medium Ævum* 47 (1978): 40-65.

Saunders, Corinne J. "Arthur's *Val merveilleux et perilleux*: A Note on the Relationship of the *Roman de Thébes* to the Alliterative *Morte Arthure*, Lines 3230-51." *Notes and Queries* ns 38 (1991): 452-54.

Shepherd, Geoffrey. *The Nature of Alliterative Poetry in Late Medieval England*. London: Oxford UP, 1971.

Strohm, Paul. "Some Generic Distinctions in the *Canterbury Tales*." *Modern Philology* 68 (1971): 321-28.

Tout, Thomas Frederick. *Chapters in the Administrative History of Mediaeval England*. 6 vols. Manchester: Manchester UP, 1920-33.

Trigg, Stephanie, ed. *Wynnere and Wastoure*. EETS os 297. Oxford: Oxford UP, 1990.

Turville-Petre, Thorlac. *The Alliterative Revival*. Cambridge: Brewer, 1977.

Twomey, Michael W. "Heroic Kingship and Unjust War in the Alliterative *Morte Arthure*." *Acta* 11 (1986): 133-51.

Vale, Juliet. "Law and Diplomacy in the Alliterative *Morte Arthure*." *Nottingham Medieval Studies* 23 (1979): 31-46.

Vance, Eugene. *Mervelous Signals: Poetics and Sign Theory in the Middle Ages*. Lincoln: U of Nebraska P, 1986.

Vaughan, M.F. "Consecutive Alliteration, Strophic Patterns, and the Composition of the Alliterative *Morte Arthure*." *Modern Philology* 77 (1979): 1-9.

Waldron, Ronald A. "Oral-Formulaic Technique and Middle English Alliterative Poetry." *Speculum* 32 (1957): 792-804.

Wilson, R.M. *The Lost Literature of Medieval England.* 2nd ed. London: Methuen, 1970.

Wright, Cyril Edward. *The Cultivation of Saga in Anglo-Saxon England.* London: Oliver and Boyd, 1939.

Wright, Thomas. *Feudal Manuals of English History.* London, 1872.

Wurster, Jutta. "The Audience." *The Alliterative* Morte Arthure: *A Reassessment of the Poem.* Ed. Karl Göller. Cambridge: Brewer, 1981. 45-56; nn161-64.

Yates, Frances. *The Art of Memory.* Chicago: U of Chicago P, 1966.